ANDREAS MA

ASK YOUR
MUSLIM FRIEND

An introduction to Islam
and a Christian's guide
for interaction with Muslims

ASK YOUR MUSLIM FRIEND

An introduction to Islam and a Christian's guide for interaction with Muslims

By Andreas Maurer
www.aymf.net

Copyright © 2008 by Andreas Maurer, Author

First edition 2008

ISBN 978-1-920212-26-1

9 781920 212261 >

Published by:
AcadSA Publishing
PO Box 12322
Edleen, Kempton Park, 1625
Rep. South Africa

Cover design, artwork and page design by:
"Atelier für Kommunikation", www.atk.ch

Cover picture:
imagepoint.biz

This is a production of AWM (Arab World Ministries)
www.awm.org

ACKNOWLEDGEMENTS

The original text of this publication was compiled in 1997 after many years of intensive personal interaction with Muslims in Southern Africa. My thanks go to my former colleagues of the SIM team (Life Challenge) in South Africa, to MERCSA, and other specialists and members of the Mondeor Methodist Church, Johannesburg.

This updated English edition includes recent developments in Islam and new insights of personal interaction with Muslims. I would like to give special thanks to the following people who have contributed substantially to this publication: Christian Bibollet, Don Heckman, David Greenlee, ML Howard, Manfred Jung, Andreas Kaplony, Carrie Lyon, Elsie Maxwell, Renato and Hala Mazzei, Gerhard Nehls, Roland Weber, Abe Wiebe and Aida Zollinger-Khalifa. Special thanks go to Greg Kernaghan who did a wonderful job with editing. Many thanks go also to Peter Schäublin and his team (www.atk.ch) who did the page design.

I encourage readers to communicate their experiences and helpful criticism in order to improve future editions of this book.

Dr Andreas Maurer
January 2008

CONTENTS

PRELIMINARY REMARKS

- Biblical texts are quoted from the New International Version, unless otherwise identified. The Biblical references are abbreviated according to standardized guidelines (see Appendix section 4.3).
- Quotations from the Qur'an, as well as the verse numbering system, are taken from the translation of A. Yusuf Ali (edition 1946, printed 4/1993). Verse numbers vary slightly between various translations of the Qur'an.
- Arabic names and terms are given in their common English spellings. They are either explained where they occur, or are listed and described in Appendix section 4.4 (Glossary of Arabic/Islamic terms). Arabic terms not yet integrated in the English language (see a standard dictionary for definition) are shown in italics.
- For reasons of simplicity, female forms such as *Muslima* are omitted in this publication. Muslim as generic terms are used instead.
- References in the footnotes are abbreviated. More bibliographic information is provided in Appendix section 4.1 (Bibliography and recommended reading).
- Since the concept of God is perceived differently in the Qur'an and the Bible, I use the term "Allah" when it appears in a Muslim context.
- For further information and resources, please contact the following websites: www.aymf.net (www.ask-your-muslim-friend.net).

PREFACE

Since World War II, Islamic nations have gradually elevated themselves to become powerful religious and political entities. Due to unprecedented migration, many non-Muslims have become neighbours to Muslims in most non-Islamic countries. Recent events like the attack on September 11, 2001 in the USA, and countless terrorist attacks elsewhere have brought Islam to the forefront of attention, naturally raising questions about this religion. By now it has become evident that Islam is not a religion in the generally accepted sense i.e. a purely personal religious conviction. To the contrary, Islam claims that as a religion it stands above individuals and nations, above all spheres of life: faith, ethics, law, societal order, art, education, economy, and politics.

In this book I endeavour to provide an overview of the religion of Islam and its rather vitriolic attacks against basic biblical faith. I will investigate how Christians can confidently and lovingly relate to their Muslim neighbours in an effort to rectify their often strange perceptions. Efforts have been made to formulate the text for easy comprehension. For a deeper study of the subject, readers are advised to contact our website (www.aymf.net) and/or use the literature recommended in Appendix section 4.1.

Four points of emphasis

1. This book is written in a structured way to give basic insight into the religion of Islam and how Muslims practice their religion. After this book, readers may realize that in many cases they know more about Islam than the average Muslim does. However, the aim is not that Christians can correct Muslims about their beliefs. Instead, Christians should demonstrate a keen interest in what Muslims have to say.
2. The information herein may contrast with statements by Muslims and help Christians to differentiate between facts and wishful thinking of Muslims.
3. On this basis, Christians are then able to formulate more effective questions to challenge Muslims to think about the relationship between themselves and the Creator. Rather than immediately present answers, it is better that Muslims are first challenged to think and find answers themselves.
4. Only later may Christians share their faith with Muslims and explain the teaching of the Bible.

The following conversations illustrate these points:

> **Conversation 1**
> Muslim: I have to pray five times a day to be a good Muslim!
> Christian: Oh, that is interesting! Would you be kind enough to show me where it is written that you have to pray five times a day?
> Muslim: It is written in the Qur'an!
> Christian: Well I would love to read it myself—can you give me the reference?
> Muslims: I have to find it first!
> ...after some time:
> Muslim: Here are some passages on prayer in the Qur'an... (Note: there is no reference in the Qur'an where it clearly says that Muslims have to pray five times. Christians should make Muslims aware of such facts in a loving and kind way, without ridicule.)
> Christian: Thank you for showing me these passages in the Qur'an. May I show you what the Bible says about the topic of prayer?

> **Conversation 2**
> Christian: Tell me how you became a Muslim.
> Muslim: Well, I was born in Saudi Arabia!
> Christian: If you had been born in Japan, would you be a Buddhist?
> This often leads to more discussion, perhaps leading to the question:
> Muslim: Well, how did you become a Christian?

The aim of this book is thus to equip Christians to be more effective in their witness to Muslims. The knowledge gleaned through the study of this book is not intended to correct Muslims in their own beliefs, but that:

1. Christians may gain confidence and dispel their fear, prejudice and wrong attitudes when meeting Muslims.
2. Christians learn to ask appropriate questions to challenge and stimulate Muslims to think about their own faith.
3. Christians learn to differentiate between wishful thinking of Muslims concerning their faith and facts.
4. Christians become capable of effectively answering Muslim objections.
5. Christians develop the art of sharing the gospel with Muslims whose religious perceptions are vastly different from Christians.

It is my conviction and experience that one of the best strategies to reach Muslims with the Good News of Christ is to ask intelligent questions. This requires a basic understanding of Islam and the Bible.

Notes
1. The purpose of asking questions is not to put the Muslim in an embarrassing position (he may not know the answer), nor to provoke an aggressive reaction. Christians need to develop approaches compatible with Christian love which encourage a deeper exchange of views and serious reflection (see sections 3.1 and 3.2). Each situation is different and unique; therefore Christians need to be wise in selecting the questions suggested in this book. Not every question applies to each situation. Often it is wise in the beginning simply to ask the general question: "What do you mean by that?" moving to specific questions if the situation warrants.
2. There are many other valid approaches to Muslims in addition to asking questions. Sharing the gospel immediately is one possibility, but in all things sensitivity to the lading of the Holy Spirit is crucial.

This book is divided into three main parts
1. **Islamic teaching:** A basic introduction to the religion is presented in a topical and structured order.
2. **Christian answers to Muslim objections:** Some common objections raised by Muslims against the Christian faith are identified and appropriate answers are given.
3. **Encounters with Muslims:** Practical guidelines for Christians to be more effective in making initial contacts with Muslims and to build long-term relationships with them.

God wants all men to be saved
and to come to a knowledge of the truth.
(1Tim 2:4)

For God did not give us a spirit of timidity,
but a spirit of power, of love and of self-discipline.
So do not be ashamed to testify about our Lord,
or ashamed of me his prisoner.
But join with me in suffering for the gospel,
by the power of God.
(2Tim 1:7-8)

1. Islamic teaching

> This chapter offers you
a) an overview of the origins and spread of Islam
b) an introduction to Muhammad's life, the prophet of Islam
c) knowledge about the importance of the Qur'an, the holy book of Islam
d) an introduction to Islamic theology and its various groups
e) additional information such as the position of women in Islam and Muslim festivals

To communicate effectively with Muslims, it is important to understand the way they think and live. Committed Christians need to be accurately informed about Islam. Popular images are often based on misinformation, kindling fear rather than offering help.

This book will largely examine orthodox Sunni Islam. However, the teachings of different Islamic groups vary.[1] It is therefore advisable to ask individual Muslims about their own particular beliefs and interpretations which may differ. It is impossible to study Islam without using a variety of Islamic expressions. These will either be explained where they occur or appear in the Appendix section 4.4.

! True story
I once went into a mosque in Africa and asked what their beliefs were. They told me different stories from the Qur'an and that Jesus though crucified did not die but swooned. "But this is contrary to Sunni belief", I said. They told me, that they knew better, calling themselves "Ahmadiyya". They showed me a Qur'an with their own translation and comments, insisting that they are the only true Muslims.

i Take note
• Do not assume that you know what Muslims believe. Ask them individually.
• There are many different Muslim groups and each thinks it represents true Islam.

---

[1] See section 1.6

1.1 The history of Islam

The Arabian Peninsula was the birthplace of Islam.[2] It was here that Muhammad, the prophet of Islam, lived and died. The cities of Mecca and Medina play a particularly important role in Islamic History. Yet little is known about Arabia before the rise of Islam, because all relevant materials have been destroyed during the time of early Islam. Much of what is assumed today is legend and the authenticities of traditions have to be critically analyzed.

 Why it is important to study history ...is this story true?
"When Muhammad fled from Mecca to Medina, he hid in a cave from his enemies. A spider spun a web over its small entrance. As men came looking for Muhammad, they saw the web over the cave's entrance, and said to themselves: "It is not possible that he can hide in here!" So they left and went further on. Is this not wonderful how Allah protected his prophet?" (told by a Muslim).

1.1.1 Arabia before Muhammad

Arabian tribal life: Muslims call the time prior to Muhammad (570 AD) the "age of ignorance" *(al-Jahiliyya)*[3]. Two great world powers controlled the Orient in the sixth century AD: the Byzantine and Sassanid[4] empires. Arabia was in a sense a world of its own, independent and at the fringes of the two major states of the day. The Arabian Peninsula bordered both realms and was therefore influenced by, and partly involved in, the power struggle between them. As a result of this ongoing struggle, both empires weakened thus creating a power vacuum.[5] Trade flourished on the caravan routes along the Red Sea linking East Africa with East Asia via the Silk Road[6] and Europe. The city of Mecca had become an important centre of trade but was also a religious centre and place of pilgrimage. The sale of idols was a significant source of income. Social inequalities and injustice were widespread. Having many daughters was considered a disgrace for a father. Therefore, girls were often buried alive immediately after birth—just one example of the way society gave women few rights and little protection.

---

[2] Many Muslims would disagree and say that Adam was the first Muslim.
[3] Muslims give a number of different reasons for this term. Chiefly, the point is that the Arabs worshiped many idols and were ignorant that there is only one God.
[4] The Sassanid Empire or Sassanian Persian Dynasty lasted from 226 to 651 AD. Its major religion was Zoroastrianism (www.zawa.asn.au). The Zoroastrians faced persecution from Arab invaders during the time of the second caliph Umar. Most were converted to Islam by force and under fear of death.
[5] See Endress (2002:111).
[6] The Silk Road is an interconnected series of ancient trade routes through various regions of the Asian continent mainly connecting China, with Asia Minor and the Mediterranean. It extends over 8,000 km (5,000 miles) on land and sea. Trade on the Silk Route was a significant factor in the development of the great civilizations of China, Egypt, Mesopotamia, Persia, India, and Rome, and helped to lay the foundations for the modern world. *Silk road* is a translation from the German *Seidenstraße*. The first person to use the term was the German geographer F. von Richthofen in 1877.

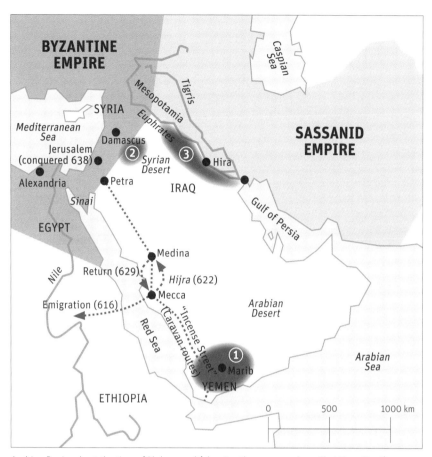

Arabian Peninsula at the time of Muhammad (showing three areas where Christians lived).

The most developed part of the Arabian Peninsula was Yemen where a network of dams had developed a rich agricultural life. The Yemeni kingdoms had partially adopted the Jewish faith. Their language was South Arabic, different but akin to the Arabic of the remaining peninsula. However, at the end of the 6th century these dams broke, and the South Arabian kingdoms collapsed. Roughly at the same time, Yemen was occupied by the Sassanid Persians.

The two other centres of pre-Islamic Arabic culture were at the desert fringes of Christian Byzantine Syria and Zoroastrian Persian Mesopotamia (Iraq). In both parts, Christian Arab kings ruled which prepared the later Muslim expansion.

Sedentary Arabs lived in Yemen and along the coast of the Arabian Peninsula, working as farmers and fishermen. Otherwise, the Arabian Peninsula was peopled predominantly by nomads and semi-nomads, apart from larger settlements in cities like Mecca and Medina. The Bedouin tribes were permanently in conflict with each other and formed shifting alliances. Unity and lasting peace did not exist. The strongest ruled; feuds were common. Raids against other tribes were part of the unwritten law of the desert. People settled at oases, which became economic centres, often visited by nomads and where markets and feasts took place. Already at that time, a long rich tradition of Arabic poetry had developed.

The religion of the Arabs: Most Arabs of the time were animists[7]. A vague notion of a "High God" ruling over everything (Arabic: "Allah") prevailed. It was essential, however, to appease a host of subordinate gods whom people believed directed their fate. In and around Mecca, for example, three goddesses were revered: *Manat, al-Uzza,* and *Allat,* the so-called daughters of Allah (Sura 53:19ff).
Nomads and townspeople believed that caves, trees, springs, and stones were inhabited by spirits, and they brought them offerings. The *Quraish* tribe (to which Muhammad belonged) had made Mecca a centre for religious activity (550–600 AD). In particular the *Ka'ba,* which housed about 360 idols was the focus of pagan worship. The *Ka'ba* (cube) was indeed cubic in shape and had various sacred stones embedded in its walls. One object of special veneration was a black stone, the objective of an annual pilgrimage which Arabs revered by kissing.[8]

Judaism during that period: Since their expulsion from Jerusalem by the Romans in 70 AD, many Jews lived in the *Hijaz,* the western part of the Arabian Peninsula. They were industrious and talented in trade, agriculture, and the manufacture of arms, and thus had considerable reputation. In *Yathrib* (Medina), they lived according to their clans *(banu)* in separate districts. The Jews saw themselves as the "chosen people". They believed in one God, and had their own book, the Torah. Perhaps for this reason Muhammad assumed that his own people also needed their special book from God. Muhammad had many encounters with Jews, discussed religious topics with them and learned many of their texts from the Talmud[9] which are found in the Qur'an today.

Christianity during that period: In the Byzantine Empire Christians were in the majority, whereas in the Sassanid Empire Christians were a significant and influential minority. In Arabia around 600 AD we find that different elements of the Christian church were well-established on the frontiers. Besides many small Christian establishments in various places, there were three major areas of Christianity on the fringes of Arabia:[10]
1. The south-western corner of the Arabian Peninsula, today known as Yemen, especially at the town of Najran. The agent of its diffusion was the Christian

---

[7] Animists are people who consider objects in nature and of human use as indwelt by a spirit.
[8] The *Ka'ba* owed its sanctity to the Black Stone. The religion of the ancient Arabs was essentially the worship of deities somehow related to particular stones, trees, etc. (see also Gibb & Kramers 1953:197).
[9] The Talmud is a record of rabbinic discussions pertaining to Jewish law, ethics, customs and history.
[10] See map on page 15, for more details see Goddard (2000:11-17).

kingdom of Axum on the opposite shore of the Red Sea (present-day Ethiopia and Eritrea).

2. To the northwest, in the direction of Jerusalem and the Mediterranean, some Arab tribes on the Byzantine frontier had accepted Christianity.

3. The north-eastern area, bordering on Iraq, was a province of the Sassanid Empire. One of its rulers, Nu'man ibn Mundhir,[11] was a convert to Christianity (583-602 AD).

In addition, numerous Arab tribes in Arabia had accepted the Christian faith. The Arabs perceived Christianity as a foreign, but nonetheless modern religion.[12] Most Christians with whom Muhammad and his Arab people had contact came from northern Yemen and neighbouring countries. Besides Christians of Jewish origins, Muhammad encountered Christians from Ethiopia and Syria. Many Christians evicted from elsewhere due to certain heretical beliefs settled on the Arabian Peninsula and preserved their own culture and language.

However, the Christianity with which Muhammad became acquainted was not a universally agreed-upon faith, but a jumble of small groupings arguing with each other.[13] These could be identified primarily by their forms of outward worship. The adoration of the Virgin Mary was similar to the idol worship of Arabs. As a result, Muhammad condemned it as idolatry.[14]

Christianity displayed no unity, but was rather marked by theological conflicts, disputes over rank among bishops and internal persecution. The Qur'an reflects the misconceptions of a fragmented Christianity. Muhammad received biblical stories, traditions and folklore by word of mouth from Jews and Christians. The way biblical themes appear in the Qur'an leads to the conclusion that Muhammad himself never read the Bible.[15]

Another important influence on the Arabs came from the spread of monasticism from Egypt. The monks often practiced their religion in ways not in accordance with the Bible. Several participated in the pilgrimage to Mecca and adopted habits from Arabian paganism. Some preached openly in the vicinity of the *Ka'ba*. Muhammad was very sympathetic towards these monks.[16]

---

[11] Nu'man ibn Mundhir was a Ghassanid King. The Ghassanids were Arab Christians that emigrated in 250 AD from Yemen to the Hauran, in southern Syria. The term Ghassan refers to the kingdom of the Ghassanids, and is the name of a spring of water in the Hauran.

[12] Like the Jews, the Christians had a "Book of God" as a basis for their religion-something the Arabs did not yet have.

[13] The main differences were views on the nature of God, the person of Jesus Christ, and the Trinity.

[14] See Sura 5:119.

[15] Biblical themes appear in the Qur'an mostly in an obscure form. It appears that Muhammad was not able to distinguish between biblical statements, traditions and folklore.

[16] See e.g. Sura 5:85 and *Sira* Ibn Hisham (Ibn Hisham, d. 833 AD, edited the biography of Muhammad written by Ibn Ishaq).

The Qur'an's statements about Christians and Jews during the first period of Muhammad's ministry in Mecca were rather positive, suggesting that they should be seen primarily as *ahl al-kitab* (people of the Book). However, statements coming from the second period from Medina are rather negative, declaring that they should be seen as being guilty of polytheism *(shirk)* or rejection *(kufr)* of the faith, and should therefore be killed. The Christian church was present and enjoyed some influence especially on the borders of Arabia, but Christianity had not become a major player in developments in the heartlands of Arabia.

The year of the Elephant - the year of Muhammad's birth[17]

Not long before the rise of Islam, Abraha, king of Abyssinia, decided to make the Christian faith dominant in southern Arabia. He had a fine cathedral built at the city of San'a to which he hoped to draw all Arabs as pilgrims. The city survives to this day in what is now Yemen, though the church he built has long since vanished.

Nonetheless he was determined to make San'a the commercial centre of the Arabian Peninsula. Soon after the completion of his cathedral he issued a proclamation obliging all Arabs to visit it annually. He was well aware of the popularity of the *Ka'ba* in Mecca and he purposed to displace it as the commercial and religious centre of Arabia. His decree generally went unheeded, however, and the Christian king of Yemenite Himyar watched with grief as hordes of pilgrims set out each year for Mecca instead.[18]

News came to the Christian king one day that a member of the Arab tribe of Kenanah had entered his cathedral and desecrated it by strewing animal dung all over its interior. Abraha was infuriated, more so when he heard that tribes in the

---

[17] See for more detail Gilchrist (1994:11-14).
[18] Mecca was already in pre-Islamic time a place of worship.

vicinity had revolted against his rule and assassinated his ally, Muhammad ibn Khuza'a, the king of Modar. He responded by leading an expedition to Mecca with the sole purpose of destroying the *Ka'ba*.

A large contingent set out with numerous soldiers and horsemen. A unique feature of the army was the inclusion of an elephant among the other animals, a circumstance which was later to give the year in which the march took place its name, the *Year of the Elephant* (570 AD). The Arabs of Mecca were highly outnumbered by this large army and fled into the nearby hills. 'Abd al-Muttalib, a leader of the people in Mecca and Muhammad's grandfather, prayed for the protection of the *Ka'ba*.

Meanwhile the elephant was brought to the front of the army, clothed in festive apparel. Legend says that the guide of the procession marching on Mecca, Nufayl, was very reluctant to proceed with the journey and, in a whispered but emphatic voice, commanded the elephant to kneel. Abraha was annoyed but was unable to persuade it to rise and march on the city with his army.

It is not known exactly how the army came to grief but something dramatic happened to decimate it and its march on Mecca. As the *Quraish* occupied the hills, they may have rained down stones and rocks on the exposed force and obliged it to withdraw. An outbreak of smallpox or some other plague could have caused Abraha to pull back without accomplishing his goal. A legend soon grew, however, that the army had been beaten back miraculously by a flock of birds which hurled down rocks and stones upon the soldiers. A record of this is found in the Qur'an itself, Sura 105 which is called *The Elephant:*

> Seest thou not how thy Lord dealt with the companions of the Elephant? Did He not make their treacherous plan go astray? And He sent against them flights of birds, striking them with stones of baked clay. Then did He make them like an empty field of stalks and straw, (of which the corn) has been eaten up (Sura 105:1-5).

The rest of the army returned to Yemen; many others died on the way (giving the impression that it was most probably an outbreak of a disease such as smallpox that caused the catastrophe).The Qur'an, however, takes the legend at face value. The deliverance of the *Ka'ba* was obviously regarded by Arabs as a miracle and sign that the shrine had divinely sanctioned significance.

Two other factors may be mentioned why Muslims claim that Muhammad owns "universal prophet hood". Firstly it was his own grandfather who took the lead and initiative in opposing the Abyssinian ruler and in assuring him that the "Lord of the *Ka'ba*"[19] would look after his own house just as the Arab chieftain had seen to his. Secondly it has always been believed by Muslim historians that Muhammad himself was born in 570 AD, the very Year of the Elephant, and it has been customary for Muslims throughout history to regard the destruction of Abraha's army as a sign of the imminent rise of a final messenger who would withstand all attempts of pagans and unbelievers to destroy the ultimate revelation of God given to him through the mediation of a divinely-inspired scripture.

↗ In conclusion the following points merit consideration
1. Muslims see this whole story as a sign from Allah, who confirmed through this historical event the significance of Mecca as the place of pilgrimage for all times and which cannot be touched or destroyed by non-Muslims.
2. At the same time, Muslims believe that through this event the "holy character of the *Ka'ba*" is confirmed and that Allah will in similar miraculous ways protect the *Ka'ba* and Islam as a whole against all future attacks by Christians.
3. The fact that it was Muhammad's grandfather, 'Abd al-Muttalib, who took the initiative and stepped forward to pray for the protection of the *Ka'ba*, is seen by Muslims as a further sign that Muhammad is indeed the true and final prophet.
4. Muslims regard this event as a sign that Christianity was defeated even before the rise of Islam—the first victory against Christianity.
5. That Muhammad is born in the "Year of the Elephant" is regarded as yet another sign that Allah brought Muhammad as a final messenger who will for all eternity make sure that the *Ka'ba* cannot be destroyed by non-Muslims.

1.1.2 Muhammad and the origin of Islam[20]

Who is this man whose name is, in the Muslim creed,[21] inseparably linked with the name of Allah? Millions of people all over the world honour Muhammad as

---

[19] The "Lord of the *Ka'ba*," or also called "Lord of the Territory", is believed to be one of the chief gods in Mecca.

[20] The main traditional biographical source for the life of Muhammad is the *Sirat Rasul Allah* (The Life of the Prophet of Allah) by Ibn Ishaq (d 750 AD).

[21] Muslim creed: "I bear witness that there is no god but God (Allah), and that Muhammad is Allah's messenger" (see section 1.5.2.).

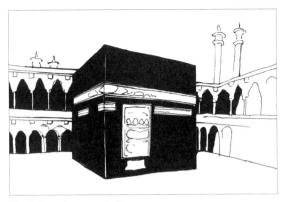

The *Ka'ba* and mosque in Mecca.

the prophet of Islam. For Muslims, he is the last and greatest prophet. He descended from a poor family and became a mighty statesman. He was destined to transform the religious and social characteristics of his people and to eventually become the founder of the only major world religion to succeed the Christian faith. A Muslim once described him as "the greatest example, combining all the virtues in one person". It is the aspiration and duty of all Muslims to imitate the life of their honoured prophet as much as possible. A short overview of Muhammad's life is presented in the following section.

Birth and childhood
570 AD It is not known for certain when Muhammad was actually born in Mecca (*Quraish* tribe). His father, Abdallah ibn Muttalib, dies before his birth. He loses his mother Aminah at the age of six. He is brought up by his grandfather 'Abd al-Muttalib and, later, by his uncle Abu Talib. Muhammad becomes a shepherd, and later a merchant.

582 AD At the age of twelve, his uncle takes him on business travels.

Marriage and visions[22]
595 AD At the age of 25, he marries Khadija, a rich widow, in whose trading company he works for some time. Through this marriage Muhammad's social status improved markedly. The marriage with Khadija, fifteen years older than Muhammad, ends 25 years later with her death. It seems to have been a good marriage. Their two sons die in childhood, causing much grief for Muhammad. Four daughters survive childhood.[23]

---

[22] Muhammad had some kind of "spiritual experience". Many scholars would not speak of "visions or pictures", but rather that he received a word from Allah: *iqra'* (recite)!
[23] The names of the four daughters are Raqiyya, Zainab, Umm Kulthum and Fatima. Fatima became later in life a highly-devoted Muslim.

21

610 AD At about the age of 40, Muhammad withdraws repeatedly to meditate in a cave on Mount Hira near Mecca. During these meditations, Muhammad is said to have received his first vision, and thus his vocation to be a prophet (Sura 96:1-5). The visions are communicated by the "angel Gabriel"[24]. Muhammad is very frightened and heavily in doubt at the first vision because he is not sure whether it comes from Allah or evil spirits.[25] Islamic tradition tells us that Muhammad was comforted by his wife Khadija, her cousin Waraqa ibn Naufal, who is stated to have been a Christian, and Muhammad's cousin Ali, and encouraged to believe in his vocation.[26] New visions occurred at several places and in various situations. They are later written down, and today form the Qur'an. As a consequence of these visions, Muhammad begins to preach in Mecca.

616 AD Muhammad's message of monotheism and its ethical consequences, at first finding little approval, contains one central point: "There is only one God, Allah, and man is obliged to submit to him". The word 'Islam' occurs for the first time, a word that is about to name the entire movement, meaning submission or surrender. Muhammad's preaching meets with increasing opposition from the Arab tradesmen because it is directed against idolatry and thus damages a flourishing trade with idols. Muhammad and his first followers are thus persecuted in Mecca. Some followers take refuge in the Christian kingdom of Abyssinia (Ethiopia).

619 AD After the deaths of his wife Khadija and his uncle and protector Abu Talib, Muhammad's situation continually worsens because of the increasing persecution. Even among his own clansmen, he no longer feels safe. Two months after Khadija's death, Muhammad marries the Abyssinian widow Sawda. He later marries other women, among them Aisha, only nine years old when Muhammad consummated their marriage. The total number of women Muhammad married is disputed, probably between 12 and 15.[27]

Emigration *(Hijra)* from Mecca to Medina

622 AD Due to increasing persecution in Mecca and an invitation from followers
0 AH in Medina, Muhammad and about 80 supporters emigrate to Medina[28]. His position changes abruptly. Here, he is no longer a persecuted preacher, but an influential leader of the townspeople who appoint him as mayor, concentrating all authority in one person. The emigration proves to be a

---

[24] In the Qur'an, Gabriel (Jibril) is a spiritual being who does not introduce himself (Suras 2:97-98; 66:4). Since the message is not in agreement with the Bible, it cannot be the same angel (cf Lk 1:26-33).
[25] See Ibn Said, Kitab al-Tabagat al-Kabir, Vol.1, p225.
[26] See Mishkat IV, p356 and 357.
[27] See Hughes 1982:399-400.
[28] Medina was then called *Yathrib*.

successful manoeuvre, representing according to Islamic chronology, the beginning of a new religion.

Change of Muhammad's position (622 AD)

Mecca	Medina (gradually assuming power)
• little power	• powerful and influential
• simple preacher	• religious leader
• persecuted at the end	• supreme military leader
• ordinary citizen	• political head
• becoming poor	• becomes wealthy

Muhammad, who in the beginning of his ministry is convinced that his faith is the same as that of Jews and Christians, seeks the support of three local Jewish tribes.[29] However, the Jews refuse to acknowledge Muhammad as a true prophet of God because he gives them no proofs.[30] Hostility arises as a consequence, and Muhammad differentiates Islam from the two monotheistic "predecessor religions".[31] Jews in Medina are forced either to emigrate, accept Islam, or be killed and their women and children enslaved. From now on, Jews and Christians living in Islamic areas are treated as subjects *(dhimmi)* who have to pay a special tax *(jizya)*.[32] During his ten-year rule from Medina, Muhammad established a small but strong empire, partly by force of arms and partly by diplomacy.

624 AD Muhammad and his followers start raiding caravans from Mecca and taking plunder for their followers. These raids lead to several open fights with Meccan citizens:[33]
- Battle of Badr: 324 Muslims from Medina defeat a force of three times that number of attackers from Mecca.
- Battle of Uhud (625 AD): The Muslims are defeated by Meccan fighters. Muhammad is wounded in this battle.

---

[29] A variety of models for the relationship between Muslims and non-Muslims can be found in Muhammad's career between 622-632 AD. Three main agreements are well known from that period. In one instance, involving the oasis of Khaybar, the Muslims reserved the right to break the agreement at any time for any reason (see Guillaume 1955:510-18).

[30] The Jews demanded a sign from Muhammad which he could not give them (see Suras 3:183-184; 6:3; 17:90-93).

[31] From that time on, as Muslims today believe, Muhammad emphasized the importance of Abraham and his son Ishmael, thinking probably they were his ancestors (though there is no proof for this assumption). He changes the prayer direction from Jerusalem to Mecca, and declares the *Ka'ba* to be a sanctuary erected by Abraham (see Suras 2:124-127; 2:142-144). The Qur'an displays this change of attitude by Muhammad: friendly verses are from the Meccan and early Medina period, such as 2:62; 3:199; 5:69, whereas hostility during the later Medina period is shown in verses such as 5:75-76; 9:29.

[32] For more details on this topic see the book by Ye'or (1985). People confronted with Islam had the following options: 1) to submit and accept Islam; 2) to retain their own faith but live as a kind of "second-class citizen" and pay a special tax; 3) to be killed by the sword.

[33] Here only the three main battles are mentioned, but there were many more hostile encounters.

- "The Battle of the Trench" (627 AD): The Muslims successfully defend Medina by digging a trench around the exposed parts of the town.

Muhammad's last years

628 AD The citizens of Mecca sign the peace treaty of al-Hudaibiya[34] with the Muslims of Medina. This allows Muhammad and his followers to make the pilgrimage to Mecca in the following year. In the twenty-two months after signing the treaty, Muhammad significantly built up his power base, making new conquests and forming alliances with powerful tribes, in particular with the Bani Khuza'a. As a result, by 630 AD he was considerably stronger vis-à-vis *Quraish* than at the time of the signing. *Quraish* did less well in terms of making new alliances, but it did ally with another strong tribe, the Bani Bakr. The Bani Khuza'a and the Bani Bakr lived near each other and had a long history of feuding. In 629 AD, some of the Bani Bakr took vengeance on a party of the Bani Khuza'a, killing several. On hearing this, Muhammad instantly opted for the most drastic response: to attack Mecca. The time had come to challenge the ultimate power base of *Quraish* in their home city.

630 AD Muhammad returns to Mecca, together with about 10,000 warriors. In the face of this superior force, the people of Mecca submit without resistance, and become Muslims.[35] Muhammad issues an amnesty for most inhabitants of his home town. The idols and images in the *Ka'ba* are removed and destroyed, and Mecca is declared a forbidden city for non-Muslims. In the following year, Muhammad leads for the first time a war of conquest against the Great Powers. Byzantium and Persia have been weakened by battling with each other. Muhammad invades the borderlands of Byzantine Syria with a large host of warriors.

632 AD Muhammad dies in Medina at 63, without designating a successor.[36] His sudden death poses a large problem for his followers: who will take his place and lead the newly founded Muslim community so that its unity remains intact?

1.1.3 The four caliphs[37]

622 AD The year of the *Hijra* is the beginning of the official chronology of the Islamic calendar.

---

[34] *Al-Hudaibiya* is the name of a well near Mecca.

[35] Muhammad's intention was to conquer the people of his home town without bloodshed. Therefore he put forward an agreement: if they submit to him and his religion, he will guarantee that Mecca remains a place of worship where all Muslims need to travel once in their lifetime, and thus securing the flow of money (Treaty of Hudaybiyya).

[36] It is not known for sure what was the cause of Muhammad's death. Scholars suggest the following theories: death by illness; having been critically wounded in battle; being poisoned by enemies; or a combination of these.

[37] The *caliph* is the head of the state, the leader of the Islamic *umma*. It means "successor" or "representative".

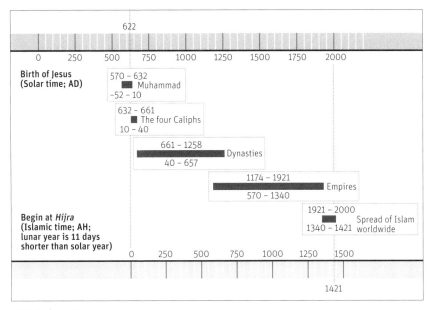

Historical survey.

630 AD

Towards the end of Muhammad's career his message became more critical towards Jews and Christians. After his death this approach predominated among Muslims, namely fighting the "people of the Book". Military raids were launched into the areas bordering Arabia.[38]

632–634 AD

Abu Bakr, the first caliph (Muhammad's successor) and father of Aisha (one of Muhammad's wives), crushes several rebellions among Arabian tribes to prevent them from leaving the Islamic community.

634–644 AD

Umar, the second caliph. After the battle at the Yarmuk (637 AD), he takes Jerusalem and acquires power over Syria. Shortly after that, Egypt and Persia are conquered under the able leadership of Khalid ibn Walid. Umar is assassinated in the mosque

---

[38] An example is the choice given to the Byzantine garrison in Gaza: they were invited to abandon their faith, deny Christ and participate in Islamic worship; when they refused they were all martyred. Further examples of antipathy against Christians in this period were the burning of churches, destruction of monasteries and blasphemies against the church and Christ (Crone & Cook 1977).

while praying. The texts of the Qur'an are collected and collated by Zayd ibn Thabit on orders of Abu Bakr and Umar.

644–656 AD   **Uthman**, the third caliph, orders the edition of the Qur'an because a number of versions had been written that caused confusion. He decrees that only the now-revised version of the Qur'an

Islamic dominion at 634 AD.

text is valid; all other texts are to be destroyed. Uthman is murdered by a rival group motivated by Fatima, the daughter of Muhammad, who was married to Ali.

656–661 AD   **Ali**, the fourth caliph, was Muhammad's cousin, adopted son, and son-in-law (and husband of his daughter Fatima). The question of succession splits the Muslims into Shiites and Sunnites. Shiites (mostly in Iran) acknowledge Ali as the first lawful caliph, and therefore reject the authority of the first three caliphs whom Sunni Muslims acknowledge. As his two predecessors, Ali is also assassinated.

1.1.4 The dynasties
661–750 AD   **Umayyad dynasty:** Ali's second son, Hussein allows the caliphate to be bought from him. Mu'awiya becomes the sole ruler and

founds a dynasty, with Damascus as its centre. The Umayyads descended from Umayya, and were a clan separate from Muhammad's in the *Quraish* tribe. By conquests, predominantly in North Africa, the young empire experiences enormous territorial growth. In 711 AD, Muslim troops cross over to Spain, and conquer four-fifths of the Iberian peninsula. The advance is stopped only at Poitiers, France by an army led by Charles Martel (732 AD).

750–1258 AD   The **Abbasid dynasty** replaced the Umayyad dynasty and had its most elaborate centre at Baghdad. The Abbasid caliphs officially

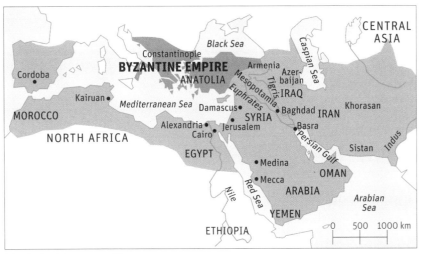

Islamic dominion at 750 AD.

based their claim to the caliphate on their descent from Abbas ibn Abd al-Muttalib (AD 566–652), one of the youngest uncles of Prophet Muhammad, by virtue of whose descent they regarded themselves as the rightful heirs of Muhammad as opposed to the Umayyads. They distinguished themselves from the Umayyads by attacking their secularism, moral character, and administration in general. The "Crusades"[39] which liberated Palestine from Islamic dominion temporarily, fall into this time. The Crusades were a series of military conflicts of a religious character which occurred from 1095–1291, usually sanctioned by the Pope in the name of Christendom. The Crusades originally had the goal of

---

[39] The crusades were a sad chapter in the history of Christendom. Up to this day, Muslims accuse Christians of having wanted to spread Christianity with the sword.

recapturing Jerusalem and the sacred "Holy Land" from Muslim rule and were launched in response to a call from the Eastern Orthodox Byzantine Empire for help against the expansion of the Muslims into Anatolia. After the Islamic expansion of the 8th century, Christianity is heavily subdued in the Middle East, the location of its origin. In 850 AD the caliph al-Mutawakkil passed laws which sought to make it manifestly clear that Jews and Christians were to be seen as second-class citizens within the Islamic world.[40] In 1258 AD the Mongols[41] killed about 800,000 people in an assault on Baghdad, resulting in the destruction of the Abbasid dynasty. The ninth century has also been called "the elaboration of Islam" in respect to disciplines of study within an Islamic context.[42] The Abbasids created an army loyal only to their caliphate, drawn mostly from Turkish slaves, known as Mamluks.

1.1.5 The empires

During the Middle Ages four Muslim empires emerged:
1. Mamluk Empire in Egypt
2. Safavid Empire in Iran
3. Mughal Empire in India
4. Ottoman Empire in much of the Middle East, Balkans and Northern Africa.

These new imperial powers were made possible by the discovery and exploitation of gunpowder and more efficient administration. By the end of the 19th century, all four had been weakened or destroyed by massive Western cultural influence and military ambitions.

1174–1811 AD   The origins of the **Mamluk Empire** of Egypt lie in the Ayyubid Dynasty that Saladin (Salah ad-Din) founded in 1174. With his uncle Shirkuh he conquered Egypt for the Zengid King Nur ad-Din of Damascus in 1169. The Mamluks defeated the Mongols in Homs in 1260 and begun to drive them back east. In the process they consolidated their power over Syria, fortified the area, formed mail routes and formed diplomatic connections between

---

[40] Some points of these laws were, for instance: wearing prescribed coloured clothes, destroying newly-built churches, wooden images of devils should be nailed to the doors of their houses, no employment where they would have authority over Muslims (see Goddard 2000:66-68).

[41] The Mongols were a group of nomadic people who in the 13th century found themselves encompassed by large, city-dwelling agrarian civilizations. However, none of these civilizations, with the possible exception of the Islamic Caliphate located in Baghdad, were part of a strong central state. Asia, Russia, and the Middle East were controlled by either declining kingdoms or divided city states. Taking the strategic initiative, the Mongols exploited this power vacuum and linked all of these areas into a mutually supportive trade network.

[42] Two important achievements were that of *al-Shafi'i* (820 AD) in the field of *Shari'a* (Islamic law) and of *al-Kindi* (870 AD) in the field of *falsafa* (Islamic Philosophy).

the local princes. Mamluk troops also defeated the last of the Crusader states in the Holy Land.

Napoleon defeated Mamluk troops when he attacked Egypt in 1798 and drove them to Upper Egypt. By this time Mamluks had added only muskets to their typical cavalry charge tactics. After the departure of French troops in 1801, Mamluks continued their struggle for independence, this time against the Ottoman Empire and Great Britain. Mamluk power in Egypt ended in 1811, when Muhammad Ali[43] invited all Mamluks to his palace to celebrate the declaration of war against the Wahhabis in Arabia. There were about 600 Mamluks on parade in Cairo. Near the Al-Azab gates, in a narrow road down from Mukatamb Hill, Muhammad Ali's forces ambushed and slaughtered them.

1502–1722 AD The **Safavid Empire** ruled Iran from the early 16th century to the early 18th century. Although claiming to be the descendants of Ali ibn Abi Talib (the fourth Caliph), the Safavids were orignially Sunni (the name "Safavid" comes from a Sufi order called *Safavi*). Their origins go back to Firuz Shah Zarrinkolah, an Iranian local dignitary from Iran's north. During their rule, the Safavids imposed Shiism as the state religion, thus giving Iran a separate identity from its Sunni neighbours. In 1524, Tahmasp acceded to the throne and revived arts in the region. Carpet making became a major industry, gaining new importance in Iran's cities. The finest of all artistic revivals was the commissioning of the *Shahnama* meant to glorify the reign of the *Shah* through artistic means. The two-volume copy contained 258 large paintings to illustrate the works of Firdawsi, a Persian poet. The Shah also prohibited the drinking of wine, forbade the use of hashish and ordered the removal of gambling casinos, taverns and brothels.

1526–1857 AD The **Mughal Empire** was a product of various Mongol invasions into Persia and India. Founded by Babur in 1526, the empire ruled most of present-day India, Pakistan, Bangladesh and Afghanistan for several centuries before it fell to the British in 1857. The empire left a lasting legacy on Indian culture and architecture. During the empire's reign, Muslim communities flourished all over India, particularly in Gujarat, Bengal and Hyderabad. Various Sufi orders from Afghanistan and Iran were very active throughout the region. Consequently, more than a quarter of the population of India converted to Islam.

---

[43] Muhammad Ali Pasha, Governor of Egypt from 1805–1849, is often cited as the founder of modern Egypt. Muhammad Ali was born in the town of Kavala (in present-day Greece) to an Albanian family. After working as a tobacco merchant in his youth, Muhammad Ali took a commission in the Ottoman army.

1301–1921 AD   The **Ottoman Empire** is not Arab but Turkish, since 1453 controlled from Istanbul (Constantinople). The Islamic world reached a new peak (albeit not comparable to the Golden Age of the Abbasids) under the Ottoman (Uthmaniah) Empire. The Turks migrated from the Central Asian steppe and at first established a tiny state in Anatolia (modern-day Turkey). In 1453, after a two-month siege, elite Ottoman soldiers and cannons overwhelmed Constantinople. The millennium-old Roman-Byzantine Empire was suddenly absorbed by the new Ottoman Empire which would extend its influence over most of the Islamic world and reach deep into Christian Europe. The empire, making great strides in the East, threatened to conquer Central and Western

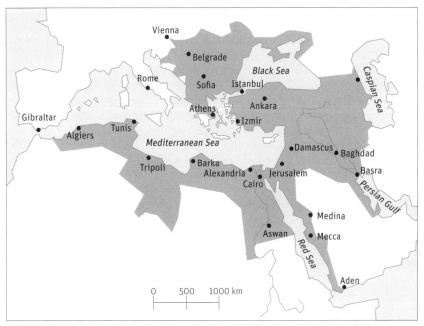

Ottoman empire at 1700 AD.

Europe. In 1529, the Siege of Vienna failed, stopping any further Ottoman advances into Eastern Europe. The Battle of Vienna in 1683 precipitated the withdrawal of the Ottoman Empire from many parts of Eastern Europe and the Balkans. The later weakness of the Ottoman Empire allowed the Europeans to extend their dominion over all northern Africa. The time of the colonial powers[44] starts with France taking power first in Algeria (1830) then Tunisia (1881), then Morocco (1912). Egypt becomes a British protectorate in 1882. In 1920, the Middle East is divided into mandates of Great Britain and France. After the Second World War, the colonial empires quickly unravel.

Mustafa Kemal Ataturk (1881-1938), the founder of the Turkish Republic and its first President, stands as a great figure of the 20th Century. Emerging as a military hero at the Dardanelles in 1915, he became the charismatic leader of the Turkish national liberation struggle in 1919. Following a series of impressive victories, he led his nation to full independence. He put an end to the Ottoman dynasty that lasted more than six centuries and created the Republic of Turkey in 1923, establishing a new government modelled on Western democracy. As President for 15 years, Atatürk introduced a broad range of new reforms in political, social, legal, economic, and cultural spheres.

1.1.6 The spread of Islam worldwide

1922–today: Due to the massive migration of people after World War II, Islam spread to many parts of the world. There is probably no country without Muslims today. Largely due to biological growth,

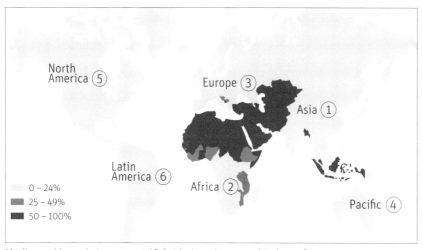

Muslim world population at 2000 AD (with six main geographical areas).

---

[44] In the Muslim view, the colonists represented the economical and supremacy of the foreign powers. Therefore, most of them had to leave Islamic countries after independence was declared. In Algeria (once actually part of France), where many French families had lived for three or four generations, the new development brought about terrible bloodshed on all sides in a war lasting from 1954 until 1962.

Islam is now the second-largest and fastest-growing religion in the world. The Islamic revolution in Shiite Iran in 1979–80, lead by Ayatollah Khomeini, kindled new self-confidence and zeal in Muslims for the propagation of Islam. Most Muslims live in countries stretching from West Africa through Central Asia to Indonesia. Their growth worldwide in the 20th Century has been significant: from 12.3% in 1900 to 20% in 2005. Growth through conversion has been greatest in West Africa, Indonesia and the USA.[45]

Muslims have increased by over 235% in the last 50 years (nearly 1.3 billion). By comparison, Christians have increased by 47%, Hinduism 117%, and Buddhism 63%.[46]

Christianity, Islam, Hinduism, Chinese folk religion and Buddhism are the largest world religions today. Approximately 69–78% of humanity adheres to one of these five religions. Christianity has the largest number of adherents, followed by Islam, Hinduism, Chinese folk religion and Buddhism respectively. These figures are necessarily approximate. The world population was in 2005 about 6.5 billion.

1.	Christianity	2 billion	(31%)
2.	Islam	1.3 billion	(20%)
3.	Non-adherent	1 billion	(16%; secular/atheist)
4.	Hinduism	780 million	(12%)
5.	Primal indigenous	380 million	(6%; 'pagan')
6.	Chinese folk religion	380 million	(6%)
7.	Buddhism	380 million	(6%)
8.	African traditional and diasporic	100 million	
9.	Sikhism	25 million	(0.4%)
10.	Juche	20 million	
11.	Judaism	19 million	(0.3%)
12.	Spiritism	15 million	
13.	Bahá'í Faith	7 million	

---

[45] See Johnstone (2001:14).
[46] These figures are estimates and include all adherents to the respective faith whether by birth or devotion. See also www.adherents.com and www.wikipedia.com.

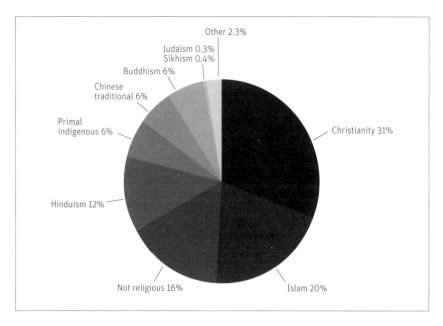

Major religious groups (percentage of world population, 2005 data).

The growth of Islam and Christian-Muslim relations
in the six main geographical areas (see map on page 31)

1) Asia
In the late 13th century, Muslim merchants and teachers began to bring Islam to Southeast Asia. By 1292, when Marco Polo visited Sumatra, most of the inhabitants had converted to Islam. The first Muslim kingdom was founded by a Javan Prince on the Malay Peninsula. Through trade and commerce, Islam spread to Borneo and Java (Indonesia). By the late 15th century, Islam had been introduced to the Philippines. As Islam spread, three main Muslim political powers emerged. Ajeh, the most important Muslim power, was based firmly in Northern Sumatra and controlled much of the region between Southeast Asia and India. The Sultanate also attracted Sufi poets. The second Muslim power was the federation of Sultanates on the Malay peninsula. The third power emerged in Java, where several Muslim powers defeated the local Majapahit kingdom in the early 16th century. After 1990 there were significant increases of Muslims converting to Christianity, despite or even because of the activities of Islamist extremism. This has mainly come through the wide spread of media.

Hot spots in Asia and the Middle East
- **Israel and Palestine:** The unresolved conflict between these powers is a matter of great concern. All international efforts for a peace deal had no lasting effects.

There are deep differences concerning land claims, especially Jerusalem itself. The Dome of the Rock[47] will continue to play a major role in the conflict.

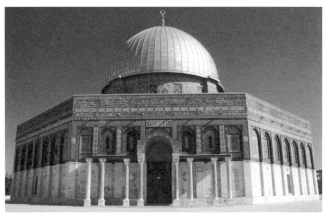

Dome of the Rock; Jerusalem.

- **Afghanistan** with decades of invasions and wars. The Taliban, an extreme Islamist movement, strives to control the country through violence and oppression. Many have died or fled the country. The Taliban export revolutionaries to many foreign nations. Afghanistan has been diplomatically ostracized.
- **Kashmir** is the focal point of the conflict between India, Pakistan and China. Territorial disputes are the cause of a number of wars and a nuclear race between India and Pakistan.
- **Indonesia:** The strength of Islam has been increasingly exercised since 1990. Muslims aim to reduce Christian influence. Persecution of Christians, including open violence, has increased.
- **Shia/Sunni mistrust:** The seven-year war between Iran and Iraq in the 1980s and the open conflict between these two groups in Iraq after Saddam Hussein has caused much misery. Millions have lost their lives and almost no family is without tragedy in the horrifying war.

---

[47] The rock in the centre of the Dome is believed by Muslims to be the spot from which Muhammad ascended to Allah, accompanied by the angel Gabriel. It was built between 687 and 691 by the 9th Caliph, Abd al-Malik. For centuries, European travelers have called it the "Mosque of Umar". During the Crusades the Dome of the Rock was given to the Augustinians, who turned it into a church. Jerusalem was recaptured by Salah al-Din in 1187 and it was reconsecrated as a Muslim sanctuary. The cross on top of the Dome of the Rock was replaced by a golden crescent. In Judaism the stone is the site where Abraham fulfilled God's test to see if he would be willing to sacrifice his son Isaac (See Ge 22:1-19). In Christianity, in addition to Jesus' actions in the temple, it is believed that during the time of the Byzantine Empire, the spot where the Dome was later constructed was where Constantine's mother built a small church, calling it the Church of St. Cyrus and St. John, later on enlarged and called the "Church of the Holy Wisdom".

- **Kurds:** 27 million people without a country of their own form a large rebellious minority likely to cause problems in the future–mainly in Turkey, Iraq and Iran.
- In **India,** Muslims number 140 million, making this the second-largest Muslim country. However, they are pressured by the Hindu majority (Muslims 12.5%, Hindu 80%, Christians 2.5%).
- **China** is experiencing an increased influence of Islam and confrontation with other religions. Many Muslims who immigrated to China began to have great economic impact on the country. Under the Ming Dynasty (1368–1644 AD), generally considered to be the golden age of Islam in China, Muslims gradually became fully integrated into Han society. Muslims claim that by 2000 there were about 33,000 mosques in the People's Republic.

Islam in Asia has become less tolerant and more militant where *Shari'a* law has replaced existing legislation in countries such as Afghanistan, Iran, Pakistan, Brunei and the Maldives. Elsewhere, as in Indonesia and Malaysia, Muslims are forcing the introduction of *Shari'a* law despite large non-Muslim populations. In 2000, 27 Asian countries had a Muslim majority. In many countries, the level of persecution of Christians and other minorities has increased dramatically.

While Muslims gain religious rights in the West, persecution of religious minorities by extreme Islamic elements in some Muslim countries in Asia and the Middle East continues unabated. Christians, especially Philippino guest workers, face harassment and intimidation. In Saudi Arabia and other Islamic countries, any attempt to convert a Muslim to another faith is subject to criminal prosecution. Public religious worship by any non-Muslim is a criminal offence. Saudi Arabia once had a large Christian population before the rise of Islam in AD 622. No Christian or any non-Muslim is permitted to set foot in Islam's holiest cities, Mecca

Mosque in Beirut.

and Medina. Every year over two million make the *hajj* or pilgrimage to these cities. Saudi Arabia has one of the world's worst records on religious freedom though its society is straining at the seams as its aged rulers find it increasingly difficult to govern between those pushing for liberalization and those demanding stricter Islamization. A massive Islamic missionary effort is going out from this country. Huge amounts of money are being spent to propagate Islam around the world by building mosques, sending Muslim missionaries, literature, radio, TV programs, internet, etc. The kingdom hosts the biggest Qur'an printing complex in the world.[48]

2) Africa

After the initial conquest of North Africa, Islam came along the East African coast in the 8th century, as part of a continuing dialogue between people on the east coast and traders from the Persian Gulf and Oman. In the early centuries of its existence, Islam in Africa had a dynamic and turbulent history, with reforming movements and dynasties clashing and succeeding each other. Gaining power depended on securing trade routes into gold-producing areas in Sub-Saharan Africa. Islamic rulers expanded north as well as south. However, sub-Saharan Islam was dominated by brotherhoods and mixed with earlier superstitious practices. In the last quarter of the 11th century, Islam dominated the Mediterranean world. From the 16th to the 19th century, much of the Maghreb[49] was under Ottoman rule. By the 1880s, Islam had taken root in many adjacent countries of the continent.

Between 1956 and 1994, all states in Africa became independent from their colonial powers. Over 17% of Africa's population is of Arab origin. The area where most Muslims and Christians live side by side stretches from Senegal across the Sahel to Ethiopia and along Africa's Indian Ocean seaboard. The potential for widened confrontations is high because of increasingly aggressive Islamist movements and African Christian evangelism gaining converts from within Muslim communities. In Sudan and Nigeria this has led to war or mass violence. Other countries such as Guinea-Bissau, Cote d'Ivoire and Chad are in danger of trouble in the future. Persecution of Christians by Muslims has increased in countries such as Egypt, Sudan, northern Nigeria and the Comores. Violent Islamist movements have deeply affected this continent from Algeria in the north to South Africa in the south. Bitter guerrilla warfare in Algeria, terrorist attacks in Kenya and *jihad* against Christians in northern Nigeria are evidences of this.

Muslims in Africa have been steadily gaining converts from traditional religions in countries west of Ghana and across the Sahel. More recently, Muslim missionary efforts have extended to nearly every country in Africa. The use of oil-funded

---

[48] See www.qurancomplex.org
[49] The Maghreb also rendered *Maghrib*, meaning "place of sunset" or "western" in Arabic, is the region of Africa north of the Sahara Desert and west of the Nile, coinciding with the Atlas Mountains. Geopolitically, the area includes Morocco, Algeria, Tunisia, Libya, Western Sahara and sometimes Mauritania, which is often placed in West Africa instead.

education, aid projects, grants and well-organised mission efforts to give Islam a role in Africa's political life has had some success. Islam tolerated some traditional African values, allowing for instance a man to have more than one wife (which the Qur'an also allows), thus making conversion to Islam easier and less upsetting than conversion to Christianity.

To South Africa Muslims came in the 17th Century, initially brought as slaves or political exiles by the Dutch colonists. As a consequence of the political climate in South Africa during the apartheid era, many black Africans looked for alternative religions since the ruling government had often been identified as the "White Christian oppressors". The reality of racism in South Africa was responsible for establishing a negative image of the Christian faith in the minds of many black people. This resulted in a growing interest in Islam as a religion of Africa. African people began to perceive Jesus as the author of racism, not the one who died to break down the dividing wall between peoples. Muslims have taken advantage of this situation and have promoted Islam as "the religion based on equal rights and justice", not only in South Africa but worldwide. Today there are many black Muslims, almost all coming from a traditional Christian background, particularly in Soweto as well as in other areas.[50] In 1957 Deedat founded the IPCI (Islamic Propagation Centre International) in Durban and started to publish literature and videos worldwide which aims to ridicule the Bible and its message, thereby counteracting Christian mission.

3) Europe

The growth of the Islamic population in the western world is mainly due to immigration from the former colonies of the great European powers and the high birth rate of these immigrants. However, the main influx of Muslims to Europe came through immigration from North African countries such as Algeria, from Balkan countries, and especially from Turkey. Most of these Muslims are, however, rather nominal though many become devout and even radical by entering the "world of the infidels" in Europe. Islam is also spread increasingly by Muslim men marrying western women. In most cases, the non-Muslim wives and their children convert to Islam or are pressured to do so. Some in the West are also accepting Islam as their new religion out of conviction. By 2000, many countries had several million Muslims: e.g. France (5 million), Great Britain and Germany (each 3.5 million). Islam is the second-largest religious group in France and Great Britain. Relatively few Muslims living in Europe ever move back to their country of origin as many of them had originally planned.

No accurate statistics exist about the composition of Muslims living in Europe. It is certain that the majority are of Sunni origin. Only a minority belong to the Shiite branch. The unorthodox Ahmadiyya[51] movement is comparatively prominent

---

[50] Maurer 1999:126.
[51] See chapter 1.6.5.

in the western world, in proportion to its worldwide size. This results from the freedom of religion in the western world, as well as the active propaganda operation of this group. Sufism seems to have a continually increasing influence and wide dispersion. Experience shows that western people are more and more interested in, and becoming followers of, this ascetic-mystic branch of Islam. However, western Sufism tends to become quite unorthodox and mixed with New Age movements.

The first generation of immigrants belonged to the lower- and middle-class in their home country. They often came to the west for simple, unqualified work. Their education was far below that of westerners. Even the acquisition of the language of their host countries could cause huge difficulties. This is different for children, however, who learn the language easily and grow up in the culture of their host country. A self-confident and more educated second and third generation exists today.[52]

Elsewhere, Muslims in the West do not form a homogeneous group but have different origins, cultures and languages. An amazing variety of opinions and behaviour with regard to their faith is found. Many only exercise their religion on important Islamic holidays, or turn to religion in crises. Others feel that being a Muslim is not easy in the West, with its Christian background but secular lifestyle perceived to be Christian. Muslims of lower social rank are not necessarily more religious than others. It is clear, however, that young Muslims are often sceptical of traditional Islam which their parents brought with them. Many are searching for a modern and enlightened form of Islam.

As in any other religion, the spectrum of religious convictions by Muslims range from fundamentalist to nominal related in part to the country of origin. Albanians, with little opportunity under communist rule to look into Islam tend to be nominal Muslims, whereas people from a strictly religious environment like Pakistan usually have deeper religious convictions. Muslims from strictly Islamic regions (Iran, Pakistan, Bangladesh, etc.) where the practice of religion is intimately interwoven with the state, have a political understanding different from that of Muslims from former communist countries. Turkey is different again because religion and state are officially separated.

Since the 7th Century a very large area of Russia has been Islamic. Since the demise of the Soviet Union these countries, like Khazakstan, Usbekistan, Turkmenistan and Kirgizstan have become independent states where Islam is now thriving

---

[52] However, new problems arise. For example in France, a large number of Muslims, second and third generations descended from North Africa migrant labourers, are unemployed. They often encounter discrimination due to their origin when hunting for work. This increases social tension and delinquency in the suburbs of the large cities where they live. Due to the rejection they experience in many places-sometimes also from Christians—many young Muslims delve increasingly into Islam.

again. It is estimated that if current trends continue, nearly 20% of Russia's population will be Muslim by 2050. Ethnic Russians have lower birth and higher mortality rates due to alcoholism, while Muslims have higher birth rates and alcohol is considered taboo. Millions of Muslims from the Caucasus and Central Asia have settled in Russia proper. Since 1989, Russia's Muslim population has increased to about 10 million (2000). There has been a growing interest in Islam amongst ethnic Russians as there appears to be a rising number of converts to the faith.

4) Pacific

Before 1950 there were hardly any Muslims in this part of the world. In Australia, Muslims have increased a hundred-fold since 1947 and now constitute 1% of the population—approximately 260,000 from over 70 different countries. Most live in the Sydney and Melbourne areas. Small numbers of Muslims were also recruited from Dutch and British colonies in Southeast Asia to work in the Australian pearling industry in the late 19th and early 20th centuries. Lebanese migrants, many of whom were Muslims, began arriving in larger numbers after the outbreak of civil war in Lebanon in 1975.

5) North America

Between 1989 and 1998 the Islamic population in the United States grew by 25 percent. By 2005, Islam was the second-largest religious group in the USA with about 4.7 million adherent.[53] Muslims moving to the USA are changing the cultural and religious landscape and are fully exercising the rights and freedoms available to them. Islam is gaining most of its US converts in prisons and on university campuses. The majority of American converts to Islam are black. Anglo women make up an another demographic sector with a surprisingly high conversion rate in the USA. Muslims represent a great many movements and identities: immigrant and indigenous, Sunni and Shi'ite, conservative and liberal, orthodox and heterodox. While there were some Muslims among the African slaves who came to work in plantations in the American South in the 18th and 19th centuries, very few retained an Islamic identity.

The earliest Muslim arrivals came between 1875 and 1912 from the rural areas of present-day Lebanon, Syria, Jordan, the Palestinian Authority, and Israel. The area then known as Greater Syria was ruled by the Ottoman Empire. Many of these arrivals were single men in search of work, intending to stay only long enough to earn enough money to support their families back home. Some were fleeing conscription into the Turkish army. Gradually, they began to settle in the eastern United States, the Midwest, and along the Pacific Coast. After World War I, the demise of the Ottoman Empire resulted in a second wave of immigration from the Muslim Middle East. This was also the period of Western colonial rule in the Middle East under the mandate system created to "govern" Arab lands. The war

---

[53] See *Encyclopædia Britannica* Book of the Year (1.5% of national population).

had brought such devastation to Lebanon that many had to flee simply to survive. Significant numbers of Muslims decided to move to the West, now for political as well as economic reasons. Many joined relatives who had arrived earlier and were already established in the United States.

The third identifiable period of immigration, from 1947 to 1960, again saw increasing numbers of Muslims arriving in the United States from areas well beyond the Middle East such as Eastern Europe (primarily Yugoslavia and Albania) and the Soviet Union; a few emigrated from India and Pakistan after the 1947 partition of the Subcontinent. While many of the earlier Muslim immigrants had moved into rural as well as urban areas of America, those in this third wave tended to be from urban backgrounds, and made their homes almost exclusively in major cities such as New York and Chicago.

The fourth and most recent wave of Muslim immigration has come after 1965, the year President Lyndon Johnson sponsored an immigration bill that repealed the longstanding system of quotas by national origin. Under the new system, preferences went to relatives of US residents and those with special occupational skills needed in the United States. The new law was a signal act in American history, making it possible for the first time since the early part of the 20th century for someone to enter the country regardless of his or her national origin. After 1965, immigration from Western Europe began to decline significantly, with a corresponding growth in numbers arriving from the Middle East and Asia. More than half of the immigrants to America from these regions have been Muslim. Among the specific events that have brought immigrants and refugees to the West seeking escape and asylum were the military defeat of Arab states by Israelis in 1967, the civil war in Lebanon and its aftermath.

The Iranian Revolution and ascent to power of Imam Khomeini in 1979, followed by nearly a decade of debilitating war between Iran and Iraq, brought Iranians westward. Many settled in America, with significant numbers relocating in California. It is estimated that there are nearly a million Iranians in the United States today. Since the Iraqi occupation of Kuwait and the Persian Gulf War, large numbers of Kurds have come to the USA. Also newly arrived for reasons of political strife and civil war are Muslims from Somalia, Sudan and other African nations, Afghanistan and Muslim refugees of ethnic cleansing in the former Yugoslavia.

For decades, various forms of strife in India and Pakistan have encouraged many from the Subcontinent to seek a calmer environment in the West. England and the United States have been especially popular destinations. While Pakistanis, Indians, and Bangladeshis have been a small part of the Muslim immigration to America all through the 20th century, in the last several decades their ranks have grown significantly and today probably number more than one million. Pakistani and Indian Muslims, many of whom are skilled professionals such as doctors and engineers, have played an important role in the development of Muslim political groups in America and in lay leadership of mosque communities. Today more and more Muslims are arriving from countries such as Indonesia and Malaysia;

many of these immigrants are also highly trained and often assume positions of leadership in American Islam.

Canada has a small but growing Muslim population. As of 2001, there were 580,000 Muslims in Canada, about 1.8 percent of Canada's population. Islam is the largest non-Christian religion in Canada. The first recorded Islamic presence in Canada was the 1871 census which found 13 Muslims among the population. The years after World War II saw a swift increase in the Muslim population, but in the 1981 census the population was still below 100,000. Since the September 11, 2001 attacks, many Muslims have begun to look to Canada as an alternative to the United States, where anti-Muslim sentiment is perceived as high. This is especially true with international students who have come to Canada in much larger numbers since the attacks.

6) Latin America

In 1900 almost the entire Spanish-speaking population was considered Catholic. In 2000 it was estimated that Brazil's Muslim population ranged from 1–1.5 million including local converts. A very large percentage are Lebanese immigrants who left their country during its civil war.

The history of Muslims in Brazil begins with the importation of African slave labour to the country. Brazil obtained 37% of all African slaves traded; more than three million were sent to this one country. Starting around 1550, the Portuguese began to trade African slaves to work the sugar plantations once the native Tupi were decimated. The Brazilian authorities began to watch the *males* very carefully and, in subsequent years, intensive efforts were made to force conversions to Catholicism in an effort to erase popular memory and affection towards Islam. Following the forced assimilation of the Afro-Brazilian Muslim community, the next period of Islam was primarily the result of Muslim immigration from the Middle East and South East Asia. Some eleven million Syrian and Lebanese immigrants live throughout Brazil; just over ten percent are Muslim while the vast majority claim to be Catholics. The biggest concentration of Muslims is found in the greater São Paulo region, presumed to be home to approximately 500,000 Muslims.

Argentina is home to one of Latin America's largest Muslim populations. Over the past century Argentina has been a centre of immigration for many Arabs, some of whom were Muslim. Other Muslims include immigrants from the Indian Sub-Continent and recent Argentine converts. Today, estimates of the Muslim population in Argentina exceeds half a million people. There is a large mosque in Buenos Aires built in 1989, but there are numerous other mosques in various parts of the country. The King Fahd Islamic Cultural Centre, the largest Islamic project in South America, was completed in 1996 with the help of the Custodian of the Two Holy Mosques, on a piece of land measuring 20,000 square metres. The total land area granted by the Argentine Government measures 34,000 square metres, and was offered by President Carlos Menem following his visit to Saudi Arabia in 1992.

? Questions

- Why was Muhammad at first unsure from which source the revelation came?
- Why did Allah not make it clear who the successor should be after Muhammad?
- Why was it necessary for Muhammad and his followers to build a huge army in order to go to war and kill people who were declared as "unbelievers"?
- Why did Muslims at Muhammad's order kill so many Jews at Medina?
- Since Muslims claim that Muhammad is the final prophet, why was Muhammad not capable of establishing everlasting peace between Muslims, Jews and Christian i.e. people on earth?
- Why did Muhammad not treat people from other faiths as equal, but instead made them second-class citizens (*dhimmi* status)?
- Why do so many Muslims emigrate from their Islamic home country into western countries?
- Why are you a Muslim? Were you born into Islam or did you convert?
- What does it mean to be a Muslim?
- What do you think of people who follow other groups/sects of Islam?

1.2 The Qur'an

1.2.1 Sources

Islam is based on the Qur'an[54] which Muslims believe to be the revelation of Allah.[55] The messages were communicated to Muhammad by an angel named Jibril (Gabriel). In Muslim understanding, the Qur'an is the verbatim revelation of Al-

---

[54] *Qur'an* means "the reading" or rather "the recitation, the discourse" (see Gibb & Kramers 1953:273). This word comes originally not from Arabic but from Syria and was a Christian term meaning "Perikope" (liturgical texts to be read). The majority view among Muslim authorities has been that Qur'an is simply the verbal noun from kara'a, "he read" or "he recited".

[55] On this topic see also Gilchrist (1995).

lah, free of any human influence.[56] Many theological terms and events mentioned in the Qur'an and the tradition[57] had already appeared in pre-Islamic time in the Arabian Peninsula. These are, for example:

- From the **Arabian-pagan tradition**: Allah, *Ka'ba, hajj* (pilgrimage)
- From the **Talmud**[58] **and the Old Testament**: *qibla* (direction of prayer, the Islamic prayer was first directed toward Jerusalem, Sura 2:142-144), stories about Abraham, Satan's refusal to worship Adam, Cain and Abel, Joseph, the Queen of Sheba's visit, seven heavens and six hells. Stories about Moses, David, and Solomon[59]—all grossly distorted.
- From the **Gospels**: Jesus born to the Virgin Mary, John the Baptist, miracles of Jesus Christ, the ascent of Jesus to heaven.
- From the **apocryphal writings of the New Testament**: childhood miracles of Jesus, the cave of the seven sleepers.
- From **eastern sources**: paradise as a sensual place, the scales of justice, the bridge over hell to paradise *(as-Sirat)*.

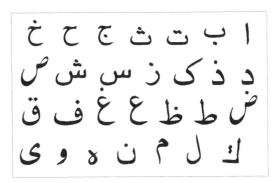

Arabic alphabet.

Since Muhammad was in contact with several religious groups, he absorbed these themes and stories. In some places in the Qur'an, the stories appear in changed form. This would imply that today's Qur'anic text can hardly be the pure "revelation of Allah", since much of its material has been taken from sources of pre-Islamic times rather than constituting the "direct words of Allah".

---

[56] This understanding of revelation is called *"tanzil"*, Arabic for "sending down" or "dictated inspiration of Allah".

[57] The tradition will be explained in section 1.3.

[58] The Talmud is a record of rabbinic discussions pertaining to Jewish law, ethics, customs and history.

[59] Over 60% of the Qur'an is biblical material but grossly distorted. There are loose resemblances rather than direct quotations: Sura 48:29 resembles Mk 4:26-28 (the parable of the seed), Sura 5:44-45 resembles Ex 21:23-25 (the Law of retaliation), Sura 21:105 resembles Ps 37:29.

1.2.2 Origin and transmission

According to Islamic tradition, Muhammad received his first vision at the age of 40 (610 AD). Until his death (632 AD) he received further visions. Bit by bit the Qur'an was revealed by the angel *Jibril* (Gabriel) over a period of 22 years, usually divided into two episodes:

1. The years in Mecca (610–622 AD). During this time, Muhammad preached mainly against idolatry and of Allah's judgment i.e. the reward for the just in paradise, and the punishment of the godless in hell. Muhammad tried to persuade Jews and Christians to vouch for his visions.
2. The years in Medina (622–632 AD). This period lays the foundation and confirmation of Muhammad's supremacy and the organization of the Islamic community (laws). Muslims now had sufficient political power, but Jews did not submit to them in the expected manner. As a consequence, conflict resulted.

Muslim scholars assume that 86 Suras or chapters were revealed in Mecca, and 28 in Medina. At first, Muhammad's words were memorized by his companions. By and by, however, some were written down on various materials e.g. on dried animal skin, stones, and palm leaves. It was not until 23 years after Muhammad's death, at the time of the third caliph Uthman, that the currently available Qur'anic text was composed. All deviating texts in existence were thereupon destroyed.[60] Most Muslims consider the existing text of the Qur'an in Arabic a perfect replica of the "primordial plates"[61], which are allegedly kept in paradise.

1.2.3 Content and important topics

The Qur'an is, for Muslims, the "adored scripture", the final and ultimate message from Allah to humanity,[62] the perfect transcript of the heavenly original, without contradictions and inaccuracies. Muslims are convinced that it also confirms and replaces all previous revelations and sacred books.[63] The Qur'an has crucially affected world history, and shaped Islamic culture. It is the basis of faith, thinking, and law in Islam. It influences the thoughts of Muslims and is the foundation of Islamic social structures. For Muslims, the Qur'an in the Arabic original constitutes the direct word of Allah. Orthodox Muslims are convinced that the Qur'an cannot be accurately translated into other languages but must be read, and learnt by heart, only in Arabic.[64] Thousands of Muslims have memorized the Qur'an; each one is called a *"hafiz"*. The recitation of the Qur'an is reputed to bring blessings and benefits. It is therefore more important to recite the text in Arabic than to understand it.

---

[60] See *Masahif by ibn Abi Dawood, Hadith: Sahih al-Bukhari,* vol.6, p479. On the compilation of the Qur'an see also Jeffery (1975), Gilchrist (1989) and Bukhari Vol. IV, Ch LXI (3) Vs. 509, p477-478 and Mishkat Vol.3 p708.

[61] These plates are also named the "Golden Plates".

[62] The Qur'an is for Muslims what Jesus is for Christians, namely God's last, perfect revelation (see Heb 1:2).

[63] See section 1.5.1 for the books mentioned in the Qur'an.

[64] Contrary to orthodox teaching, liberal Muslims today translate the Qur'an into many languages.

Al-Fatiha, the Opening, (Sura 1) in Arabic and English

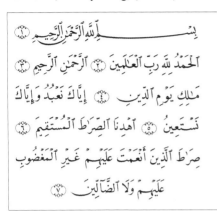

1. In the name of Allah, Most Gracious, Most Merciful.
2. Praise be to Allah, the Cherisher and Sustainer of the Worlds;
3. Most Gracious, Most Merciful;
4. Master of the Day of Judgment.
5. Thee do we worship, and Thine aid we seek.
6. Show us the straight way,
7. The way of those on whom thou hast bestowed thy Grace, those whose is not wrath, and who go not astray.

Many passages of the chapters of the Qur'an supposedly received during Muhammad's time in Mecca are written in a poetic style, and often as the direct speech of Allah. It is divided into 114 Suras (chapters). These are not listed chronologically, but rather by length—with the exception of the first Sura, *Al-Fatiha*, considered the most important and part of the obligatory prayer to be recited 17 times daily. Concerning length, the Qur'an is slightly shorter than the New Testament. Non-Muslims find reading and understanding the Qur'an rather difficult. Yet it is advantageous to read to acquaint oneself with the style and content. Important sections are:

• The sovereignty, dignity and unity of Allah, Sura 2:255.
• The "most beautiful names of Allah", Sura 59:22-24.
• The creation, Suras 3:189-191; 13:2-4; 31:10-11; 32:4-9.
• Heaven and hell, Suras 2:14-25; 38:49-60; 44:47-57.
• Prophets, Sura 2:124-134.

Besides these sections, a whole chapter could be read, e.g., Sura 2 (*al-Baqara*, the cow)[65]. The Qur'an does not go into detail on legal issues, often raising a topic by a short or abstract reference. Besides a few Arabics, some of the most important Biblical characters mentioned are Noah, Abraham, Moses, David, Solomon, Zechariah, Jonah, Jesus and Mary.[66]

---

[65] Each Sura (chapter of the Qur'an) is named for a word or name mentioned in an *ayah* (section), of that ‚Sura'.
[66] It is interesting to note that Mary is the only woman mentioned by name in the entire Qur'an.

1.2.4 The problem of abrogation

The Islamic *Fiqh*[67] teaches also the doctrine of abrogation[68] i.e. earlier revealed verses of the Qur'an are annulled by the revelation of later verses:[69]

> None of Our revelations do We abrogate or cause to be forgotten, but We substitute something better or similar: knowest thou not that Allah hath power over all things? (Sura 2:106)

This principle is often used to explain the validity of the Qur'an over the revelations of previous prophets i.e. the Bible. Few Muslims are actually aware that this doctrine concerns contradictions within the Qur'an. The number of annulled verses is unspecified. An Islamic scholar, *Jalalu'd-Din*, gives a number up to 500.[70] Today, different scholars would identify a maximum of 240 and a minimum of 6 abrogated verses. An important change (abrogation) was, for example, the change of the direction of prayer *(quibla)* from Jerusalem to Mecca (cf Sura 2:142-144), the law of retaliation, inheritance, the punishment of adulterers and many more. The problem is compounded by the fact that in many cases both the abrogated verses *(mansukh)* and their replacement *(nasikh)* are in the Qur'an and, in certain instances, it remains uncertain which is which. It should be noted also that a verse which forbade *jihad* during the "holy months" (Sura 9:5) was abrogated by not less than 124 other verses.

Besides, the doctrine of abrogation is in contradiction to the claim of the Qur'an that the word of Allah (or revelation) cannot be changed (see Suras 6:34; 10:64). One would have to raise the question why Allah deemed it necessary to replace portions of his 'divine' revelation within a very short space of time with "something better"—the situations addressed had not changed.

1.2.5 The "Satanic Verses"

Some recorded traditions *(hadith)* report that Muhammad longed to convert the people of Mecca (who were, after all, his kinsmen and neighbours) to Islam. In order to make his message more palatable, he recited *Al-Najm* (Sura 53), not as revealed to him by the angel Gabriel. Satan had tempted him to utter the following lines after verses 19 and 20 ("Have ye seen Allat and al'Uzza and another, the third (goddess), Manat?"): "These are the exalted Gharaniq, whose intercession is hoped for."

Allat, al'Uzza and Manat were three goddesses worshiped by Meccans. Gharaniq is a *hapax legomenon,* a word found only here. Commentators note that it means Numidian cranes, which fly at a great height. The subtext to this allegation is that

---

[67] *Fiqh* is Islam's verdict or dogmatic theology (see Hughes 1982:128).

[68] Abrogation is a technical term meaning invalidation, rejection, cancelation.

[69] See also Suras 16:101; 17:86; 22:52. The Arabic terms are *mansukh* (annulled; verse that was replaced) and *nasikh* (annulling; verse that replaces another).

[70] See Hughes (1982:520) where a list of 20 verses is given that have been replaced.

Muhammad was backing away from his otherwise uncompromising monotheism by saying that these goddesses were real and their intercession effective.

According to *at-Tabari*,[71] an early Islamic historian, the Meccans were overjoyed to hear this and ceased persecuting Muhammad and his flock, even to the extent of joining the Muslims in ritual prostration. Muslim refugees who had already fled to Abyssinia[72] heard of this and started to return home. The angel Gabriel is reported to have then come to Muhammad and chastise him for adulterating divine scripture, at which point Allah reveals Sura 22:52 to comfort the prophet, reminding him he is no different from those prophets who came before him who were also tempted by Satan. Yet Allah promises to ensure the integrity of his revelation by abrogating what the Devil cast in, which he does by revealing the actual versions of verses 53:21-26, in which the goddesses are belittled. Muhammed takes back his words and the persecution by the Meccans resumed.

Salman Rushdie published in 1988 a novel, *The Satanic Verses*. He was inspired in part by the life of Muhammad and an attempted interpolation in the Qur'an described by *Ibn Ishaq* in his biography of Muhammad (the oldest surviving biographical text). The novel caused much controversy upon its publication, as many Muslims leaders insisted that it contained blasphemous references (which it actually did). Ayatollah Ruhollah Khomeini, the Supreme Shi'a Leader of Iran, issued a *fatwa* (judicial sentence) calling for the death of Rushdie and claimed that it was the duty of every Muslim to obey and kill him, despite never having read the book. On 14th February 1989, the Ayatollah broadcast the following message on Iranian radio: "I inform the proud Muslim people of the world that the author of *The Satanic Verses* book, which is against Islam, the Prophet and the Qur'an, and all those involved in its publication who are aware of its content are sentenced to death." India was the first country to ban the book.

Rushdie's book is a transformed re-narration of the life of Muhammad (called the "Messenger" or "Mahound") in Mecca ("Jahilia" in the novel). At its centre is the episode of the Satanic Verses, in which the Messenger first pronounces a revelation in favour of the polytheistic deities of pre-Islamic Mecca in order to placate and win over the population, but later renounces this revelation as an error induced by Satan. The narrative also presents two fictional opponents of the Messenger: a demonic heathen priestess, Hind, and an irreverent sceptic and satirical poet, Baal. When the Messenger returns to the city in triumph, Baal organises an underground brothel where the prostitutes take on the identities of the Messenger's wives. Also, one of the Messenger's companions claims that he, doubting the Messenger's authenticity, has subtly altered portions of the Qur'an as the Messenger narrated it to him.

---

[71] At-Tabari; born 839, Tabaristan [Iran] died 923, Baghdad, Iraq. Full name: Abu Ja'far Muhammad Ibn Jarir At-tabari. Muslim scholar, author of enormous compendiums of early Islamic history and Qur'anic exegesis who made a distinct contribution to the consolidation of Sunni thought during the 9th century.
[72] Muslim migration to Abyssinia (Arabic: *Habasha*) or modern-day Ethiopia.

? Questions
- Who wrote the Qur'an?
- When and how was the Qur'an written down?
- Why is the Qur'an not written in chronological order? (It would be much easier to understand).
- What is the actual message of the Qur'an? (ask for references—Suras/verses)
- What happens to you as a Muslim, if you do not follow all the teachings of the Qur'an?
- Why are there contradicting verses in the Qur'an?
- Why did Allah not himself make it clear in his word which verses are mansukh (annulled; verse that was replaced) and *nasikh* (annulling; verse that replaces another)? Why did Allah leave this difficult task to the Muslims?
- Is the Qur'an eternal? If yes, how can something eternal be nullified (see law of abrogation)?
- Could Allah not send a final edition of the Qur'an with no need of a law of abrogation?
- What is your point of view on the "Satanic Verses"?
- Why is Mary, the mother of Jesus, the only woman mentioned in the Qur'an? Why is the mother of Muhammad not mentioned?

1.3 The traditions[73]

1.3.1 Necessity

While Muhammad lived, many important questions were resolved on the basis of his visions and judgments. It is said that often these came with perfect timing, i.e. shortly after a problem had occurred. These prophetic visions ceased with his death, since Muhammad is considered to be the last prophet sent by Allah. But the growing Islamic community *(umma)* continued to face new decisions, especially when encountering other cultures. The Qur'an often had no clear answer to these issues. How should such questions be answered, since Muhammad was no longer available to answer through new revelations and as final authority? How should Muslims behave "Islamically" in real life situations? Believing Muslims realized that their prophet's way of life, and the actions of his contemporaries of which he approved, were role models. This way of life was to be imitated as closely as possible. Since these stories from Muhammad's way of life, not found in the Qur'an, had not been collected and written down, scholars found it necessary to do so.

Another problem the Muslim community faces is how to make a *tafsir,* an interpretation of the Qur'an. Many passages are very difficult to comprehend. Other texts need to be interpreted to match unfamiliar situations. Since the Qur'an was

---

[73] In Arabic: as-Sunna, (the tradition).

given to only one person, Muhammad, it is reasoned that he alone was equipped to explain and interpret it. The second important reason for collecting the sayings and acts of Muhammad was thus to preserve these explanations and interpretations for posterity.

1.3.2 Collection of the *hadith*

To preserve the knowledge of Muhammad's way of life, Muslims began after his death to collect and write down his sayings and those events in his life not included in the Qur'an. These mostly orally transmitted anecdotes and incidents are known in English as the "traditions" and may be subdivided into *"hadith"*[74] (sayings, story) and "Sunna"[75] (custom, habit). Today, they are handed down in collections of texts.

The Sunna comprises three categories of actions:
1. Muhammad's actions or omissions.
2. Actions that were performed by a group of Muslims in Muhammad's presence, and therefore considered to be approved by him.
3. Actions that were performed by third parties in Muhammad's presence, of which he approved or did not forbid.

The *hadith* and Sunna contain the transmitted words and actions of Muhammad and his contemporaries and are considered authoritative. However, many traditions were expediently forged to promote a certain doctrine or even personal advantage. Muslim scholars tried to identify false traditions from authentic ones. Muslims soon recognized that many alleged traditions did not trace back to Muhammad or his companions and were therefore not acceptable. About 200 years after Muhammad, some Muslim scholars began to collect and collate them in an effort to identify authentic and false traditions .

Criteria for acceptance as an authentic tradition were:
1. The tradition had to have an irreproachable, complete chain of narrators *(isnad)*.
2. Each narrator in the chain had to be accepted as a reliable and trustworthy informant.
3. The content of the text *(matn)* had to be attested in several places, and contradict no other authoritative tradition.

---

[74] *Hadith* are reports relating to the words and deeds of Muhammad. The Arabic plural is *ahadith*. In English academic usage, *hadith* is often both singular and plural. The terms Sunna and *hadith* are described differently in the literature but in the vernacular are often closely inter-related or used as synonyms. The word *hadith* in its singular form, is also used for the collections of traditions in this publication. (See Hughes 1982:639-645; Gibb & Kramers 1953:116-120).

[75] Sunnah means "way" or "custom", or "the way of the prophet". The word ‚Sunnah' in Sunni Islam means the deeds, sayings and approvals of Muhammad during the 23 years of his ministry. Whatever he did during his ministry as a prophet and messenger of Allah is considered a Sunna, which Muslims received through consensus of companions of Muhammad *(sahaba)* (cf Hughes 1982:622f).

The two most famous collectors of Sunni traditions are *al-Bukhari* (died 870 AD) and *Muslim* (died 875 AD). *Al-Bukhari* collected about 600,000 traditions of the deeds and sayings of Muhammad of which, after examination, he considered only about 7200 to be authentic. Since a good number of these are very questionable, critics today doubt even these. To compensate for this, Muslim researchers have tried to corroborate them; Islamic theology has divided them into categories such as "healthy", "beautiful" or even "weak". The importance of these traditions grew over the course of time and are, for many Muslims, as significant and directive as the Qur'an itself.

1.3.3 Important topics attended to in the *hadith*
The traditions *(hadith)* talk about various issues of daily life:
• Religious matters: prayer, pilgrimage, fasting, holy war, God's predestination.
• Family life: inheritance, marriage, and divorce.
• Economic matters: contracts, commerce, banking.
• Personal hygiene: cleanliness, shaving, use of perfume, brushing one's teeth.

Different interpretations of the *hadith* and disagreements about its detailed practical application exist between various Islamic groups. Time and again, this leads to conflicts and tensions.

Some examples of *hadith*[76]

1) A *hadith* relating to a rather amazing part of the process of compiling the Qur'an:

   Narrated Anas bin Malik: Uthman sent to every Muslim province one copy of what they had copied, and ordered that all the other Quranic materials, whether written in fragmentary manuscripts or whole copies, be burned (6:479; 61.3.510).

   The Islamic leadership had spoken, but this *hadith* shows an extreme act of destruction of evidence! Who can be sure that these human beings at that time of history acted within a framework of absolute inerrancy? Islamic vulnerability seems quite obvious to most Western scholars.

2) Another *hadith* reports on sin and forgiveness:

   Narrated Aisha: I heard the Prophet and listened to him before his death while he was lying supported on his back, and he was saying, "O Allah! Forgive me, and bestow Your Mercy on me, and let me meet the highest" (5:511; 59,81.715).

   The Qur'an has a number of references to Muhammad repenting from sin.[77] It also appears that his salvation was dependent on repentance of sins, asking

---

[76] These examples are taken from the book by Parshall (1994), using Al-Bukhari's collection. The citation used is as follows: (6:479; 61.3.510): Six is the volume; 479, the page number. The book is 61, the chapter is 3, and the number of the tradition is 510. This style of citation should enable the reader to find any *hadith,* no matter which Al-Bukhari collection is used.
[77] See Suras 47:19; 48:2.

for forgiveness, on good deeds and the mercy of Allah-a formula followed by most Muslims throughout the centuries. And yet it is almost unanimously accepted by Muslims that Muhammad was sinless.

3) There are also many *hadith* on fasting. One shows the seriousness of missing one day of fasting (although this is quite common among Muslims).

> Narrated Abu Huraira from the Prophet: "Whoever did not fast for one day of Ramadan without a genuine excuse or a disease, then even if he fasted for a complete year, it would not compensate for that day" (3:88; 31.29.155).

4) Concerning the pilgrimage *(hajj)*, the following *hadith* explains why Muslims aim to kiss the black stone at Mecca: simply because Muhammad did:

> Narrated Abis bin Rabi'a: Umar came near the Black Stone and kissed it and said, "No doubt, I know that you are a stone and can neither benefit anyone nor harm anyone. Had I not seen Allah's Apostle kissing you I would not have kissed you" (2:390;26.49.667).

5) There are also many *hadith* on *jihad* and violence. The next two explain why the followers of Muhammad are highly motivated to wage battle against non-believers: Muhammad himself is reported to have killed people. As one reads these words of emotional intensity, one cringes at the devastating potential of religious devotion. Fighting and killing is portrayed as a beloved activity!

> Narrated Ibn Abbas: Allah's Wrath became severe on him whom the Prophet had killed in Allah's cause. Allah's Wrath became severe on the people who caused the face of Allah's Prophet to bleed (5:277; 59.23.401).
> Narrated Hisham: My father informed me that Aisha said, "Sa'd said, 'O Allah! You know that there is nothing more beloved to me than to fight in Your Cause against those who disbelieved Your Apostle and turned him out (of Mecca)" (5:309; 59.29.448).

6) In the next *hadith,* Muhammad has a prophetic vision relating to the day of judgment and observed that the majority of people in hell are women:

> Narrated Usama: The Prophet said, "I stood at the gate of the Fire and found that the majority of the people entering it were women" (8:363; 76.51.555).

7) Paradise is described by the Qur'an as well as many *hadith* with picturesque language. There will be no unclean bodily functions and no illness. It is written as if there will only be men in paradise to enjoy these special privileges. Each man will possess two wives. Other non-Bukhari *hadith* mention 72 wives for each man. These are the *hur* (houris) who are said to be special creations of God for the eternal enjoyment of Muslim men.

> Narrated Abu Huraira: Allah's Apostle said, "The first group of people who will enter Paradise, will be glittering like the full moon, and those who will follow them, will glitter like the most brilliant star in the sky. They will not urinate, re-

lieve nature, spit, or have any nasal secretions. Their combs will be of gold, and their sweat will smell like musk. The aloes-wood will be used in their censers. Their wives will be houris. All of them will look alike and will resemble their father Adam (in stature), sixty cubits tall" (4:343; 55.1.544).

8) There are all kinds of other *hadith* where Muhammad gives certain orders. A rather strange one is reported where his followers are ordered to drink the milk and urine of camels and thus become healthy. This *hadith* is repeated several times in the Al-Bukhari collection.

Narrated Anas: The climate of Medina did not suit some people, so the Prophet ordered them to follow his shepherd, i.e. his camels, and drink their milk and urine. So they followed the shepherd and drank their milk and urine until their bodies became healthy (7:399;71.6.590).

9) Towards the end of his life, Muhammad became more and more bitter against Jews and Christians. Just before his death, he cursed them:

Narrated Aisha: When the last moment of the life of Allah's Apostle came he started putting his khamisa (blanket) on his face and when he felt hot and short of breath he took it off his face and said, "May Allah curse the Jews and Christians for they built the places of worship at the graves of their Prophets." The Prophet was warning (Muslims) of what those had done (1:255;8.55.427).

1.3.4 Differences between Sunni and Shi'a traditions
The different Islamic groups have different opinions concerning the authenticity of various traditions which appear authentic and reject the others. Here only the two major groups are briefly discussed:

1) *Hadith* **accepted by Sunni Muslims:** The Sunni canon of *hadith* took its final form close to three centuries after the death of Muhammad. Later scholars may have debated the authenticity of a particular *hadith*, but the authority of the canon as a whole was not questioned. However, in recent times the number of scholars and intellectuals who question that authority is growing rapidly. This canon, called the *Six major hadith collections*, includes:
1. Sahih Bukhari, collected by al-Bukhari (d. 870), included 7275 *ahadith*
2. Sahih Muslim, collected by Muslim b. al-Hajjaj (d. 875), included 9200
3. Sunan Abi Da'ud, collected by Abu Da'ud (d. 888)
4. Sunan al-Tirmidhi, collected by al-Tirmidhi (d. 892)
5. Sunan al-Sughra, collected by al-Nasa'i (d. 915)
6. Sunan Ibn Maja, collected by Ibn Maja (d. 886).

Sahih Bukhari and Sahih Muslim are usually considered the most reliable of these collections. There is some debate among scholars over whether the sixth member of this canon should be Ibn Maja or the *Muwatta* of Imam Malik.

2) *Hadith* accepted by Shi'a Islam: Shi'a Muslims trust traditions transmitted by Muhammad's descendents through Fatima, or by early Muslims who remained faithful to Ali ibn Abi Talib. Shi'a distrust traditions transmitted by early Muslims who were hostile to Ali-Muslims such as Aisha, Muhammad's widow, who opposed Ali at the Battle of the Camel.

There are various schools within Shi'a Islam, each with its own traditions of scholarship and framework for accepting and rejecting *ahadith*. Four prominent Shi'a collections are known as "The Four Books".[78]

? Questions
- How were the *hadith* collected?
- Why is it necessary for Muslims to consult the *hadith* (traditions) in respect of questions of faith? Is the Qur'an not comprehensive enough?
- Is the Qur'an alone, the *hadith*—or both—the eternal word of Allah?
- How do you know which *hadith* is authentic and trustworthy?
- Who determines which *hadith* are to be followed today?
- Which main tradition do you follow (Bukhari, Muslim, Tirmizi, ...)?
- What happens if you do not observe essential traditions?

1.4 Islamic law *(Shari'a)*

1.4.1 Origin
The Arabic word *Shari'a* denotes the way one should follow or the "way to a place rich in water". It is the way that Allah himself showed through Muhammad. Muhammad died without making arrangements for the future leadership of the Muslim community, nor did he give an all-embracing body of rules for the solution of legal questions to his followers. With the expansion of the Islamic empire and the growing time distance from Muhammad, new questions of legal practice arose. Judicial issues in the Qur'an were insufficient to procure a legal code. To solve this problem, Muslims have adopted over the course of time the view that all of Muhammad's life style and behaviour (Sunna) were determined by Allah's inspiration. Therefore, only those traditions (*hadith*) which could be traced back to Muhammad himself were accepted as binding. This is why the traditions stand, for many Muslims, on an almost equal footing with the Qur'an as Allah's revelation. If Muhammad really is the role model of the Islamic community, it is only logical that his sayings and his behaviour are binding for all Muslims. The Sunna, as defined at that time, became, in addition to the Qur'an, the second authoritative source of Islamic law.

---

[78] "The Four Books" (Arabic *Al-Kutub Al-Arb'ah*) is a Shi'a term referring to their four best-known *hadith* collections: 1) Kitab Al-Kafi of Kulayni, 2) Man la Yahdhuruhu'l Faqih of Shaikh Saduq, 3) Tahdhibu'l Ahkam by Abu Ja'far al-Tusi, 4) Al-Istibsar by Abu Ja'far al-Tusi.

During the 19th and more so the 20th century, the history of Islamic law changed due to new challenges facing the Muslim world. The West had grown into a global power and colonized a large part of the world, including Muslim territories. Many societies underwent transition from the agricultural to the industrial stage. New social and political ideas emerged and social models slowly shifted from hierarchical towards egalitarian. The Ottoman Empire in particular, but also the rest of the Muslim world was in decline. Calls for reform became louder. In Islamic countries, codified state law started replacing the role of religious legal opinion. Western countries sometimes inspired, sometimes pressured, and sometimes forced Muslim states to change their laws. Secularist movements pushed for laws deviating from the opinions of the Islamic legal scholars who remained the sole authority for guidance in matters of ritual, worship, and spirituality, but they lost authority to the state in other areas. The Muslim community divided into groups that reacted differently to the changes:

- **Secularists** believe the law of the state should be based on secular principles, not on Islamic legal theory.
- **Traditionalists** believe that the law of the state should be based on traditional legal schools. However, traditional legal views are considered unacceptable by most modern Muslims, especially in areas like women's rights or slavery.
- **Reformers** believe that new Islamic legal theories can produce modernized Islamic law and lead to acceptable opinions in areas such as women's rights.
- **Salafis** believe that the traditional schools were wrong, and therefore failed; they strive to follow the generation of early Muslims.

1.4.2 The four authorities

How should Muslims decide when problems arise for which neither the Qur'an nor the *hadith* reveal a solution? A way out is found in the principle of *ijtihad* (usage of human reason) i.e. the formulation of a decision or a rule of conduct based on the authoritative sources of law (the Qur'an and the Sunna). As a consequence, *qiyas* and *ijma* became the third and fourth method of finding justice. In the three centuries after Muhammad's death, Islamic jurists[79] built an all-embracing legal system whose principles of jurisprudence emerged from a mixture of tradition and legal practice. They consist of four elements:

1. **Qur'an:** This first source is considered to be the most important base of Islamic law.
2. **Sunna:** The customs and sayings of the Prophet, as available in the collections of *hadith*.
3. **Qiyas:** Newly arising cases are solved via conclusion by analogy, using the rules of logical deduction and following known cases.
4. **Ijma:** If there are still cases that cannot be solved by the Qur'an, the *hadith* or via conclusion by analogy, the consensus of the Islamic community is au-

---

[79] The main founder of this jurisprudence is the famous jurist Muhammad ibn Idris as-Shafii (d 820 AD).

thoritative. In practice, this consensus is limited to the agreement of Muslim theologians.[80]

These four basic components are used in descending order to resolve any legal question. Opinions on interpretation and application, however, differ among theologians and Muslim communities. The Sunni, for example, have developed four schools of law. Each Sunni Muslim belongs to one of these schools and adheres to its rules. The schools are named by students of the classical jurist who taught them and are commonly found in these regions:

- **Hanafites:** Turkey, the Balkans, Central Asia, Indian subcontinent, China and Egypt.
- **Malikites:** North Africa, West Africa and several Arab Gulf States.
- **Shafi'ites:** Indonesia, Malaysia, Egypt, East Africa, Yemen and southern parts of India.
- **Hanbalites:** Arabia.

These four schools share many laws, but differ on the particular *hadiths* they accept as authentic and the weight given to analogy or reason *(qiyas)* in deciding difficult questions. The Jaferi school (found in Iran, Iraq, Lebanon, Bahrain, Pakistan, and parts of Afghanistan and Saudi Arabia) is associated with Shi'a Islam. *Fatwas* are taken more seriously in this school, due to the more hierarchical structure of Shia Islam, ruled by the Imams. They are also more flexible, in that every jurist has considerable power to alter a decision according to his own opinion.

1.4.3 Practical application

The *Shari'a* contains not only religious commandments but aims for public acceptance and joint realization.[81] In fact, it can only be applied in a country governed by Islam. Muslims in the West become grievously aware of this and pressure groups push aggressively to incorporate *Shari'a* law into Western law or, alternatively, to apply the *Shari'a* to all Muslims in those countries. Wherever the ritual commandments on prayer, food or marriage and family life are concerned, time and again they notice that, in the West, they are a minority in a non-Islamic secularized society. Three possibilities are open to them:

1) **Islamists:** They live in a segregated way and try to obey the laws as well as they can. Contact with the western world is avoided as much as possible (ghetto mentality). This type of Islam is also called radical Islam, political Islam, Islamism or Islamic fundamentalism.

---

[80] This teaching is based on a *hadith* that determines the following: When the vast majority of Muslims agree about a certain matter, this is correct, and corresponds to Allah's will. There are differences between Sunni and Shi'a Muslims concerning establishing the law.

[81] The *Shari'a* rules virtually all behaviour patterns of practical day-to-day life e.g. marriage, dietary laws, posture and pattern of prayer, etc. According to Muslim scholars, Islam can be divided in five areas: faith *(I'tiqadat)*, ethics *(Adab)*, piety *('Ibada)*, business *(Mu'amalat)*, punishments *('Uquhat)*. The law consists of the latter three terms (see also Hughes 1982:285-292 and Gibb & Kramers 1953:524-529).

2) **Liberalists:** They live according to the view that the *Shari'a* is valid only on a limited scale in a non-Islamic country. Liberal Muslims choose freely which laws they want to obey and which ones are inconvenient to keep in their present situation.

3) **Modernists:** Without questioning the place of the Qur'an and Sunna, they try to find a new interpretation of the *Shari'a*. This is considered to be a contemporary advancement of the law based on the principle of *ijtihad*.[82] Modernist Muslims justify for instance the use of computers, although Muhammad never had one![83]

There are great differences between points of view of Islamists, Liberalists and Modernists in respect of application of the law which contribute further to the struggle within and amongst Muslim groups.

1.4.4 Contemporary practice

Sunnis and Shi'as disagree on the authority to issue fatwas and how each side views the *hadith, Shari'a, Fiqh* (Islamic jurisprudence and authority structures). As a result, there is tremendous variance in the interpretation and implementation of Islamic law in Muslim societies today. Liberal movements have questioned the relevance and applicability of *Shari'a* from a variety of perspectives. Several countries with the largest Muslim populations, including Indonesia and Bangladesh, have largely secular constitutions and laws, with only a few Islamic provisions in family law. Turkey has a constitution that is (still) strongly secular. India is the only country so far which has separate Muslim civil laws, framed by the Muslim Personal Law board and wholly based on *Shari'a*, though criminal laws are uniform. Some controversial laws are thought to favour men over women, including rejection of alimony and polygamy (one man having up to four wives).

Most countries of the Middle East and North Africa maintain a dual system of secular courts and religious courts, which mainly regulate marriage and inheritance. Saudi Arabia and Iran maintain religious courts for all aspects of jurisprudence, and religious police enforce social compliance. Laws derived from *Shari'a* are also applied in Sudan, Libya and Afghanistan. Some districts in northern Nigeria have reintroduced *Shari'a* courts, meaning most often the re-introduction of relatively harsh punishment without respecting the much tougher rules of evidence and testimony. Punishments include amputation of one or both hands for theft, stoning for adultery, and execution for apostasy.

Many consider the punishments prescribed by *Shari'a* as barbaric and cruel; Islamic scholars argue that, if implemented properly, the punishments serve as a deterrent to crime. In international media, practices by countries applying Islamic

---

[82] However, in Sunni Islam, the *bab al ijtihad* (door to the finding of justice) is deemed to have been closed in the 10th century.

[83] Though it must be said, that the "radicals" also use modern things, at least temporarily, in order to spread Islam.

law have fallen under considerable criticism particularly when the sentence carried out is seen as opposite to standards of morality and internationally accepted human rights. This includes the death penalty for adultery, amputations for theft and flogging for fornication.

1.4.5 *Adat* law

Adat[84] law is a set of local and traditional laws and dispute resolution systems in Islamic countries. It has been developed and instituted in many parts of Indonesia. In older Malay language, *adat* refers to the customary laws and unwritten traditional code regulating social, political, and economical as well maritime laws. One of the most important scholars of *adat* law was Cornelis van Vollenhoven.

Derived from the Arabic *'ada*, is generally use for "custom, practice, use and wont". The application of the word is extended to all that an individual or a community has become accustomed to. Animals too have their *adat*. An *adat* can never be neglected without misgivings from the community. The Muslim peoples of Indonesia are often conscious of the difference between the Islamic parts of their *adat* and the native *adat*. Differences between them have led in several instances to fanatical outbursts and conflicts.

Adat law is not easy to discover and collect. The native written sources are basically edicts of the local chiefs. Law books are not to be judged according to Western thinking. They come from jurists laying down their own opinions, not always in agreement with customary law. Often an *adat* law is added to the Sunni *Shari'a* law. For example, a marriage may be contracted according to the *Shari'a* and then followed by a celebration in *adat* law. From an Islamic point of view, the validity of the marriage is completely secured by following the *Shari'a*. In practice, the omission of the celebration often results in invalidity of the marriage.

 Questions

- What does *"Shari'a"* mean?
- Of what elements does the *Shari'a* consist?
- Is the *Shari'a* made by men or by Allah?
- How do you know which laws are sent by Allah and which are made by men?
- Why are there such great differences in applying the law amongst Islamic countries, such as Tunisia compared to Saudi Arabia?
- Why is the *Shari'a* in most cases to the advantage of men and to the disadvantage of women?
- How do you know what is *Shari'a* and what is *adat* law?

---

[84] See also Gibb & Kramers (1953:14).

1.5 Islamic teaching on faith and duty

The Arabic word "Islam" connotes "submission, surrender and obedience".[85] The verb is *aslama*, meaning "to surrender". Allah expects humans to acknowledge him in his greatness and majesty, to submit to him and obey him. Islam means self-surrender, which includes the expectation that, by this surrender, man gains peace. The word Muslim (meaning the person who surrenders his life to the will of Allah) is also formed from the same root *(slm)*. A Muslim is not following a religion but a complete way of life, with guidance provided by Allah which governs all aspects of individual and corporate living.

Islam, like other religions, has a classification of things its followers are supposed to believe and do. In Islamic theology, this is very distinct; the teaching of faith *(iman)* comprises six articles, and the practice of religion *(din)* contains five duties.

1.5.1 The Six Articles of faith

Five of the six articles of faith (iman) are mentioned in Sura 2:177:
> "It is not righteousness that ye turn your faces towards East or West, but it is righteousness to believe in Allah and the Last Day, and the Angels, and the Book, and the Messengers…"

Each Muslim is obliged to believe in the following six articles:[86]

1) **Allah (God):** There is only one true and unique God, and there are no other gods beside him *(Tawhid)*: Allah (Sura 112). "He has no partner in his divinity, no son and no wife, he has not, and was not, conceived. Allah is eternal. Allah is separated from the created; he resembles the creatures in no way." Allah is almighty and omniscient. In Islam, the oneness and uniqueness of Allah is strongly emphasized: there are 99 wonderful names which denote Allah.[87]

2) **The Angels** *(malak*; plural: *mala'ika)*[88]: An unknown number of angels exist, among them four archangels[89]. The devil (the Satan, *Shaitan*) is a fallen angel. The *jinn*[90] are beings that have a status between angels and humans and are either good or bad. Angels have different functions. Two are assigned to each human—one records good deeds, the other records bad deeds. It is the task

---

[85] Other literal meanings from this root word *(slm)* are "safe, secure, peace".

[86] Though there are similarities, one has to be aware that as a whole the Christian teaching on these concepts are different!

[87] See Hughes (1982:141-142) and Gibb & Kramers (1953:33-37) for the 99 names of Allah, further explanations and corresponding Qur'an verses.

[88] The Qur'an offers no information from what angels and *jinns* are created. Fire or light are given in the traditions (cf Hughes 1982:134).

[89] The names of the four archangels in the Qur'an are: Gabriel (bearer of the revelations), Michael (guardian angel), Israfil (will announce the Last Judgement), Izrail (angel of death); cf Suras 2:97-98; 19:19; 32:11; 35:1). The *hadith* names more angels.

[90] The vague ideas of old Arabic paganism about these desert spirits are, in orthodox Islam, clarified, systematized, and coordinated with the other statements of faith.

of the two angels of interrogation, *Munkar* and *Nakir*, to ask each human being after death examination questions that will decide his immediate future fate.[91]

3) **The Books of Allah** (*Kutub* Allah): It is assumed that Allah has sent many revelations via various prophets throughout history. Some of the writings are mentioned in the Qur'an: the pages of Abraham (considered lost), the Thora (*Taurat*) of Moses, David's Psalms *(Zabur)*, the Gospel *(Injil)* of Jesus, and the Qur'an of Muhammad (Suras 4:163; 7:157; 17:46). According to Muslim perception, the Thora, the Psalms, and the Gospel have been corrupted by Jews and Christians. Only the Qur'an, as the final revealed word of Allah is authentic and thus superior to all other books (Sura 4:47; 5:15).

4) **The prophets** (Sura 35:24): According to the *hadith*, about 124,000 prophets have existed. The Qur'an mentions about 25 prophets by name, 21 of whom are biblical.[92] Islamic theology distinguishes between two types of "prophets": 1) *Nabi* (literally: prophet), one who receives a revelation; 2) *Rasul* (literally: apostle, emissary), one who receives a book of Allah, and the task to pass it on to a specific people group. The last and greatest of all Allah's prophets is according to Islamic teaching Muhammad who was both *nabi* and *rasul*.[93]

5) **The Last Day** (Suras 2:62; 4:55-57; 56:50): This is the day of judgment (*Yaumu'd-Din*) and resurrection (*Yaumu'l-Qiyama*) when it is determined, on the basis of deeds performed, who is going to paradise and who is going to hell. Those who have obediently followed Allah and Muhammad are supposedly accepted into Islamic paradise, a place of sensual pleasures.[94] Regarding hell, the Qur'an gives no consistent teaching. Sura 19:71-72, the *hadith* and many commentators say that people go to hell for a short time, to pay for their sins.[95] Other Qur'an verses, such as Sura 74:26-30, seem to indicate rather that hell is final.

6) **Predestination** *(Qadar)*: The question of the degree of human free will versus the predestination by Allah of man's destiny was heavily disputed, especially in the first three centuries of Islam. The Qur'an teaches an all-embracing Allah

---

[91] The four questions are: Who is your God? What is your religion? Who is your prophet? What is your direction of prayer? If the believer gives the correct answers (Allah, Islam, Muhammad, Mecca), he is left alone, but he is tormented for wrong answers.

[92] Six prophets are distinguished in the Qur'an with honorary names: Adam, Allah's chosen one; Noah, Allah's preacher; Abraham, the friend of Allah; Moses, the one who talked with Allah; Jesus, the word and the spirit of Allah; and Muhammad, the messenger of Allah.

[93] The *Ahmadiyya* group, however, has another, greater prophet: their founder *Mirza Ghulam Ahmad.*

[94] The Islamic understanding [of paradise] can be mainly called a "paradise for men", who lie on soft couches and drink wine served by heavenly virgins. In paradise, each man is allowed to marry as many of these virgin women as he wants (Suras 55:54-56; 56:27-40). According to one tradition, most women go to hell (Sahih Muslim, Vol 4, *hadith* 6597, p1432).

[95] In the Qur'an, hell is usually talked of as "fire". The place of torture is supposed to have seven gates and departments (cf Hughes 1982:170-173).

ordained predestination of all events in the world (Sura 9:51). The intention is to uphold the absolute sovereignty of God under all circumstances. Therefore, Islam (submission) is the primary virtue of pious humans, and "*in sha' Allah*" (if God is willing) is a common expression.[96] The question arises how just Allah is when he holds humans accountable for their trespasses, since whatever they think, say or do is predetermined by Allah. The Qur'an teaches clearly that man has no choice in determining his life:

"Allah leads astray whom he pleases and he guides whom he wills, *but you will surely have to account for all your actions* (verbal translation)...He sends whom he will astray...He forgives whom he pleases and he punishes whom he pleases" (Suras 5:18, 14:4, 16:93).

The *hadith* confirms this in no uncertain terms:
"When he creates a servant for hell, he keeps him engaged in the actions of the inmates of hell till he dies (Mishkat III page 107)...Verily Allah has fixed the very portion of adultery which a man will indulge in, and which he of necessity must commit" (al-Bukhari LV ch 27 v 621, or Vol IV p410).

1.5.2 The Five Duties of Islam

The five duties[97] are the "rope of Allah", to which one has to cling if one wants to be considered an orthodox Muslim. They are the practical ritual duties a Muslim must obey, a kind of identity card.

1) **The profession of faith** (*Shahada*, also called *kalima*): "I bear witness that there is no god but God (Allah), and that Muhammad is Allah's messenger". The intentional[98] repetition of this sentence in front of two witnesses makes a person irrevocably a Muslim. This creed is repeated many times during the five daily ritual prayers. Its repetitive proclamation is the most important rite in Islam.

2) **Prayer** (*salat*, Sura 17:78-79, also called *namaz*): Every Muslim is obliged to pray five times daily,[99] repeating a cycle of prescribed prayers accompanied by a *rak'a*, an exactly prescribed prostration. In all, 17 of these liturgical prayers are recited daily. Preparatory ritual washing is required for salat, performed alone or in company with others. If space is available, a separate prayer room is provided in the mosque for women.[100] Often, however, women pray at home. Personal, spontaneous prayer *(dua)* is of no legal consequence as a fulfillment

---

[96] Hence the proverbial fatalism of Muslims, which incites them on the one hand to fearless bravery, and on the other hand to inactive acceptance of the status quo, with a resistance or apathy towards change.

[97] These duties are called "the five pillars of Islam", or simply "the pillars" (*arkan al-Islam*).

[98] That is, with the intention to avow oneself a Muslim.

[99] Prayer times: at first light, at mid-day, in the afternoon, shortly after sunset, two hours after sunset.

[100] The requirement is not to be seen by men while women pray. In Islamic countries, few mosques have prayer facilities for women, whereas in the West it is more common that mosques allow for women to pray.

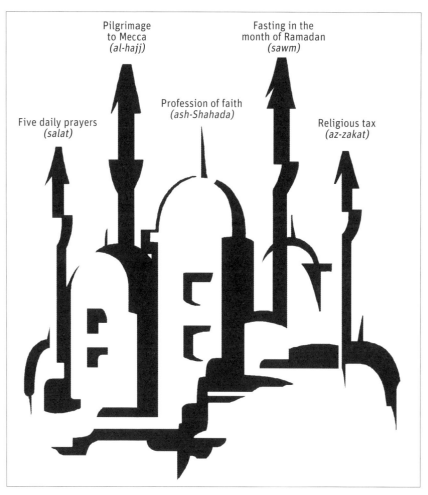

Pilgrimage
to Mecca
(al-hajj)

Fasting in the
month of Ramadan
(sawm)

Profession of faith
(ash-Shahada)

Five daily prayers
(salat)

Religious tax
(az-zakat)

The five Pillars of Islam.

of religious requirements, nor does it gain merit with Allah. The required ritual prayer *(salat)*, on the other hand, consisting of prayer formulas and recitations from the Qur'an, is considered a good deed before Allah. People pray in exactly prescribed postures, facing Mecca.[101] The call of the muezzin *(adhan)* summons Muslims to prayer. On Friday, at the time of the mid-day prayer, the imam gives an address *(khutba)*, a kind of sermon.

---

[101] In the mosque, the *imam* leads the prayers. His movements are repeated by all believers and his words are echoed by all.

3) **Religious tax** (Almsgiving, *zakat*, Sura 2:177): The religious tax of Muslims has been partly transformed into a "tax for the poor". The Qur'an emphasizes "giving"[102] but makes no detailed statements regarding the amount. That depends on the wealth and annual income of the male head of the family. There are provisions for peasants and farmers to give animals. 2.5 percent (e.g. for items of trade) is a general guideline, but it can be up to 20% of net profit in particularly successful situations.[103]

4) **Fasting** (*sawm*, Sura 2:183-187): During the month of Ramadan[104], fasting is compulsory for all Muslims except sick persons, travelers, menstruating and pregnant women, nursing mothers and small children. The fast is from sunrise until sunset.[105] It includes abstinence from smoking and sexual intercourse during daylight hours. A breach of fasting is considered a serious offence, but can be made up by good deeds or by paying a certain amount of money. Children usually start fasting at puberty after the age of nine. Fasting is meant to promote self-discipline, devotion to Allah and a better understanding of the lot of the poor.

5) **Pilgrimage** (*hajj*, Sura 2:196-197): All Muslims with sufficient financial means have to undertake the pilgrimage to Mecca at least once in their lifetime.[106] This pilgrimage takes place in the twelfth month *(Dhu l-Hijja)* of the Islamic lunar calendar. During the stay in Mecca, strictly prescribed rituals have to be

---

[102] See Suras 2:271-273; 92:5-11.
[103] If, for example, someone finds a treasure, he has to pay 20% *zakat* (see Hughes 1982:699-700).
[104] Ramadan is the ninth month of the Islamic lunar calendar.
[105] Eating and drinking is permitted during nighttime. Many Muslims hold social gatherings at their home at night, so that in many cases more is eaten and drunk in this month than in any other.
[106] The number of Muslims has so increased worldwide that it became necessary for the Saudi government to endorse restrictions: each country has a certain quota of pilgrims to be sent each year.

performed.[107] The most important is standing on the Arafat plain, where Muslims spend time in meditation and invocations to Allah. Another highlight of the *hajj* is the seven-fold walk around the *Ka'ba*, which is dressed in precious coverings. It is assumed to have first been built as a sanctuary by Adam. It was then reconstructed by Abraham and his son Ishmael. If possible, the pilgrims should kiss the black stone built into one corner of the *Ka'ba*.[108] Further obligations are the symbolic stoning of the devil with seven pebbles and the slaughter of a sacrificial animal in remembrance of Abraham's sacrifice.[109]

> **! Basic sequence of challenging questions to Muslims:**
>
> 1) While Muslims are often eager to share how they practice their faith, you may pick a topic and ask: **"Why are you doing this?"** e.g. pray five times daily, go to Mecca, keep the fast during Ramadan, etc. Challenge Muslims and let them find an answer.
>
> 2) Muslims will give different answers, but I would pose a second question: **"Where is it written? What is the basis for that?"**
>
> 3) Muslims usually reply that it is written in the Qur'an. Then I ask: **"Can you please give me the exact reference, chapter and verse, where this is written?"** (You may say that you have yourself access to a Qur'an and are interested to read it for yourself).
> The Muslim is then encouraged to find out (by himself or through a learned person) what the truth is. In my experience, many things Muslims claim are written in the Qur'an are in fact not there but perhaps in the *hadith* or elsewhere. This encourages many Muslims to research further and think more carefully.

1.5.3 *Jihad* in Islam

In addition to the five duties of Islam, *jihad* is sometimes listed as a sixth duty. This word is usually translated as "holy war"[110] by the Western media. The Arabic term (verb: *jahada*) means "effort in Allah's way", or "striving in faith". Some Muslims make the following distinction:

1) Greater *jihad*: Inner striving for personal perfection imposed by the Qur'an and the *hadith*.

2) Lesser *jihad*: Effort to propagate Islam worldwide and introduce the *Shari'a* in every country.

---

[107] The rituals are similar to those Muhammad performed during his last pilgrimage in 629 AD and which are declared canonic for all time.

[108] The stone is most likely a meteor. Muslims say that it was, in former times, white, but it turned black because of the sins passed on by the Muslims who kissed it.

[109] For more detailed descriptions of the *hajj* see Hughes (1982:155-159), and Gibb & Kramers (1953:121-125).

[110] In the Medina era (622-632 AD), marked by numerous warlike conflicts, the term *"jihad"* is to be equated with *"fight"* (cf Suras 9:41; 49:15; 66:9).

For most Muslims keeping the "greater *jihad*" basically means aiming to perform the "Five Duties of Islam" in praxis as well as possible and to believe in the "Six Articles of faith". But it also means to know the teachings of the Qur'an and the *hadith* and to keep its commands, summed up in the *Shari'a*.

The "lesser *jihad*" concept includes the territorial spread of Islam. It is important to understand the fundamental difference between Islam and the Christian faith. The Muslim concept of Allah's kingdom on Earth is that he must rule the world. Islam is not primarily concerned with leading people to a trust and faith in Allah; Allah wants submission, which can happen only when people live under the rule of the *Shari'a*. That can only happen in a state governed by Muslims. It is therefore of crucial importance that Muslims gain control over each country on Earth, as the Qur'an teaches:

> And fight them on until there is no more tumult or oppression, and there prevail justice and faith in Allah altogether and everywhere ... (Sura 8:39; cf 2:193).

This text is understood to be Allah's command to promote Islam. In Muslim eyes tumult and oppression, unbelief and injustice prevail in every country not under Islamic control. Militant Muslims use every means at hand to spread Islam, including physical force. Their world is divided into two parts:[111]

- **Dar al-Harb** (house of war): Areas of the world that are not yet Islamized are to be "conquered" for Islam with all available means.
- **Dar al-Islam** (house of Islam): These are the areas of the world where Islam rules.

The state of war will continue until all the world belongs to the "House of Islam".[112] It is impossible, from a radical/orthodox Muslim point of view, that other religions can co-exist side with Islam on an equal footing.[113] Peace in Islam is only achieved when all territory on Earth has been conquered for Islam.[114]

According to the Qur'an, fighting in the name of Allah is a command given to all Muslims (Sura 4:74; 4:95-96). Those who fight in the name of Allah will receive a higher reward in heaven than those who don't.

> Let those fight in the cause of Allah who sell the life of this world for the hereafter. To him who fighteth in the cause of Allah—whether he is slain or gets victory—soon shall We give him a reward of great (value). (Sura 4:74)

---

[111] This distinction originated with Muslim theologians; it is found neither in the Qur'an nor in the *hadith*, but in the *Sharia*. Some younger Muslim intellectuals question this geopolitical view and would prefer to speak of "Dar al-Da'wa" instead of "Dar al-Harb".

[112] The Qur'an promises that those who lose their lives in holy war immediately enter into paradise (Sura 61:11-13).

[113] Monotheistic religions that submit to Islam usually get limited autonomy and are in many cases not persecuted. They may, however, not share their faith with Muslims. Judaism and Christianity are therefore in a special category.

[114] This in contrast to Christianity, where peace is established when a person has accepted Christ as Lord and Saviour (Col 1:19-20).

The war against those not accepting the political rule of Islam can be interrupted by a truce for a defined time, for example when the adversaries are of such superior strength that there is no chance of victory. A brutal call to kill the heathen, i.e. non-Muslims, can be found in Sura 9:5:

> But when the forbidden months are past, then fight and slay the Pagans wherever ye find them, and seize them, beleaguer them, and lie in wait for them in every stratagem (of war); but if they repent, and establish regular prayers and practise regular charity, then open the way for them: for Allah is Oft-forgiving, most Merciful.

The expansion of Islam may also be achieved with peaceful means. There are, however, different opinions among Muslims as to how this war has to be performed in practice.[115] History shows that, excepting Muslim communities in Southeast Asia and East Africa, military advance was an essential part of the expansion of Islam.[116]

The Saudi-Arabian flag: Shahada and sword

1.5.4 The Islamic understanding of mission

Is there then no mission by persuading people in Islam? Are Muslims clearly instructed to proclaim Islam, similar to the command to do mission that Christians

---

[115] Opinions differ predominantly on the question of whether and how much violence may be used. The interpretation often depends on the military strength of the Muslims. Hughes (1982:243) writes: "When an infidel's country is conquered by a Muslim ruler, its inhabitants are offered three alternatives: 1) *The reception of Islam*, in which case the conquered become enfranchised citizens of the Muslim state. 2) *The payment of a poll-tax* (Jizyah), by which the unbelievers in Islam obtain protection, and become Zimmis *(dhimmi)*", provided they are not the idolaters of Arabia. 3) *Death by the sword*, to those who will not pay the poll tax."

[116] A study done by Marshall (1999), which investigates the Qur'anic verses in respect of the development towards "unbelievers" shows, that the verses from the Meccan period assert that judgment will befall them through direct intervention by Allah. However, the verses from the Medina period display an increasing conviction that divine judgment will be mediated through the community of believers i.e. the Muslims.

received?[117] Different opinions and uncertainties prevail among Muslims in this regard. Each Muslim, however, has the obligation to proclaim and bear witness to his faith.[118]

Missionary activities in Islam are generally described with the Arabic word *da'wa*. As a verb, it means "to call, collect, invite". In the Qur'an, an invitation to embrace Islam *(da'wa)* can, for example, be found in Sura 16:125:

Invite (all) to the Way of thy Lord with wisdom and beautiful preaching; and argue with them in ways that are best and most gracious: For thy Lord knoweth best; Who have strayed from His Path, and who receive guidance.

Verses from the Qur'an and the traditions *(hadith)* regarding this topic are interpreted and applied differently by different Muslims. Today there are many different da'wa organizations worldwide.

1.5.5 Qur'anic injuctions for a viable survival

Despite the harsh and intolerant Qur'anic views towards Jews and Christians, being the "others", there are injunctions in the Qur'an that enable the Islamic community to disguise, play down, and if necessary deny the intensity and the validity of these anti-Semitic and anti-Christian teachings. This particular injunction is called *taqiyya*.[119] It literally means "caution, fear, disguise". It permits the suspension, as the need arises, of any religious requirements.

Any Muslim may practice *taqiyya* if he can justify it for the spread and advantage of Islam. It legitimises all activities in words and deeds contrary to what one might think is the right belief or conduct e.g. to display love outwardly but inwardly to hate, or to evince loyalty outwardly but inwardly to feel enmity—all for the cause of Allah. It can even been practised if necessary under oath. *Taqiyya* is practised by all Muslims, but has been considered by some to be an exclusively Shiite doctrine because of the aggressive vocal nature of Shiite teaching.

1.5.6 Apostasy from Islam

The act of apostasy, *irtidad*, means literally "turning back", leaving Islam for another religion or secular lifestyle. During Muhammad's and the Caliphs' lifetimes, a number of Muslims left the faith and were either killed outright, or given a few days to turn back to Islam. The Qur'an and the *hadith* both teach that the punishment for apostasy is death. The *hadith* is even clearer than the Qur'an on that issue. According to Sunni Sharia, a male apostate *(murtadd)* has three days to reconsider the decision; if he does not recant he must be killed. A female apostate is not subject to capital punishment, but may be kept in confinement until she recants. If a boy under age apostatises, he is not to be put to death, but is imprisoned until he comes to full age. If he continues in unbelief, he must be put to death.

---

[117] The Bible teaches global mission: to go, be witnesses, to preach, teach, baptize and make disciples (Mt 28:18-20; Mk 16:15; Lk 24:47; Ac 1: 8).
[118] Cf Suras 22:75; 22:78; 25:52; 48:28; 61:9.
[119] See Suras 2:225; 3:28; 5:92; 16:106.

There are more guidelines concerning this issue.[120] However, Muslim scholars and schools differ in some details. This law of apostasy is cruel and against human rights. As such, it is usually not applied by the Islamic state directly, but rather through religious leaders or family members!

The conflict concerning religious freedom:
Article 18 of the Universal Declaration of Human Rights says:
> Everyone has the right to freedom of thought, conscience and religion; this right includes freedom to change his religion or belief, and freedom, either alone or in community with others and in public or private, to manifest his religion or belief in teaching, practice, worship and observance.

In contrast, Article 306 of the Mauritanian Constitution says:
> If a Muslim is found guilty of the crime of apostasy, either through words or through actions, he will be asked to repent during a three-day period. If he has not repented within this time limit, he will be sentenced to death as an apostate and his property will be seized by the Revenue Office. Every Muslim who refuses to pray will be asked to comply with the obligation to pray within the prescribed time limit. If he persists in his refusal, he will be punished by death.

The Qur'an seems to proclaim religious freedom:
> Let there be no compulsion in religion: Truth stands out clear from error... (Sura 2:256)

Yet it also says that Allah will not forgive those who change their religion:
> Those who believe, then reject faith, then believe again, and again reject faith, and go on increasing in unbelief, Allah will not forgive them nor guide them on the way. (Sura 4:137)

Sura 9:5 shows another picture: "pagans" shall be killed:
> But when the forbidden months are past, then fight and slay the pagans wherever ye find them, and seize them, beleaguer them, and lie in wait for them...

> **! True Story**
> I once met an Islamic religious teacher in Switzerland and we got into a discussion. He mentioned how wonderful Islam is, since there is "absolute religious freedom". As in Islam things are understood differently, I asked my Muslim friend: "What do you mean by that? How do you understand this?"
> He then explained that, in Islam, all people have absolute freedom to embrace Islam! "Well, that is wonderful" I said, but continued, "Imagine if I would accept Islam today but after six months would say: 'Well, during

---

[120] See Hughes (1982:16), and link for an article that provides examples of Qura'nic verses and *hadiths*: http://answering-islam.org.uk/Silas/apostasy.htm

these months I realised that this is not the religion I want to be part of. I have decided to leave Islam and join another religion such as Buddhism."' My friend was shocked at this and said: "If you leave Islam, then you have three days to reconsider; if you do not come back to Islam, you have to be killed!" My Muslim friend had no problem to put his definition under the term "absolute religious freedom"! I then posed the question: "Do you really believe this is just? This is religious freedom in a one-way direction, isn't it?" He started thinking...

This story proves the following points:

• In most cases Muslims have completely different conceptions of religious terminology.
• It is therefore wise to clarify by asking: "What do you mean by that?"
• It is better to challenge Muslims with questions than engage in an argument!
• It is good that Muslims start explaining their faith and try to find answers—it makes them think.

1.5.7 The Islamic theocracy

Since the *Hijra* in 622 AD, there has been no separation between religion and state in Islam, nor any separation between religion, politics or any other secular affairs. Politics and religion were already united in Muhammad's time in the 7ᵗʰ century. Muhammad was both a religious and political leader of the first Muslim community. His direct successors (caliphs, *al-khalifa*) also combined both offices in one person. This aim of a religious state, stemming from Muhammad, is demanded by fundamentalists today. The ultimate object of Islam is the submission of the entire world to Islam. Accordingly, each state of the world has to become an Islamic theocracy based on the *Shari'a*, the religious law. Muslims will find "peace" only when this ultimate object is achieved.

According to the Muslim view, life should be governed by Islam and its laws. Such Islamic governmental practice is often authoritarian and dictatorial. However, parliaments do exist in many Islamic nations that have included only parts of the *Shari'a* into their legislation, and are thus in opposition to fundamentalists. An Islamic state, governed by the *Shari'a*, is not a democracy (Greek, "rule of the people") because these are not the real holders of authority, but Allah. Besides, Islam does not acknowledge the basis of democracy, which is the equality and liberty of all citizens.

Various Islamic states worldwide have implemented the *Shari'a* to different degrees. Saudi Arabia, one of the strictest, forbids women to drive cars, while Tunisia has introduced much more liberal laws.

Questions
- Explain how you picture Allah?
- What do you know about the functions of angels?
- According to your point of view, which books did Allah send through prophets to people?
- Name those prophets who are important to you.
- What do you think will happen on the day of judgment?
- If Allah predetermines everything, then how can man be held accountable for his actions?
- Have you come any closer to Allah by observing Islamic rituals, such as daily prayers, fasting in the month of Ramadan, going to Mecca, saying the creed, etc.? If yes, please explain!
- What spiritual experience do you have after the pilgrimage to Mecca?
- How do you think you will be able to enter paradise?
- What is your understanding of "peace"?
- What is your understanding of "religious freedom"?
- What is your understanding of *jihad*?
- Do you think the apostasy law in Islam is just?
- Do you think people from different religions have the same right to do mission work?

1.6 Islamic groups

Muslims have emphasized the unity of the worldwide Islamic community *(umma)* repeatedly. In general, they do not like to discuss groupings[121] and avoid mentioning the innumerable divisions of Islam *(firqa,* sect). Muslims often overlook the fact that all attempts to question the credibility of Christianity serve no purpose, unless they apply the same criteria to their own faith.

Muslims use the word "sect" *(firqa)* differently from Christians. Primarily the word is used for the division of Muslims into Sunni and Shiites, and only secondarily for the numerous divisions within these main groups. Muhammad himself predicted that his followers would fragment into many sects.[122]

---

[121] This book does not intend to describe all groupings. It is only intended to be a short introduction to the topic.

[122] See Hughes (1982:567-569): "Abdu 'llah ibn Umar relates that the Prophet said: "Verily it will happen to my people even as it did to the children of Israel. The children of Israel were divided into 72 sects, and my people will be divided into 73. Every one of these sects will go to Hell except one sect." The Companions said, "O Prophet, which is that?" He said: "The religion which is professed by me and my Companions." (Mishkat, book i. ch vi. pt 2.). Today the number has, however, far exceeded Muhammad's predictions.

1.6.1 Origins of Sunnites and Shiites

The word Sunni comes from the word *Sunna*, which means the tradition of the Prophet of Islam, Muhammad. About 90% of all Muslims are Sunni. The rest are distributed between Shiites[123] and other groups that emanated from the conflict between Sunni and Shiites. The difference between the two large groups of Islam was originally merely dynastic: early Muslims fought about the succession from the prophet Muhammad, who left no instructions regarding his succession. While the Sunni accepted the political (and thus religious) leadership of early Islam, the Shiites rebelled and rejected the first three caliphs. Shiites only accepted Ali, Muhammad's son-in-law, and his bodily descendants as the lawful heirs of the political as well as religious leadership of Muslims.

The Shiites have quarrelled endlessly which led to schisms regarding, for example, the question of whether the Qur'an was created or existed eternally, and Allah's predestination versus human responsibility.[124] Shiites also believe that Allah made a special revelation to Fatimah, Ali's wife, while Sunni Muslims reject these traditions. Shi'a Muslims believe that the study of Islamic literature is a continual process, and is necessary for identifying all of Allah's laws. Unlike Sunni Muslims, Shi'a Muslims believe that they can interpret the Qur'an and the Shi'a traditions with the same authority as their predecessors: that the door to *ijtihad* was never closed. Because Islamic law is based also on the *hadith*, Shi'a rejection of some Sunni *hadith* and Sunni rejection of some Shi'a *hadith* means that the versions of the law differ. For example, while both Shi'a and Sunni pray Friday (*jum'a*) prayers, the exact prayer times differ. Some Shi'a also practice temporary marriages (*mut'a*), which can be contracted for months or even days. Shi'a also follow different inheritance laws and celebrate different festivals.

Shiite groups living in a minority situation developed a mentality of suffering and a pronounced cult of martyrdom as a consequence of their fight against the political establishment of the Sunnis. Therefore, in addition to the pilgrimage to Mecca, they also make pilgrimages to gravesites of their Shiite leaders whom they have declared to be "saints", though is not exclusive to Shi'a. The Shiites are convinced that their *imams*[125] are directly appointed by Allah and that, at the end of the world, a *Mahdi* will come who will build a divine realm of justice. Shiite groups developed mainly in Persia, Yemen and East Africa. Today, Shiite groups can be found all over the world, but their centre is Iran, where the Twelver-Shiites[126] have dominated since the beginning of the 16th century. Over the centuries of Islamic history, Sunni dynasties usually represented orthodox power, while Shiites were the opposition.

1.6.2 The Kharijites, Wahhabis and Mu'tazilites

The *Kharijites*, *Wahhabis* and *Mutazilites* are splinter groups rather than self-contained Islamic sects. The *Kharijites* date back to the early days of Islam as a small

---

[123] See Tabataba'i (1975) for a detailed study on Shiite Islam by a Muslim scholar.
[124] These subjects are discussed in other groups as well, though perhaps to a lesser degree.
[125] Shi'a religious leaders.
[126] Followers of twelve imams or spiritual leaders after the prophet Muhammad.

group that refused to give up an utterly radical puritanical form of Islam. They held the opinion that one had to take drastic action against any compromise, and held, inter alia, "free will" as an article of faith. The only surviving branch of the Kharijites are the Ibadi Muslims, distinguished from Shiism by their belief that the *imam* (Leader) should be chosen solely on the basis of his faith, not on descent, and from Sunnism in its rejection of Uthman and Ali and a strong emphasis on the need to depose unjust rulers. Ibadi Islam is noted for its strictness but, unlike the Kharijites proper, Ibadis do not regard major sins as automatically making a Muslim an unbeliever. Most Ibadi Muslims live in Oman and Algeria.

The *Wahhabis* are a militant, puritan group in Saudi Arabia. They form an extremely fundamentalist branch of the Sunni group and are of recent origin. During the 18th century, Muhammad ibn Abd al Wahhab (1703–1792) led a religious movement (Wahhabism) in eastern Arabia that sought to purify Islam. Abd al Wahhab wanted to return Islam to what he thought were its original principles as taught by the *al-aslaf as-saliheen* (the earliest converts to Islam)[127]; he rejected what he regarded as corruptions introduced by *bid'*a (religious innovation) and *shirk* (polytheism). He allied himself with the House of Saud, which eventually triumphed over the Rashidis to control Central Arabia, and led several revolts against the Ottoman empire. Initial success (the conquest of Mecca and Medina) was followed by ignominious defeat, then a resurgence which culminated in the creation of Saudi Arabia.

Wahhabis prefer to be called *Salafis* (movement *Salafiyyah*). One of its foremost principles is the abolition of "schools of thoughts" (legal traditions), and the following of Muhammad directly through the study of the sciences of the *hadith* (prophetic traditions). The Hanbali legal tradition is the strongest school of thought from which the Islamic law in Saudi Arabia is derived, and has had a great deal of influence on the Islamic world because of Saudi control of Mecca and Medina, the Islamic holy places, and because of Saudi funding for mosques and schools in other countries. The majority of Saudi Islamic scholars are considered Wahhabis by other parts of the Islamic world.

Mu'tazilite theology originated in the 8th century in Basra (Iraq) when Wasil ibn Ata (d. 131 AH/748 AD) left the teaching lessons of al-Hasan al-Basri after a theological dispute. As a result he and his followers, including 'Amr ibn 'Ubayd (d. 144 AH/761 AD), were labelled *Mu'tazili*[128]. Later, Mu'tazilis called themselves *Ahl al-Tawhid wa al-'Adl* ("People of Divine Unity and Justice") based on the theology they advocated. Though Mu'tazilis relied on logic and different aspects of Greek philosophy, the tenets of Islam were their starting point and ultimate reference. The accusations levelled against them by rival schools of theology—that they gave absolute authority to extra-Islamic paradigms—reflect more the fierce polemics between various schools of theology than any objective reality. For instance,

---

[127] *"al-aslaf as-saliheen":* Wehr (1979) translates this with "the venerable forefathers".
[128] The name Mu'tazili originates from the Arabic root (*i'tazala*) meaning "to leave", "to withdraw".

Mu'tazilis unanimously adopted the doctrine of creation *ex nihilo*, contrary to Muslim philosophers who, with the exception of al-Kindi, believed in the eternity of the world in some form or another. They also rejected the Islamic doctrine of predestination and for that reason were eventually phased out of existence.

From the early days of Islamic civilization, intra-Muslim conflicts and interfaith debates raised several questions for debate by Muslim theologians: was the Qur'an created or eternal, was evil created by Allah, predestination versus free will, the interpretation of Allah's attributes in the Qur'an allegorically or literally, etc. Mu'tazili thought attempted to address these issues.

1.6.3 Sufism: mysticism in Islam

Generally, Islam is a legalistic religion which can produce a reaction among those who seek relief from impersonal legalism. *Sufism*[129] has developed over the course of centuries as a reaction to "dry" orthodox Islam. It encompasses a diverse range of beliefs and practices. *Tariqas* (Sufi orders) may be associated with Shi'a Islam, Sunni Islam, other currents of Islam, or a combination of multiple traditions. Sufi thought emerged from the Middle East in the eighth century, but adherents are now found worldwide. The conventional view is that the word originates from *suf*, the Arabic word for wool, referring to the simple cloaks the early Muslim ascetics wore. However, not all Sufis wear cloaks or clothes of wool. Another etymological theory states that the root word of Sufi is the Arabic word *safa*, meaning purity. This places the emphasis of Sufism on purity of heart and soul.

Around 1100 AD, *Al-Ghazzali*[130] tried to prevent Islamic theology and jurisprudence from fossilising by emphasizing the spiritual interpretation of human obligations. But Sufism has even earlier roots. One key mystic was a woman, Rabia of Basra[131]. She aimed at bringing the "pure love of Allah" and a rigid asceticism together.[132] Islamic mystics have heavily borrowed concepts from other religions, particularly Hinduism, Buddhism and Christianity, from which they developed much of their concept of Allah. They consequently teach their followers certain meditation techniques and breath control with the thousand-fold repetition of Allah's names or other religious formulas.[133] The goal of this exercise is to become wholly one with Allah. Muhammad is considered by the Sufis as a mystic, too. Many Muslims perform mystic practices and simultaneously considers themselves as Sunni. Many *Sufi* leaders are revered as saints today, and their gravesites are visited as places of pilgrimage. Muslims expect a special blessing (*baraka*) from such visits.[134] It goes without saying that the occult plays a significant role in Sufism.

---

[129] Sufism (Turkish: *Tasavvuf*; Persian: *Sufi gari*, Arabic: *ta_awwuf*) is a mystic tradition of Islam.
[130] Al-Ghazzali is one of the most important Islamic theologians, who tried to combine the teaching of classic, orthodox Islam with mystic dimensions.
[131] Rabia of Basra died in the year 801 AD.
[132] Strict fasting, little sleep, nightly prayers, meditation of the Qur'an.
[133] These constant repetitions are called *dhikr*, remembrance of Allah. It is supposed to be a practical application of Sura 13:28: "...now surely by Allah's remembrance are the hearts set at rest."
[134] See also section 1.6.10 "Popular Islam".

Sufis congregate in small, personal groups, believing the interaction of the master is necessary for the growth of the pupil. They make extensive use of parable, allegory, and metaphor, and hold that meaning can only be reached through a process of seeking the truth, and knowledge of oneself—an esoteric perception. Although philosophies vary between different Sufi orders, Sufism as a whole is primarily concerned with direct personal experience, and as such may be compared to various forms of mysticism such as Scholasticism, Zen Buddhism and Gnosticism.

The following metaphor, credited to an unknown Sufi scholar, describes this line of thought:

> There are three ways of knowing a thing. Take for instance a flame. One can be told of the flame, one can see the flame with his own eyes, and finally one can reach out and be burned by it. In this way, we Sufis seek to be burned by Allah.

A significant part of Persian literature comes from the Sufis, who created great books of poetry. The Sufi orders engage in ritualized *dhikr*[135] ceremonies. Each order or lineage within an order has one or more forms for group *dhikr*, the liturgy of which may include recitation, singing, instrumental music, dance, costumes, incense, meditation, ecstasy, and trance. *Dhikr* in a group is most often done on Thursday and/or Sunday nights as part of the institutional practice of the orders.

There are also various *Dervish*[136] fraternities (Sufi orders), almost all of whom trace their origins from various Muslim saints and teachers, especially Ali and Abu Bakr. They live in monastic conditions, superficially similar to Christian monk fraternities, though some of them might be married. Various orders and suborders have appeared and disappeared over the centuries.

Whirling dance, the practice of the *Mevlevi* Order in Turkey, is just one of the physical methods to try to reach religious ecstasy *(majdhb, fana')*. *Mevlevi* comes from the Persian poet Mawlana al-Rumi whose shrine is in Konya in Turkey and who was a *Dervish* himself. After reaching a certain state of ecstasy *(Fana)*, they are unaware of the world around them, and claim to have made a connection with Allah. Rifa'is, also called the "howling dervishes", pierce themselves with knives, handle red-hot iron and eat hot coals or live serpents, depending on the subsect.

1.6.4 Tablighi Jamaat

Tablighi Jamaat[137] is a Muslim missionary and revival movement. They usually limit their activities to within the Muslim community itself, their main aim be-

---

[135] Remembrance of Allah. *Dhikr* as a devotional act includes the repetition of divine names, supplications and aphorisms from *hadith* literature, and sections of the Qur'an.

[136] The word *Dervish* refers to members of Sufi Muslim ascetic religious fraternities, known for their extreme poverty and austerity, similar to mendicant friars.

[137] Tablighi Jamaat "Proselytizing Group" also called *Tabliq*. Tabligh in Arabic means "to deliver (the message)".

ing to bring spiritual awakening to Muslim communities in the world. They have committed themselves to the following:

- Devote their lives, time and money for the cause of Islam.
- Visit and approach Muslims in a systematic way to try to make them better Muslims.
- Educate and train other Muslims in the teaching of Islam (using their own teaching material).
- Win them to become *tablighi* Muslims themselves.

The movement can be compared in respect of its format and structure to the Sufi movement; it can be described as a 'faith and practice' movement. It was founded in the late 1920s by the Deobandi cleric Maulana Muhammad Ilyas Kandhalawi in India. The inspiration for devoting his life to the preaching of Islam came to Ilyas during his second pilgrimage in 1926. Maulana Ilyas put forward the slogan: "O Muslims! Be Muslims!"

The group originally started out with the aim of being a non-political movement working at the grass roots level among Muslims across the economic and social spectrum. Yet, with increasing and alarming frequency, the name of Tablighi Jamaat is cropping up in the worldwide fight against terrorism. The Jamaat claims that it does not solicit or receive donations. Links with Saudi Wahhabi funding, however, have emerged. While Tablighi Jamaat in theory requires its missionaries to cover their own expenses during their trips, in practice, Saudi money subsidises transportation costs for thousands of poor missionaries.

Any Muslim can easily join in their spiritual journeys. There is no 'membership' and no background check for newcomers. Almost any Muslim can join the group in a mosque. Unlike the men, women stay outside the mosque in the house of a well-known tablighi worker following full *Shari'a* rules, including the wearing of a *pardah* (*hijab, burqu'*, Islamic dress for women). They also teach the women of that locality to join them. In addition to this core, there are the traveling Tablighis who undertake proselytizing missions of varying durations. Apart from preaching, followers are also encouraged to spend 2.5 hours every day serving others.

The Jamaat as a missionary organization is popular in South Asia and has many adherents internationally. A strong grassroots support for the movement can be found in India, Pakistan, Malaysia, Thailand, Bangladesh, Sri Lanka, Fiji, Central Asia, East Asia, North and Central Africa, South America and the Gulf. In Pakistan the movement is based in Raiwind, near Lahore. The annual Tablighi congregation in Bangladesh, the Biswa Ijtema, attracts over three million devotees from around the world. Significant participation in Tabligh efforts is also seen in Europe, North America, South Africa, North Africa and East Asia. Tablighi Jamaat undeniably has a huge social impact. The current European headquarters Tablighi mosque is based in the Savile Town area of Dewsbury, West Yorkshire in the United Kingdom.

1.6.5 The Ahmadiyya movement

At the end of the 19th century, Mirza Ghulam Ahmad[138] of Qadian proclaimed himself to be the "Reformer of the age" Mujaddid, Promised Messiah, Mahdi and Prophet of the age. Initially he wrote books to defend Islam against Christian missionaries. In 1879, while staying in the village of Qaidan in Punjab, India, he appeared before the public with the claim of being the promised *Mahdi* (a kind of messianic figure). As such, he considered himself a new emissary of Allah. Thus he became the founder of the *Ahmadiyya* (or Ahmadi) movement. Contrary to Sufism, the Ahmadiyya movement is rationally minded. Although this group is relatively small, its followers are very active worldwide, claiming to have established offices in 200 countries with a population of over 200 million. Ahmadiyya beliefs are considered heretical and outside of Islam by most mainstream Muslims. In Pakistan, Ahmadiyya followers are persecuted, which led to the group's strong establishment in western countries where freedom of religion is granted.[139] The Ahmadiyyas want to spread Islam with peaceful means.

Today Ahmadiyyas use rational arguments against Christianity. They not only reject the death of Jesus on the cross but also his virgin birth and sinless nature.[140] The group tries to take away from Christ any superior or supernatural rank that could raise him above Muhammad. Ahmadiyya followers believe that Jesus migrated as a religious teacher to India, where he died like any ordinary human. Ahmediyyas display a grave of Jesus in Kashmir.

Mirza Ghulam Ahmad claimed to have fulfilled the prophecy of the return of Jesus. He was to bring the followers of all religions under the banner of Islam. In 1889 Mirza Ghulam Ahmad laid down the foundation of his community, which was later given the name of "Ahmadiyya Muslim Jamaat" after the second name of the prophet of Islam, Ahmad. Soon after the death of the first successor,[141] in 1914, the movement split into two sects over the question of the finality of prophethood. The Lahore Ahmadiyya Movement affirmed the orthodox Islamic interpretation that there could be no new prophet after Muhammad and viewed itself as a reform movement within the broader *umma*. The Ahmadiyya Muslim Community, however, claimed that Mirza Ghulam Ahmad had indeed been a prophet in accordance with, as they believe, the correct interpretation of the Qur'an and Sunna.

Although the central values of Islam (prayer, charity, fasting, etc.) are shared by all Muslims, distinct Ahmadi Muslim beliefs include:
- The Qur'an has no contradictions (or abrogations), and has precedence over the *hadith* or traditions i.e. that one verse of the Qur'an does not cancel another and

---

[138] *Ahmadiyya* Muslims are followers of Mirza Ghulam Ahmad (b1835-d1908).
[139] Today their international headquarters is a huge centre in London .
[140] Sunnis believe, according to the Qur'an (Sura 19:19-22), in the virgin birth of Jesus and his sinlessness.
[141] First Ahmadi caliph: Maulana Hakeem Noor-ud-Din (b1841-d1914).

that no *hadith* can contradict a verse of the Qur'an. *Hadith* that contradict the Qu'ran are not accepted by Ahmadi Muslims.
- Jesus (called Yuz Asaf) was crucified and survived the four hours on the cross, then was revived from a swoon in the tomb. He died in Kashmir of old age whilst seeking the ten lost tribes of Israel. He also clearly foretold the coming of Muhammad after him, which Christians have misinterpreted.
- That *jihad* is for the defence of Islam, not for use in political conflicts or an excuse for rulers to invade neighbouring territories. Today this means *jihad* with the pen as Islam is being attacked through the media, and *jihad* against the self, is when the personal Islam of every Muslim is threatened by negative aspects of the self.

1.6.6 The Druze

The Druze are a small, distinct religious community based mostly in the Middle East.[142] They refer to themselves as an Islamic reformatory sect, although they are not considered Muslim by orthodox Muslims. They speak Arabic and follow a social pattern very similar to the other Arabs; most Druze consider themselves Arabs, though influenced by Greek philosophy and other religions. They were formed in 1017 as a splinter group from Shiite Isma'ilis. The Druze call themselves *Ahl al-Tawhid*, "the People of Monotheism" or *Muwahhidun*, "Monotheists". The origin of the name Druze is traced to Muhammad ad-Darazi, a heretic of the sect's incipient years. They held the view that Allah was incarnated in human forms and that the final incarnation was the Fatimid Khalif Hakim (996–1021) who did not die but is still living hidden in a secret place.

The main actors of the early years were the pious Fatimid ruler *Tariqu l-Hakim* and the Persian immigrant *Hamza ibn Ali ibn Ahmad*, the main architect of the movement. It was Hamza who first publicly proclaimed that Hakim was the "Ruler in the Name of Allah". The Druze believe that Hakim went into hiding and will return at the end of days as the Qa'im, "Ariser" or *Mahdi*, "Guided One". After the disappearance of Hakim, the Druze were forced to move and use the (accepted) practice of *taqiyya* "dissimulation". They conceal their true beliefs and outwardly accept the religious beliefs of those amongst whom they live. The faith of the Muwahhidun (the unitarians), as Druze call themselves, centres around a hierarchy of individuals who are the sole custodians of a religious doctrine hidden from the rest of the world and written down in their own book "The Wisdom".

Druze do not fast, go on pilgrimage or attend prayers in mosques. They do not propagate their faith, as no one can become a Druze by conversion but only by birth. Marriage outside the community can mean ostracism. Druze have a strong community feeling even across borders and countries. There is a widespread be-

---

[142] The Druze reside primarily in Lebanon, Israel, Syria (where they have official recognition as a separate religious community with its own religious court system) and Jordan. Small communities of expatriates also live in other parts of the world. The Druze played a major role in the Lebanese Civil War (1975–1990) and organized one of the strongest militas in the War.

lief in reincarnation, where souls are reborn as humans, good as well as bad. Good people have a more fortunate rebirth than bad people do. Many Druze have strange stories to tell of young children giving extremely accurate details of a previous life. Horoscopes are also important and there appears to be an ability to tell the future. As far as outsiders know, Jethro, father-in-law to Moses, is their most revered prophet. Druze are forbidden to smoke, drink alcohol or eat pork but many young Druze do not strictly adhere to these prohibitions. Their main feast day is 'Ashura, which recalls the martyrdom of Imam Hussein. This grandson of the Prophet Muhammad was slain in a doomed battle against a rival Muslim force over 1300 years ago. 'Id al-adha, the Feast of the Sacrifice, is also celebrated.

The Druze are very hospitable and are particularly curious about new people. Most of the Druze are from the *juhhal*[143] and have a kind of folk religion based around reincarnation, fate and horoscopes. There is a saying, "eat in a Druze home, sleep in a Christian one" which reveals a mistrust of the Druze from other sections of the community.

The principles of the Druze faith are: guarding one's tongue (honesty), protecting one's brother, respecting the elderly, helping others, protecting one's homeland, and belief in one God (hence their preference for the name "Monotheists"). They are not influenced by Sufi philosophy, as many believe. Druze have a fervent belief in human-only reincarnation for all members of the community. They reject polygamy, tobacco smoking, alcohol or consumption of pork, although pork and alcohol may be consumed in many non-religious and/or *al-Juhl* households. Their religion does not allow them to intermarry with other Muslims, Jews or members of any other religions. However, these rules are often disregarded in modern societies.

1.6.7 The Bahá'í

The Bahá'í faith, beginning in Iran during the mid-1800s as an outgrowth of the Shiite version of Islam, has attracted a great deal of attention in recent years by its claim to be a universal religion. It promises to offer hope for all who long for world peace, equality among races and sexes, independent religious thinking, and a responsible integration of faith and science.

---

[143] The Druze are split into two groups. The outer group, called *al-Juhhal*, "the Ignorant", are not granted access to the secret Druze holy literature. They form the Druze political and military leadership and generally distance themselves from religious issues. They comprise perhaps 90% of the Druze. The inner group are called *al-Uqqal*, "the Knowledgeable Initiates". Women are considered especially suitable to become *Uqqal;* they are even regarded to be spiritually superior to men, a belief that greatly contrasts with the surrounding Christian and Muslim communities.

Bahá'ís regard the period from the Báb's[144] 1844 declaration in Shiraz, to the 1921 passing of 'Abdu'l-Bahá[145] as the Heroic Age of the Faith. During this period its foundations were established in several countries and its early believers experienced great persecution. Shoghi Effendi, the appointed head of the faith from 1921 to 1957, wrote the following summary of what he considered to be the distinguishing principles of Bahá'u'lláh's teachings:

The independent search after truth, unfettered by superstition or tradition; the oneness of the entire human race, the pivotal principle and fundamental doctrine of the Faith; the basic unity of all religions; the condemnation of all forms of prejudice, whether religious, racial, class or national; the harmony which must exist between religion and science; the equality of men and women, the two wings on which the bird of humankind is able to soar; the introduction of compulsory education; the adoption of a universal auxiliary language; the abolition of the extremes of wealth and poverty; the institution of a world tribunal for the adjudication of disputes between nations; the exaltation of work, performed in the spirit of service, to the rank of worship; the glorification of justice as the ruling principle in human society, and of religion as a bulwark for the protection of all peoples and nations; and the establishment of a permanent and universal peace as the supreme goal of all mankind—these stand out as the essential elements.[146]

Bahá'í house of worship (Lotus Temple); New Delhi, India.

---

[144] Siyyid 'Alí Mu_ammad (20. Oct. 1819–9. July 1850) was the founder and prophet of Bábism. He was a merchant from Shíráz who, at the age of twenty-five, claimed to be the promised Qá'im (or Mihdí). After his declaration, he took the title of Báb meaning "Gate".

[145] 'Abdu'l-Bahá 'Abbás Effendí (23. May 1844–28. Nov. 1921) commonly known as 'Abdu'l-Bahá was the son of Bahá'u'lláh. At the age of 28, 'Abdu'l-Bahá received a messenger telling him of the Báb, whose message he accepted, becoming a Bábí. In 1892, 'Abdu'l-Bahá was appointed in his father's will to be his successor and head of the Bahá'í Faith.

[146] Effendi, Shoghi (1944). *God Passes* By. Wilmette, Illinois, USA: Bahá'í Publishing Trust, p 281.

However, the main tenet of Bahá'í teaching which angers other Muslims most is that they do not consider Muhammad as the last and greatest prophet, but only one in an unending series of prophets. Furthermore, the Qur'an is not the last and greatest revelation from Allah, but one in a series of revelations, among which are the scriptures of the Bahá'í who came along after Islam.

The following 12 principles are frequently listed as a quick summary of the Bahá'í teachings. The list is not authoritative and a variety of such lists circulate. The first three of this list are commonly referred to as the "Three Onenesses" and form a fundamental part of Bahá'í beliefs.

1) The oneness of Allah
2) The oneness of religion
3) The oneness of mankind
4) Gender equality
5) Elimination of all forms of prejudice
6) World peace
7) Harmony of religion and science
8) Independent investigation of truth
9) The need for universal compulsory education
10) The need for a universal auxiliary language
11) Obedience to government and non-involvement in partisan politics
12) Elimination of extremes of wealth and poverty

Although it concentrates on social and ethical issues as well, Bahá'í Faith's foundational texts might be described as mystical. The purpose of life in Bahá'í scriptures is to acquire virtues, know Allah, develop spiritually, and help carry forward an ever-advancing civilization. Personal development is conceived as an organic process, like the development of a foetus, assisted by Allah's messengers. Bahá'u'lláh taught of an afterlife in which the soul may progress infinitely through ever-more-exalted spiritual realms. Heaven and hell are perceived as a reference to an individual's proximity to Allah, not as exclusive or physical places.

Bahá'ís claim to have seven million adherents worldwide (by 2005), but they continue to be persecuted in countries with radical Muslim rule, especially Iran. Since the Islamic Revolution of 1979, Iranian Bahá'ís have regularly had their homes ransacked or been banned from attending university or holding government jobs, and several hundred have received prison sentences for their religious beliefs, most recently for participating in study circles.

1.6.8 Fundamentalism or Islamism

Islamic fundamentalism is an ideology which advocates:
• literal interpretations of the sacred texts of Islam
• the implementation of the *Shari'a*
• an Islamic state.

Islamic fundamentalism is the older, less preferred term for Islamism[147], a set of political ideologies that confirm that Islam is not only a religion, but also a political system that governs the legal, economic and social imperatives of the state according to its interpretation of Islamic law. Thus Islamism is a modern version of Islam which attempts to interpret Islam into the modern world.[148]

To understand the Islamist mindset one must understand recent history. Islamism developed afresh during the 19th and 20th centuries across North Africa, the Middle East, and Central and Southeast Asia, where any countries were colonized by Western states. Islamism has often been described as a reaction to colonialism or, alternatively, an effect of post-colonialism. This is only one side of the coin. Most Muslims are Orientals whose value system is not based on right or wrong, righteousness or sin, but on honour and shame as well as power and fear. Thus it is not important to act righteously, but to appear so. To be found out is the tragedy, for that brings dishonour and shame to oneself and the family, nation or even Islam. It was an overwhelming shame to all Muslims that Muslim lands were subdued and governed by nations that were infidels in their sight. That dishonoured not only Muslims, but also Allah.

Consequently *Islamism* is a modern movement that developed during the twentieth century in reaction to the perceived disgrace of being ruled by infidels. Following World War I, the dissolution of the Ottoman Empire and the subsequent dissolution of the Caliphate through the instrumentality of Mustafa Kemal Atatürk (founder of Turkey), many Muslims perceived that Islam was in retreat. They felt that Western ideas were spreading throughout Muslim society. This became the cause for the rise of Islamic fundamentalism or Islamism. This is a movement which bred a number of organizations with a number of characteristics:

1) They are convinced that Islamic law *(Sharia)* is valid for all aspects of social life, politics, and economy.
2) They strive for the unity of the Islamic community.
3) They hold that scholars are at liberty to interpret the Qur'an and tradition for current situations.
4) They believe that the revelations passed to Muhammad are the only connection between Allah and man.
5) They assert that the present Islamic nations are not compatible with Muhammad's original teachings.

In general, fundamentalists declare that the original Islam of Muhammad's time is the ideal, and demand a return to those ways. Islamists emphasize the foundations of their faith yet little of this original society is researched by Islamic

---

[147] This usage is controversial. Islamists themselves may oppose the term because it suggests their philosophy to be a political extrapolation from Islam rather than a straightforward expression of Islam as a way of life. Some Muslims find it troublesome that a word derived from "Islam" is applied to organizations they consider radical and extreme.
[148] See Roy 2006.

scholars. No clear notion of the characteristics of this "original Islam"[149] exists. It is merely emphasized that in those days Islam was "perfectly" realized. Moderate Muslims claim that true Islam is "Muhammad at Mecca," whereas radical or militant Muslims claim that true Islam is "Muhammad at Medina".

Egypt's military inferiority in the wars with Israel, together with Israel's protection by the West, has incurred the wrath of fundamentalist movements which form secret societies with a strictly hierarchical organization. Their members practice self-denial and are willing to make great personal sacrifices, including the offering of their lives (martyrdom), if need be. By their unquestioning religious obedience, the individual hopes to contribute to the transformation of society.

Two trends in Islamism can be defined as follows:
1) Islamic groups who aim for religious reform with peaceful means.
2) Islamic groups who want reform by using all means at hand, including terrorism.

Main events leading to Islamic fundamentalism:
1) At the end of World War I (1918) the Ottoman Empire which had ruled all the Islamic countries of the Middle East and North Africa collapsed and was divided by the League of Nations, in some cases arbitrarily, into a number of states. Most were under the control of Britain and France, which the Muslim world deemed intolerable.
2) In 1924 Ataturk established a secular state in Turkey, replacing the Islamic system with a Westernized system. Many Muslims reacted negatively to this.
3) These events in Turkey propel Egypt towards Islamic fundamentalism. A spiritual leader, *Sheikh Hassan al-Banna*, began the Muslim Brotherhood movement in 1928, referred to as *El-Kharij*. His aim was to reapply Islamic law in Egypt. The Brotherhood was very militant, aggressive and full of hatred toward the leadership of the country and anyone not complying with Islamic law. They used terrorism to shake up society and pursue their agenda of bringing back the "original glory of Islam".
4) After Israel was established as a nation in 1948, radical fundamentalist groups flourished even more. The fundamentalist groups created many cells of rebellious, hateful Muslims willing to die for their cause. This passion was directed at the Jews, leaders of Egypt and any who were not "true Muslims"! They focused their activities on assassinations.

Profile of a Jihad group:
• Purification within: eliminate all sources which compete with Allah and the Qur'an. This includes destroying books and man-made Islamic commentaries.
• They accept no authority but Allah in all matters.
• They expect resistance from authorities and society.

---

[149] "Original Islam"; also called "real Islam", "true Islam" or "correct Islam".

- They use armed forces to overthrow governments and any systems against them, just as Muhammad did by using physical violence.
- There should be no mercy or compromise in this war.
- The start will be difficult but soon true believers will hear the call and they will multiply.
- *Jihad* should be enforced: Islam should change from a religion of talk to action.
- They aim to establish a great Islamic nation stretching across the world. The only political system will be Islamic law.

Sayyid Qutb, the father of modern *jihad:*[150]
- Sayyid Qutb was chosen by the Egyptian government in 1948 to study in the USA.
- He came back filled with both envy and hostility toward the USA.
- After his return he joined the Muslim Brotherhood movement.
- He wrote more than seven books and is seen as the founding father of modern *jihad.*
- The book *Signs Along the Road* earned him the death sentence from the government.
- He was sentenced to death in 1965 during the presidency of Nasser.
- The authorities tried to burn all his books, but they survived and are available on the black market.
- *Qutb* and his books have become the heartbeat of the radical Islamic movements of today.
- He is the philosopher and spiritual leader of today's Islamic terrorist groups.
- He followed mainly the teaching of *Ibn Taymiyyah.*[151]
- He felt that the world had regressed to the way it was before Muhammad's teachings, becoming pagan and idolatrous.
- He also felt that Allah is the only ruler over Earth and rejected all man-made systems of government: democracy, socialism, dictatorship and communism.
- His logic was: Good and evil cannot live together, so they should destroy the way of man (which is evil) and follow the way of Allah.

What is the true face of Islam?
Is the original Islam to be interpreted from Muhammad's role model in Mecca (570-621 AD) or in Medina (622-632 AD) or some kind of mixture? In other words, is the real Islam moderate or radical? Muhammad during his time in Mecca was a warner, a preacher and peaceful citizen. In Medina, however, he was the leader of the army and used physical force to spread Islam; he was militant.

Muslims disagree as to which form of Islam is true. An Islamic scholar in Zürich, Switzerland, was confronted with the question: "Why are women not allowed to

---

[150] See also Gabriel (2002:ch15).
[151] Taqi al-Din Ahmad Ibn Taymiyyah (1263-1328), was a Sunni Islamic scholar. He lived during the troubled times of the Mongol invasions. As a member of the school founded by Ibn Hanbal, he sought the return of Islam to its sources: the Qur'an and the Sunna. He is also a primary intellectual source of the Wahhabi movement.

drive cars in Saudi Arabia?" His answer was: "Well that form of Islam in Saudi Arabia is not the correct one. Our form of Islam in Zürich is the only correct form!"

1.6.9 Various other groups and movements
• Muslim Brotherhood
• Islamic *jihad* movements
• Ibadi Islam

These groups and others are not explained here. Readers are encouraged to find information through literature or online (for instance www.wikipedia.org).

1.6.10 Popular Islam
Islam has many faces. Large differences exist between individual religious branches and the character of Islam in individual countries. Various styles of piety and crucial differences in doctrine can be found. The Qur'an is the highest authority for doctrine and life for all these groups, yet its exegesis and subsequent application is determined by the *hadith* and the *ijjma*.[152]

Beyond these differences in "orthodox" faith, are other differences in belief and practice called "popular Islam" or "folk Islam"[153] in Western literature describing the type of Islam Muslims actually practice in everyday life.[154] In pre-Islamic times, popular belief and practices in Arabia were strongly shaped by the occult. People felt helplessly under the control of the spirit world and sought relief and assistance from diviners that were able to influence these powers. The occult practitioners *(shamans)* were power brokers themselves. When Islam emerged, even Muhammad is reported to have suffered under these forces and sought popular remedies against these. Tolerating superstition and occult practices compromised the new faith. When Islam spread to countries with differing occult practices, the local population kept these alongside the new religion of Islam. In practical terms, this means that the official, highly visible religious practice is Islam with its uniformity, but real problems or calamities are addressed on the secondary, less visible level of the occult world.

A gap has developed between Islam as theologically defined and the way people live it. Popular belief deals with the current problems of daily life and adapts to people's requirements and customs. These include events like illnesses, floods, bad harvests, and accidents—things hardly ever mentioned by orthodox Islam. Folk belief is wrapped in myths, folklore, proverbs, and poems. Grandparents hand down the secrets of their experience to younger members of the family. Magic or astrology can be further components of popular belief.

---

[152] See section 1.4.2.
[153] The terms "popular Islam" or "folk Islam" are unknown in the Islamic world.
[154] A similar complexity exists among Christians. Churches house various forms of religious expressions, and Christians live their faith in different ways in everyday life.

The relation between popular belief and orthodox belief is tense. Islamic scholars fight popular Islam as false doctrine, but are often forced to tolerate it to some extent. Elements of popular Islam, frequently in contradiction to orthodox Islam, are, for example:[155]
• sacred spiritual exercises (e.g. visiting shrines and places of pilgrimage)
• practice of mysticism
• superstition or heretical views
• occult practices and spells (including animal sacrifices, rites and rituals).

Islamic history knows no councils or official doctrinal decisions about the basic dogmas of faith. It is therefore impossible to determine precisely where popular Islam differs from orthodox faith. The question of what unbelief *(kufr)* means in individual cases has been answered differently, too. Since this kind of piety can develop very differently in various times and cultural (ethnic) groups, it is not possible to describe the phenomenon of "popular Islam" in a comprehensive way.

The following figure shows the five main elements of Islam that influence the way Muslims practice their faith. Muslims live in permanent tension: the five elements show not only similarities, but also contradictions.

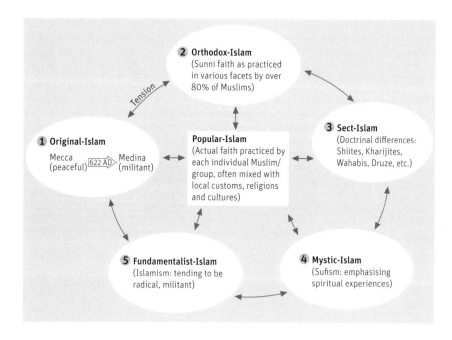

---

[155] Musk (1992) deals with the topic of "popular Islam" in detail, with examples of Muslim everyday life.

Popular Islam

Each individual Muslim lives out the kind of faith he is born into and which he adapts during his life. It is often mixed with local customs and culture, taking elements from the following faces of Islam in various, often changing, degrees:

1) Original-Islam[156]

This is Islam as practiced by Muhammad and his companions, roughly divided into the two periods of Mecca (610-622 AD) and Medina (622-632 AD). Muhammad was mainly peaceful in Mecca and more militant in Medina. The question is: What is true Islam: "Mecca Islam" or "Medina Islam" or some kind of mixture?

2) Orthodox-Islam[157]

This form of Islam can be named "Sunni Islam" followed by over 85% of all Muslims, a faith interpreted and prescribed by local religious leaders to their respective community from the time of Muhammad until today. Within Sunni Islam there are many divisions.

3) Sect-Islam[158]

Numerous religious divisions over questions of succession, doctrinal statements, implementing the *Shari'a*, opinions on the authority of *hadith*, etc.

4) Mystic-Islam[159]

Called *Sufism* with its emphasis on spiritual experiences, these practices are in contradiction to Orthodox Islam yet in many cases tolerated. There are many subdivisions within Sufi Islam.

5) Fundamentalist-Islam[160]

A growing percentage of Muslims are becoming more radical and prepared to use physical force to spread Islam—it is the face of Islam most discussed in the media. It is also called "Islamism" (going back to the roots). Islam as practiced during the time of Muhammad. Islamism tries practice what they believe is true Islam. However, various groups differ in ideology and often fight each other.

---

[156] See section 1.1.2.
[157] See section 1.6.1.
[158] See section 1.6.
[159] See section 1.6.3.
[160] See section 1.6.8.

Questions
- Do you both regard Sunni and Shiite Muslims as true Muslims?
- What are the marks of a true Muslim?
- What would you describe as "true Islam"?
- How did Shiite Islam came into being?
- Do you think Muhammad was a Sufi?
- What is your view on the Ahmadiyya Movement?
- Why do many Arab and Turkish Muslims not regard each other as true Muslims?
- Do you regard radical/militant Muslims as representing true Islam?
- What is your opinion on terrorist attacks by Muslims in recent times?
- How do you interpret verses in the Qur'an which promote the killing of people? (i.e. Sura 9:5)

1.7 Religion, culture and customs

1.7.1 Religion and culture

Like Judaism, Islam is a religion with cultural features which its followers cannot escape. The countries into which Islam expanded had ancient and significant cultures which Islam incorporated and developed in new directions. The Islamic faith mixed with societal culture in those countries to which it expanded. Its followers practice Islam differently than during Muhammad's time.

The history of Muslim people in these countries is a case study of the way a religious belief mixes with various cultures. This cultural adaptation often separates Islamic groups as much as doctrinal differences. On the other hand, the Arabic language unites Muslims over and above doctrinal orthodoxy. A wealth of Arabic poetry and prose exists that glorifies the Islamic faith.

1.7.2 The role of the mosque in society

The world today is confused about what they see in the name of Islam. Many Muslims are also troubled especially in the area of human rights, freedom of choice and whether Al-Qaida represents core Islamic values. In Islam, life and religion are deeply intertwined and inseparable. The mosque is the central point for the dissemination and application of the rulings of Islamic law, the main institution with a central role in the Muslim community, directing almost everything related to life. The mosque is the meeting place for liberal as well as radical Muslims.

The word mosque *(masjid)* is derived from the root word *"sajad/sujud"* meaning "to prostrate", which is normally viewed as worship. Worship in Islam is upholding and implementing the revealed law of Allah. The other Arabic word in this context is used usually for the central mosque in town: *"jami'"*, meaning the "gathering mosque" or the "Friday mosque".

Every mosque attempts to be modelled on the first mosque built and directed by Muhammad in Medina which he built before his own house to demonstrate its utter importance.[161] As the *Shari'a* unfolded in Medina, the mosque was to become not only a building where religious teachings were taught but also for the cultural life of the Muslim community.[162] However, since the time of Muhammad, Muslim communities suffer from internal divisions and religious denominational fragmentation stemming from the clash of various schools of thoughts and factions.

Most Muslim scholars agree that "Islam Rises Above All", a basic principle of the Islamic *Shari'a* which permeates all aspects of Islamic jurisprudence. On this principle, a mosque building must be the highest, widest and grandest of all edifices, especially in the land of the unbelievers (non-Muslims) in order to demonstrate power and superiority.[163]

1.7.3 Women in Islam

The position of woman in Islam differs from country to country, and within individual countries between urban and rural areas.[164] The Qur'an proclaims man's superiority over woman, who is required to obey him (Sura 4:34):

> Men are the protectors and maintainers of women, because Allah has given the one more than the other, and because they support them from their means. Therefore the righteous women are devoutly obedient and guard in absence what Allah would have them guard. As to those women on whose part ye fear disloyalty and ill-conduct, admonish them, refuse to share their beds, beat them; but if they return to obedience, seek not against them means: for Allah is most high, great.

---

[161] Since Muhammad is the highest and most venerated model for the Muslim community, they are ordered to imitate him (See Suras 4:80; 33:21; 48:8-10; 59:7; 68:4).

[162] See also Belteshazzar & Abednego (2006).

[163] See Suras 3:110; 4:95; 32:18.

[164] For this topic see also Brooks (1995); Glasser (1998); Mernissi (1985); Tucker (1993).

On this strong position of the man, a patriarchal system is built. The veil, exclusion from public life (either total or partial) and polygamy are signs of the repression of woman, and of her subordinate role. Interpretation of Qur'anic statements have always led to fierce arguments.[165]

The family is of high importance for the internal well-being of Islam. Each Muslim is recommended to marry and have many children. A male Muslim may marry up to four women, given that he treats them all alike, and provides them with accommodation, food and clothing in like manner.[166] In addition, he may have as many concubines as he likes. The Qur'anic order that originally prohibited marriage with persons of other religions (Sura 2:221) was later modified in favour of men: a male Muslim was later allowed to marry Jewish or Christian women (Sura 5:6). Men also have privileges in divorce.

Polygamy is not an obligation, but an option.[167] In recent times, more and more Muslim men choose monogamy, especially in western countries. Besides, Islamic rules are not always observed, particularly in non-Islamic countries, and often a rather liberal attitude towards the legal position of women in society prevails.[168] Many practices regarding women are, moreover, not based on religion, but on culture or can even be traced back to pre-Islamic common law (e.g. pharaonic circumcision)[169].

There is no doubt that women in Islam have a subordinate position, and hardly appear in the public life of many Islamic nations. This is primarily due to the allocation of traditional roles, which means that men are responsible for earning a living, while women are responsible for the household and children.[170] Even today there are women in the Islamic world who never leave the house after marriage because their husbands consider that indecorous. This clear hierarchy and role allocation are seen differently by Muslims and non-Muslims. The former refer to the stability of Muslim families and the protection of women. The latter consider it to be a kind of enslavement of women who are degraded to second-class humans. In Saudi Arabia, women are not even allowed to drive cars or travel without

---

[165] Veil: Suras 24:31; 33:59; exclusion: Sura 33:53-55; polygamy: Suras 4:3; 4:129.
[166] It is virtually impossible for a man to treat several wives equally. Such marital communities are therefore often prone to problems.
[167] Some countries e.g. Turkey, prohibit polygamy in national law.
[168] In some cases the woman is the core of the family. As a result, she often has much influence and catalyzes what her man later does. Although generally less educated than men, women are sometimes also more orthodox than men.
[169] Pharaonic Circumcision is a term used in literature and by the Sudanese and is synonymous with such western technological terms as female circumcision and infibulation. During Pharaonic circumcision, the clitoris and labia minora are removed and then the labia majora is sewn closed while leaving a small opening at the vulva for urination and release of menstrual blood.
[170] This role allocation does not explicitly follow from the Qur'an.

the permission of their husband; they must be escorted by a relative. Further examples showing the inferior position of women in Islam are:
- A woman inherits only half of what a man inherits (Sura 4:176).
- The evidence of two women counts as much as the evidence of one man (Sura 2:282).[171]
- Certain verses in the Qur'an appear to describe women as unclean (Sura 4:43, 5:6).
- Women are to stay quietly in their homes, be modest in appearance and, if they go out of the home, are to wear a veil (hijab) (Sura 33:33).
- Women are not to look at men and are not to display any parts of their bodies to anyone except close family members (Sura 24:31).
- Adultery is forbidden except with captive women (Sura 4:24).
- A man may divorce his wife by repeating a divorce formula three times (Sura 2:224-230).
- A man may marry up to four wives (Sura 4:3).
- The impossibility of treating multiple wives all equally (Sura 4:129).
- Any indecent woman should be locked away until her death (Sura 4:15).
- How men should approach women: *"Your wives are as a tilth unto you; so approach your tilth when or how ye will ..."* (Sura 2:223).
- Women are deficient in intelligence, religion and gratitude (Bukhari Vol1 No. 301).
- Most inhabitants of hell are women (Bukhari Vol1, pp 48 and 301).

Quotations from the *hadith* in this regard:
- Narrated by Abu Hurayrah: Allah's Messenger (peace be upon him) said, "If I were to order anyone to prostrate himself before another, I should order a woman to prostrate herself before her husband." (Al-Tirmidhi Hadith 3255).

- Abu Huraidah reported that the Messenger of Allah was asked: "Who among women is the best? He replied: She who gives pleasure to him (husband) when he looks, obeys him when he bids, and who does not oppose him regarding herself and her riches fearing his displeasure." (Mishkat I, p 216).

- Narrated by Mu'awiyah ibn Haydah: "I said: Apostle of Allah, how should we approach our wives and how should we leave them? He replied: Approach your tilth when or how you will, give her (your wife) food when you take food, clothe when you clothe yourself, do not revile her face, and do not beat her." (Sunan of Abu-Dawood Hadith 2138).

- Abu Huraira (Allah be pleased with him) reported Allah's Messenger (may peace be upon him) as saying: "By Him in Whose hand is my life, when a man calls his wife to his bed, and she does not respond, the One Who is in the heaven is displeased with her until he (her husband) is pleased with her." Abu Huraira (Allah be pleased with him) reported Allah's Messenger (may peace be

---

[171] Legally, a woman is "worth only half" as much as a man.

upon him) as saying: "When a man invites his wife to his bed and she does not come, and he (the husband) spends the night being angry with her, the angels curse her until morning." (Sahih Muslim II, p. 723).

It appears that Muhammad did nothing to improve the plight of women in his day. However, today not all women in Islam are treated badly; some are strong in character and have a great influence on the men in the household. There are even Muslim women who applaud these laws and see them as protective.

1.7.4 Islamic chronology and feasts

The Islamic year is adjusted to the phases of the moon, and is therefore eleven days shorter than the solar year. Thus the months and feasts happen ten or eleven days earlier each year. An Islamic century is thus some three years shorter than a Christian/Common Era one.[172] The first year of the Muslim calendar is 622 AD, the year of the *hijra*, Muhammad's emigration from Mecca to Medina. The lunar year has 354 days and is divided into 12 months of 29 or 30 days each.

A convenient summary is as follows:[173]
• Start of the Islamic calendar: 622 AD = 1 AH
• 20 September 1300 AD = 700 AH
• 2000 AD began in 1420 AH

The names of the twelve Islamic months are:
1. Muharram
2. Safar
3. Rabi' al-Awwal
4. Rabi' ath-Thani
5. Djumada al-Ula
6. Djumada al-Akhira
7. Rajjab
8. Sha'ban
9. Ramadan
10. Shawwal
11. Dhu l-Qa'da
12. Dhu l-Hijja.

Muharram is the Islamic month of mourning (for Shiites only), *Ramadan* is the month of fasting, and *Dhu l-Hijja* is the month of pilgrimage.

---

[172] Full conversion tables can be found in G.S.P. Freeman-Granville, *The Muslim and Christian Calendars*, 2nd edn., London: Collings, 1977 (which goes up to 2000 AD).

[173] AD = Anno Domini (Latin), in the year of the Lord; counting of years starts with birth of Jesus. AH = Anno Hegirae, "after the *Hijra*", counting of years starts with emigration of Muhammad from Mecca to Medina in 622 AD.

Different Islamic groups celebrate different feasts. In orthodox Islam, the following feasts are important:

Day/Month	Name	Description
1 Muharram	New Year's Day	A holiday in many countries. The new year day of Hijrah reminds Muslims of the *Hijra* (migration) of Muhammad from Mecca to Medina in 622 AD.
10 Muharram	*'Ashura*	Shi'a observation of the martyrdom of Imam Hussein.
12 Rabi' al-Awwal	Milad-e Nabi Mawlid an Nabi	The birthday of Muhammad. Not celebrated by all Muslims.
27 Rajjab	Night of Ascension Laylat al-Mi'rajj	Remembers Muhammad's Night Journey into heaven in a dream. Some Muslims believe he was physically transported.
1 Ramadan	Beginning of month of fasting	Believers abstain from food, drink or tobacco from sunrise to sunset, and abstain from intimate relations. The beginning of the fast starts at the dawn prayer *Sahar* and, at the end, the sunset prayer *Iftaar* when a meal is enjoyed with family and friends.
27 Ramadan	Laylat al-Qadr Night of Power	Night of destiny. This is the night of the revelation of the Qur'an starting with the first five verses of Sura 98 to Muhammad. Muslims pray throughout the night, seeking Allah's glory.
1 Shawwal	Eid al Fitr Breaking the Fast	This feast marks the end of Ramadan, the month of fasting. This is a specially great feast where new clothes are bought and presents are given to the poor and friends. Known as Seker Bayram in Turkish, Hari Raya Puasa in South East Asia.
10 Dhu l-Hijja	Eid al Adha Feast of Sacrifice	The greatest feast in Islam. For most Muslims, this is the remembrance of Abraham being expected to sacrifice his son Ishmael. Families slaughter a sacrificial animal, usually a sheep. At the conclusion of *hajj* (holy pilgrimage), celebrations can last up to four days. Known as Kurban Bayram in Turkish, Hari Raya Hajj in South East Asia and Tabaski in parts of Africa.

In the Islamic calendar, the month of fasting,[174] *Ramadan,* takes a special position. Although it is merely counted as the ninth month, it is nonetheless the middle of the religious year and is a "holy month" of Islam when Muhammad is said to have received his first visions. Even those Muslims who have abandoned the daily practice of their faith have to return to the source of their identity, the Qur'an, in *Ramadan.* They take their place in the community of those who remind themselves and others that there is but one Allah. As well as fasting, it is customary to recite the whole of the Qur'an during this month and to carefully observe all prayers. Deeds and rituals done during this month are considered worth more than in any other month.

1.7.5 Customs and dietary laws
At the beginning of any action, even a car ride, the pious Muslim says the words *"bismillah"* (in the name of Allah), and at the end he says *"Alhamdu lillah"* (praise to Allah). This applies also to actions in the workplace and to meals.[175]

When someone intends to do something, or give a promise, the formula *"Insh'allah"* (Allah willing) is added in most cases. If a Muslim meets a fellow-believer, he offers the greeting *"Assalamu alaikum"*, whereupon the other answers, *"Wa alaikum assalam"* (peace be upon you; with you, too, be peace). Before going to sleep and before rising from bed, Allah is glorified with the slogan *"subhanallah"* (Allah be praised). There are many more formulas which are considered to protect against the devil and evil *"jinn"* (demons).

Islam has catalogued nearly everything, food and drink included, into two categories: *halal* (permitted), and *haram* (forbidden). Strict obedience to dietary laws is indispensable for a practicing Muslim,[176] an important part of their religious identity. It is generally valid that all good things whose consumption is medically and morally harmless are allowed. Forbidden food can be placed into three categories:

1) Intoxicating substances that disturb consciousness (wine and other alcoholic beverages in particular, but also drugs).
2) Blood, or meat of animals that did not bleed completely. The consumption of pork is equally forbidden. All meat slaughtered without the formula *basmala*[177] is unclean *(haram).*
3) Noxious and spoiled food.

---

[174] With regard to fasting, see Sura 2:183-187. See also section 1.5.2.
[175] Generally, these formulas *(al-basmala)* are spoken in Arabic. Exceptions exist, however e.g. in Germany, where more than 70% of the Muslims are of Turkish descent. There, the slogans are similar, albeit with Turkish accentuation and spelling.
[176] The terms *halal* (allowed or permitted) and *haram* (forbidden or taboo) are used in this connection. See also Sura 5:5.
[177] The saying *"bismillah"*, usually translated with "in the Name of Allah", is named as *"basmala"* or *"tasmiya"*.

? Questions

- What is the message of Islam?
- Why do women in Islam not have the same rights as men?
- Why do women in Islam often have to wear clothing which covers them totally?
- Why do you think that Mary, the mother of Jesus, is the only woman mentioned in the Qur'an by name?
- What spiritual benefits do you gain by observing the month of fasting, Ramadan?
- Do you celebrate Muhammad's birthday? If yes, why?
- Which Islamic festivals do you celebrate?
- The "feast of sacrifice" is in remembrance of Abraham. What exactly does this feast mean to you? Who was the son to be sacrificed? Can you show me in the Qur'an where it is written?
- The Islamic calendar starts with 622 AD. Was the time prior to this (Muhammad in Mecca) unIslamic?
- Can you explain to me the terms *"halal"* and *"haram"*? How does this affect your life?

2. Christian answers to Muslim objections

> **This chapter provides information about**
> a) the most common Muslim objections and ways of thinking
> b) the doctrinal differences between Christianity and Islam[178]
> c) the way Christians provide answers that Muslims can understand

Islam's challenge to biblical teaching began with Muhammad. The Qur'an, in which Muhammad's supposedly revealed texts are recorded, contains many polemical statements that contradict Christian teachings. Do Christians have reasonable and well-founded answers for these objections? Yes indeed! Christians can give truthful answers to each objection. This chapter is intended to sketch a selection of the most popular Muslim objections.[179]

A good knowledge of the Bible and of Christian teaching are an important prerequisite for discussions with Muslims. Christians are encouraged to study and discuss the material of this chapter with each other in order to become confident in sharing with Muslims. Answers from the Bible should be given with much patience and love. The point is not only to explain *what* Christians believe, but also *why* they believe it. In cases where a Christian does not know the answer offhand, it is better to admit this rather than to give an ill-considered answer. Enough time should then be taken to prepare for a follow-up meeting by researching the point raised, in the spirit of 2Ti 2:15:

> Do your best to present yourself to God as one approved, a workman who does not need to be ashamed and who correctly handles the word of truth.

The answers should challenge Muslims to think about their relation to God and finally accept the truth.[180]

2.1 Theological areas of conflict

Differences between Christians and Muslims, the objections of Muslims and the answers given by Christians are described in the following section. We begin by examining similarities between the two religions, which can serve as entry points for conversations between Christians and Muslims.[181] The following table lists ex-

---

[178] Very few Muslims have a clear understanding of the Christian message and teaching. This is proven, for example, by the Islamic accusation that Christians worship three gods.

[179] There are more Muslim objections against Christianity. See, for example Gilchrist 1999.

[180] It has to be kept in mind that Muslims are, as a rule, not used to questioning religious matters but rather accepting and reciting the Qur'an unconditionally. It is a sin to question Muhammad or the Qur'an.

[181] For this topic, see also the explanations in chapter 3.4.

amples of topics in Christianity and Islam where there are similarities to a certain degree but also differences:

Topic	Similarities	Differences
God is one	The belief that there is only one God.	The Bible and the Qur'an portray God differently.
God as ruler	God lives eternally and rules the world.	The way God rules the world.
Revelation	God has revealed his word to humans.	The method of revelation and which books actually contain God's word.
Sin	Humans commit sin.	The definition of sin is fundamentally different.
Forgiveness	God can forgive human sins.	The way God forgives.
People mentioned	The Qur'an and the Bible talk of the same characters e.g. Abraham, Moses, Noah, Mary, Jesus[182] etc.	Who these people and their missions actually were.
Judgement Day	The fact that there will be a Judgment Day.	What exactly will happen on this day.
Eternity	Existence of heaven (paradise) and hell.	The whole concept differs.

As seen above, many people and topics are mentioned in both the Bible and the Qur'an. But the mission of their adherents and their teachings differ considerably. The Qur'an, for example, tells about Adam's transgression in paradise, but the detail of the story and the importance of the fall of man are totally misunderstood and different from that recounted in Genesis. In Islam, the sin committed by Adam has no further consequence to mankind and therefore Muslims reject the biblical concept of original sin. It ought therefore be clarified that we will not be condemned for Adam's sin, but we have inherited the sinful nature from Adam and thus have a strong inclination to sin.

Jesus holds an important position among the prophets in the Qur'an but, from the Christian point of view, the crucial point is missing: in Islam, Jesus is not the Son of God who died on the cross for the sin of the world. A closer investigation shows that there are more differences than similarities. These will be clarified in the following sections.

---

[182] In the Qur'an, the name of Jesus appears as "Isa". The correct Arabic spelling, however, would be *Yasu'*. A clear reason for this discrepancy cannot be found.

2.2 Muslim objections to the Bible

2.2.1 "The Bible is not God's revelation"

> **Muslim objection**
> "The Bible is not Allah's true revelation. Only the Qur'an is the last and best revelation from Allah."

Firstly, it is important to understand the differences in the doctrine of revelation:

Christianity	Islam
God reveals himself through his creation, in history, and especially through a chosen people, Israel. God reveals his nature and his name (Ex 20). In Jesus, he comes into the world to bring reconciliation and draw people to him. Jesus is the final and essential word of God (Jn 1:1-14; Heb 1). God reveals himself in Jesus. The Bible is the inspired evidence of God's self-revelation. God selected authors who, by inspiration of the Holy Spirit, wrote down the words of Scripture (2Ti 3:16; 2Pe 1:16-21). These people wrote Scripture in their own style. Therefore the Bible has a dual authorship, God through the power of his Spirit and some chosen people. Thus, although humans wrote the Bible, God was in control and ensured that the truth is revealed.	Allah does not reveal himself, only his will. He sends prophets to various nations at different times. Besides a few Arabs, some important Biblical characters are mentioned by name in the Qur'an: Noah, Abraham, Moses, David, Solomon, Zechariah, Jonah, Jesus. Muslims claim that Muhammad is the last prophet and that he was given the Qur'an piece by piece through the archangel Gabriel *(Jibril)*. The original Qur'an, in Arabic, is said to be kept in the seventh heaven and is the "mother of the book". It contains Allah's orders for all the actions of mankind. Muhammad is said to have passed on the revealed text directly and without changes. This means that no human elements are present in the Qur'an and so it is claimed to be the pure word of Allah. Although Muslims maintain that Allah alone addresses mankind in direct speech, it is evident already in the first Sura that portions of the Qur'an are written in the third person (Sura 1:5 "Thee do we worship, and Thine aid we seek").

Christians believe that the Bible is the inspired word of God and the only clear message to mankind regarding the remission of sin, redemption, and the certainty of salvation.

Any human work can never be perfect. The Islamic assertion that today's written Qur'an, passed on by word of mouth and written down 23 years after Muhammad's death by a scribe, is a perfect copy of Allah's original, is therefore difficult to uphold.[183] Muslims believe that the written book, the Qur'an, is Allah's word in an absolute perfect form.

In contrast to this, Christians believe that God's word became human in Jesus Christ,[184] the Son of God who is perfect in the divine sense. So, Muslims have a *book* as their ultimate revelation, whereas Christians were given *a person* as divine revelation. The question is then: which is the more valuable revelation from God, a book or a person?[185]

2.2.2 "The Bible is not the Word of God"

> ⟫ **Muslim objection**
> "The Bible can no longer be the word of God: it was changed and falsified by Jews and Christians *(tahrif)*."

From the Muslim viewpoint, the Qur'an contains everything that had been written down in previous revelations from God.[186] Muslims take the view that these earlier writings have been falsified, and now only the Qur'an contains the true word of God. The Qur'an mentions many biblical topics, but most are presented in shorter, highly distorted, misunderstood and superficial ways.

Since the Qur'an contradicts many biblical statements, Muslims assume that the Bible has been falsified. They declare this without a thorough critical investigation of the Qur'an. Their position actually contradicts Qur'anic statements about the Bible.[187] This means that not everything the Muslims say is in agreement with the Qur'an. The following table illustrates this:

Qur'anic teaching	What today's Muslims believe	What Christians believe
Regarding the origin of the Bible		
The Bible comes from Allah (Sura 5:47).	The Biblical writings were originally revealed by Allah to humankind via prophets.	People chosen by God wrote the Bible under the guidance of the Holy Spirit (2Pe 1:21; 2Ti 3:16).
Regarding the authority of the Bible		
In the Bible is guidance and light from Allah (Suras 5:46; 10:94; 32:23).	The Bible is no longer the word of Allah because Jews and Christians falsified it.	The Bible is the written word of God, which shows us the way of salvation (Jn 20:31).

---

[183] Muslims claim that nothing is perfect and holy except Allah! So how can a book, like the Qur'an, on Earth be perfect?

[184] See Jn 1:14. That Jesus himself should have been a revelation of God, that the word of God has thus come to humans in a human shape, does not fit in the Islamic idea of how Allah reveals himself.

[185] See the story in section 3.3.4.

[186] These books are listed in section 1.5.1.

[187] The Qur'an, however, never mentions the word "Bible", it refers to sections of the Bible like the books of the Law *"Taurat"* and the Gospel *"Injil"*.

The following table gives an explanation of two challenging verses in the Qur'an:[188]

Verse | Arabic	English	Explanation
Sura 32:23 وَلَقَدْ ءَاتَيْنَا مُوسَى ٱلْكِتَٰبَ فَلَا تَكُن فِى مِرْيَةٍ مِّن لِّقَآئِهِۦ ۖ وَجَعَلْنَٰهُ هُدًى لِّبَنِىٓ إِسْرَٰٓءِيلَ ﴿٢٣﴾	"We did indeed aforetime give the Book to Moses: Be not then in doubt of its teaching: and We made it a guide to the Children of Israel."	The Qur'an speaks positively about the OT books of the Bible. It does not say that they have been changed, as Muslims claim.
Sura 10:94 فَإِن كُنتَ فِى شَكٍّ مِّمَّآ أَنزَلْنَآ إِلَيْكَ فَسْـَٔلِ ٱلَّذِينَ يَقْرَءُونَ ٱلْكِتَٰبَ مِن قَبْلِكَ ۚ لَقَدْ جَآءَكَ ٱلْحَقُّ مِن رَّبِّكَ فَلَا تَكُونَنَّ مِنَ ٱلْمُمْتَرِينَ ﴿٩٤﴾	"If thou wert in doubt as to what We have revealed unto thee, then ask those who have been reading the Book from before thee: the Truth hath indeed come to thee from thy Lord: so be in no wise of those in doubt."	This verse actually says that any Muslim who is in doubt about any revelation from Allah should ask the people who have been given the Book before: Jews and Christians!

The authority of the Bible is nowhere questioned in the Qur'an, but is positively emphasized. In Sura 3:3 for example, the Gospel *(Injil)* and the *Taurat* (Law of Moses) are described as being "a guide to mankind". Further, the Qur'an also states (Suras 6:34; 10:64) that nobody can alter the word of Allah. The legitimate question is therefore: why do Muslims today hold a different view that contradicts their Qur'an?

To prove their claim of biblical falsification, Muslims are challenged to answer the following pertinent questions:
1) When and why was the Bible falsified?
2) Who falsified the Bible?
3) How did other believers react, who did not participate in the falsification?
4) How does one know that an "original Bible" existed, unless there is some proof of this allegation?

The trustworthiness of the Bible is confirmed by four foundational truths:
1) **Fulfilled prophecy:** Many can be found in the Bible. Often, events were predicted of several hundred years beforehand. No critic can deny this. This is

---

[188] Further verses from the Qur'an where the autority of the Bible is positively confirmed: Suras 2:136; 3:3; 4:136; 5:68; 10:37.

unique in the whole of history, and occurs in no other religion with such clarity. Examples of prophecies and fulfillment are given in the following table:[189]

Event about Jesus (and when predicted)	Prophecy	Fulfillment
The Messiah's birthplace and pre-existence (700 BC)	Mic 5:2	Lk 2:4-7
His virgin birth (700 BC)	Is 7:14	Mt 1:18-23
His divinity (700 BC)	Is 9:6	Mt 1:23
His arrival in Jerusalem riding on a donkey (480 BC)	Zec 9:9	Mt 21:1-9
He would come to save and to heal (700 BC)	Is 53:3-6	Mt 1:21; Lk 18:40-43; 19:10
The name of the Messiah (700 BC)	Is 49:1-8	Mt 1:21
His suffering and crucifixion	Is 53; Ps 22:1-18	Mt 27:33-50; Jn 18:36-19:37
His burial	Is 53:9	Mt 27:60
His resurrection	Ps 16:8-11	Ac 2:25-32
His ascension	Ps 110:1	Ac 1:6-11; Heb 1:13

2) **Eyewitnesses:** The events recorded in the Bible occurred in public; all Israel was witness. The apostles repeated time and again their call to contact eyewitnesses for confirmation of the truth (Lk 1:2; Ac 2:22-24; 5:30-32; 26:25-26; etc.):
   ... just as they were handed down to us by those who from the first were eyewitnesses and servants of the word. (Lk 1:2).

3) **Archaeology:** Numerous archaeological findings corroborate the credibility of the Bible, confirming its historical truth and accuracy.[190] When compared to other religious books, the Bible is unique as the oldest, testified to by the places, people, titles, and events mentioned therein, and the language and literary formats used to compose the Bible. The discoveries of archaeology can be helpful in removing doubts about the historical trustworthiness of the Bible. When the truth of Scripture is challenged by skeptics, archaeology can be used to demonstrate that the people, places, and events of the Bible are real. There are many highlights concerning archaeological findings; one example is recorded just after 1967:
   Following the capture of the Western Wall and the Temple Mount during the Six-Day War, archeologists conducted more extensive excavations within the

---

[189] See also Nehls (1985) and www.answering-islam.org
[190] See, for example Free (1992) or websites such as www.christiananswers.net which shows via many excavations, solid proof of the Bible's truthfulness.

city limits of modern Jerusalem. One highlight in particular came just southwest of the Old City: two small silver scrolls which uniquely preserved Biblical texts older than the Dead Sea Scrolls were discovered. Both of these amulets contain the Priestly Blessing from the Book of Numbers; one also contains a quote found in parallel verses of Exodus (20:6) and Deuteronomy (5:10 and 7:9). The same verses appear again even later in Daniel (9:4) and Nehemiah (1:5).

4) **History:** Historians of the time, such as Tacitus or Josephus,[191] who were often non-Christians, also confirm biblical accounts. We have therefore no reason to doubt the Bible, because the events described actually happened. Josephus, for instance, wrote in 93 AD:[192]

Now there was about this time Jesus, a wise man, if it be lawful to call him a man, for he was a doer of wonderful works, a teacher of such men as receive the truth with pleasure. He drew over to him both many Jews, and many of the Gentiles. He was the Christ (= Messiah). And when Pilate, at the suggestion of the principal men amongst us, had condemned him to the cross, those that loved him at the first did not forsake him; for he appeared to them alive again the third day; as the divine prophets had foretold these and ten thousand other wonderful things concerning him. And the tribe of Christians so named for him, are not extinct at this day (Antiquities of the Jews, Book 18, Ch 3:3 in *The Works of Flavius Josephus* translated by William Whiston, Milner and Sowerby, London, p392).

2.2.3 "Christians have Bibles with contradictory texts"

Muslim objection
"The Christians have various Bibles that differ in content in several places. God is surely not the author of contradicting Bibles."

This argument is based on the assumption that there are differing Bible texts. Obviously Muslims have never investigated this claim. What they actually mean is that there are differing translations which applies also to the Qur'an. They must learn that various translations address people of different intellectual backgrounds and periods. Since language is dynamic and changes from generation to generation, translations need upgrading. Bibles, however, are all translated from the original Hebrew and Greek texts! It is difficult for most Muslims to understand that it is possible to translate the Bible into various languages without changing its content.

---

[191] Cornelius Tacitus (54–117 AD) was the greatest historian of the Roman Empire. Josephus (shortly after 100 AD) who became known, in his capacity as a Roman citizen, as Flavius Josephus, was a first-century Jewish historian and apologist of priestly and royal ancestry who survived and recorded the destruction of Jerusalem in 70 AD. His works give an important insight into first-century Judaism.

[192] For further scientific proofs to the truth of the Bible, see Stoner (1969).

Concerning the Qur'an in the context of the Islamic teaching on revelation,[193] Muslims take the view that the word of Allah has to be verbatim. This theory is unrealistic, since minor discrepancies necessarily spring up when a text is passed on orally, written down, and copied manually over centuries. This is an assumption with little argumentative power. Muslims assume that the Qur'an is "perfect" without looking critically at the text and its transmission. However, the Qur'an is by no means as "perfect" and homogeneous as Muslims think.[194] In contrast, it can be said that no other book has been so thoroughly investigated, so critically examined as the Bible—and it has passed the test!

Christians can be at ease because, of all books, the Bible has the best proofs of authenticity. No other ancient book has so many ancient manuscripts. Among more than 5000 ancient manuscripts or parts thereof we find three major manuscripts which were written prior to Islam. These show that the Bible we have today is the same as the one the ancient Jews and Christians had used:[195]

1) The **Codex Alexandrinus** was written in the fifth century AD. It contains the entire Bible, with the exception of a few pages of the New Testament, which were lost.[196] The entire text of the manuscript is contained in today's Bible. This manuscript is situated in the British Library in London.

2) The **Codex Sinaiticus** was written at the end of the fourth century AD. It contains the entire New Testament and parts of the Old Testament. It was kept in the library of St. Petersburg, Russia, later sold, and is also now in the British Library in London.

3) The **Codex Vaticanus** is probably the oldest manuscript containing the entire Bible. It was written in the fourth century AD, and is today kept in the Vatican Library in Rome. The last part of the New Testament was written in a different hand than the first.[197]

Regarding alleged changes in the Bible, it must be categorically stated that the above-mentioned manuscripts predate Muhammad. There is no way that changes could have been introduced to the Bible after that time, for Bibles today do not deviate from the above texts. The Qur'an clearly states that the Bible at the time of Muhammad was considered to be divine revelation and that no man can change that. Therefore it must be assumed that Muslims who argue that the Bible has been corrupted are ignorant of these facts.

---

[193] This theory is explained in chapter 2.2.1.
[194] See Gilchrist 1999:23-40.
[195] There are many more manuscripts that prove the integrity and homogeneity of the Bible e.g. the Masoretic text in Hebrew, the Dead Sea scrolls, the Septuagint, the Latin Vulgate (see also Gilchrist 1999:20-23).
[196] The lost texts in Codex Alexandrinus are Mt 1:1-25; Mt 6; Jn 6:50-8:52; 2Co 4:13-12: 6.
[197] From Heb 9:14 till the end of Revelation.

The following table gives an interesting comparison in respect of revelation and book given from God to mankind:

Subject	Christianity	Islam
Perfect, final Revelation from the Creator	Jesus = a living person	Qur'an = a book
Written guidance to mankind	Bible = written word of God	Qur'an and *hadith* = word of Allah

Thus the difference is that in Christianity "The Word became flesh and lived for a while among us..." (namely Jesus, Jn 1:14) whereas in Islam the "Word of Allah" became a book, namely the Qur'an. In Christianity the perfect final revelation is Jesus, a living person, whereas in Islam it is a book, the Qur'an. Thus, in discussing the perfect final revelation between Christianity and Islam, one needs to compare Jesus with the Qur'an.

Questions
- How did the Qur'an become a written text as it exists today?
- Why do Muslims today claim that the Bible has been falsified, while on the other hand the Qur'an confirms the authority of the Bible?
- What evidence do Muslims have concerning the alleged corruption of the Bible?
- At what time in history do Muslims claim the Bible was changed?
- Why do Muslims not follow the advice of the Qur'an according to Sura 10:94–namely, if they are in doubt on the meaning of the revelations, to ask Jews and Christians?
- Since the Qur'an gives credibility to the scripture of Jews and Christians, why do Muslims not consult the Bible for spiritual answers?
- Muslims claim that nothing is perfect and holy except Allah! So how can a book, like the Qur'an, on Earth be perfect?

2.3 Muslim objections to Jesus Christ

2.3.1 "Jesus is no more than an ordinary prophet"

Muslim objection
"Jesus is a prophet like any other. Jesus came only to the Israelites. Muhammad is the greatest and last prophet who came to all mankind", (cf Suras 4:171; 5:75; 33:40; 43:59; 43:63-64).

Muslims acknowledge Jesus as no more than a prophet. Muhammad, on the other hand, is presented as the last, most important and greatest prophet. However the

Qur'an does ascribe a very high and indeed unique position to Jesus.[198] Although he is mentioned in 15 of the 114 Suras of the Qur'an,[199] none of these Suras is exclusively about his person or his work. So a picture of the Qur'anic Jesus must be constructed from the 93 scattered verses which mention him. The most important statements about Jesus and the names given to him are listed below:

Sura	Statement
3:45	He is highly esteemed in this world and in the hereafter.
4:158	He was taken up to heaven (literally: to himself i.e. to Allah) by Allah.
4:171	He is the Messiah (Christ)[200], the word of Allah,[201] a spirit from Allah.
5:113	He created life, healed the sick, and resurrected the dead.
19:19	He was faultless (without sin).[202]
19:20	He was born of a virgin.
19:21	He is a sign to mankind.
19:34	He is the word of truth.
21:91	He is a sign for all the peoples of the earth.
43:61	He has "knowledge of the hour" (of judgment).
43:63	He came with clear proofs.

Most Muslims ignore these remarkable statements in the Qur'an which make Jesus unique. It is significant, however, that the Qur'an never—not even in places where it turns against Christian teachings most fiercely—attributes any sin to Jesus.[203] In addition, it is noteworthy that the Qur'an uses the term Messiah[204], although one would expect it to reject this particular title strongly. So, even the Qur'an describes Jesus as a unique, unequaled person who is more than a prophet. Muslims argue all the same that Jesus was only a prophet sent to his people, the Israelites, basing this statement on the verse of the Bible: He answered, "I was sent only to the lost sheep of Israel." (Mt 15:24; see also Mt 1:21; 10:5-6).

The answer to this is that Jesus' mission must be seen in its entire context.[205] At first, Jesus concentrated his preaching on the Jews, and later extended it to

---

[198] Christians do not need the Qur'an to portray Jesus' uniqueness. But it can be pointed out to Muslims that they should recognize, by carefully studying the Qur'an, that Jesus is more than just a prophet: he is unique and unrivaled.

[199] Regarding Jesus in the Qur'an, see e.g. Parrinder 1965.

[200] Explanation on the topic of "Messiah" see section 3.4.3.

[201] Al-Bukhari (6:200-201; 60.178.236) confirms this title "Allah's Word" for Jesus.

[202] The Qur'an also says that John the Baptist was holy in Sura 19:13. All other prophets except Jesus had to ask for forgiveness of their sins, including Muhammad (Sura 4:106; 40:55; 47:19). The *hadith* by Al-Bukhari (6:324; 54.10.506) confirms that Jesus was spared of the touch of Satan and sin.

[203] Reports exist that all other prophets sinned and asked for forgiveness. Muslim tradition, too, confirms Jesus' sinlessness.

[204] The Qur'an offers no explanation of this title.

[205] Muslims frequently take Biblical verses out of context which leads them to false conclusions. Christians should therefore always be keen to explain the entire context.

the Gentiles. This becomes clear in the numerous encounters Jesus had e.g. with the woman at Jacob's well (Jn 4)[206]. The Great Commission (Mt 28:18-20) and the promise of the Holy Spirit to the disciples (Ac 1:8) show clearly that Jesus' message applies to all mankind.

Jesus' strategy is rooted in God's blessing for Abraham (Ge 12:1-3): '...and in you shall all families of the earth be blessed." This blessing was transferred to Isaac, and so to Jesus. Jesus confirms this with the words, "...for salvation is from the Jews" (Jn 4:22). Thus, Jesus begins his mission with preaching to the Jews because God's blessing comes through the Jews to all mankind.

The Muslim objection that Jesus was sent only to the Israelites contradicts statements of the Qur'an. Sura 19:21 says that Jesus was "a sign to men".

2.3.2 "Jesus is not the Son of God"

 Muslim objection
"It is impossible for Allah to have a son, otherwise he could have daughters and wives, too. Allah is one!" (cf Sura 19:35).

As previously emphasized, Jesus holds a special position in the Qur'an by bearing extraordinary titles and doing extraordinary deeds. On the other hand, fundamental differences certainly do exist:

Statement regarding	Bible	Qur'an
Jesus' position	Son of God	Prophet, emissary *(rasul)*
Jesus' mission	Redemption[207] of mankind	Preaching and healing

Muhammad misunderstood the Christian doctrine of Jesus being the Son of God to mean this in a biological sense, as if God had had a wife, and had a son with her. This misunderstanding is shown in various Qur'anic verses.[208] The position and mission of Jesus in Islam is defined solely according to the Qur'anic concepts of prophet and emissary. The Christian teaching of Jesus, being the Son of God and Saviour of the world, contradicts the Muslim view of God i.e. their concept of the unity and uniqueness of Allah *(Tawhid)*. It is therefore very difficult for Muslims to accept that Allah and Jesus have a father-son relationship. Since, therefore, Allah has no son, he cannot be understood as father either to Jesus or to Muslim believers. The term "father" is consequently strange and unacceptable to Muslims. The statement that God is the father of all Christians, however, is one of the core statements of the Bible (2Th 1:2; 1Pe 1:17).

---

[206] Here, Jesus talks to a Samaritan woman from the village of Sychar. Afterwards, he addresses many people from the same village. As a consequence of this encounter, many believe in Jesus.
[207] Redemption is discussed in chapter 2.4.3.
[208] See Suras 6:100-101; 10:68; 19:88-92.

In the New Testament, the "Son of God", or simply "the Son", is the predominant messianic designation for Jesus. God himself calls Jesus his Son and acknowledges him before the people.[209] Jesus avows himself as the "Son of God" and thus reveals his origin from God and his unique relationship with God, the father.[210] When Jesus calls himself the Son of God, this includes the claim of absolute precedence over all of creation.[211] He is before all things. Through him, everything exists. Thus, the term "Son of God" equates with the term "the Lord". To acknowledge Jesus as the Son of God is to accept and believe the revelation that came through him (Mt 16:16). Even the demons recognized Jesus as the Son of God, showing the cosmic dimension of his revelation.[212]

> **! How to explain the concept of "Son of God"**
>
> When meeting a Muslim man for the first time, you may ask him where he is from and then greet him and say (as the case may be), "Ah, a son of Pakistan" or "Ah, a son of the Nile" or "Ah, a son of Iraq."
>
> But, then you say, "But Pakistan (or what ever) never had a wife/consort, yet YOU are a SON of Pakistan (or whatever)". It has helped several men to remember that "son" does mean other beings besides physical sons born of sexual activity.

2.3.3 "Jesus cannot be God"

> **⨯ Muslim objection**
>
> "Jesus was not God. He was a human like we all are. God is one; he has no partner!" (cf Sura 5:19-20).

In orthodox Islam, it is perceived that Allah will not and cannot reveal himself as a human person. Allah's revelation is just a message that, according to Islam, was revealed through the angel Gabriel to Muhammad and then recorded word for word in writing. That the man Jesus Christ is God's revelation, and thus the eternal word of God in bodily form, does not fit into the Islamic concept of revelation. It is perceived as idolatry (shirk) which is in Islam the worst form of unbelief.

The Biblical statements, however, are clear: the Old Testament predicts that one will come who will be God, and the New Testament shows how this was fulfilled.[213] The Bible states clearly that Jesus is "God with us" (Immanuel; Mt 1:23).

---

[209] See Mt 3:16-17; 17:5; Lk 9:35.
[210] Cf Mt 11:27; Jn 14:20.
[211] Cf Col 1:15-16; Jn 1:3.
[212] Mt 8:29; Mk 3:11; Lk 4:41.
[213] See the following verses in the Bible: Da 7:13-14; Is 7:14; 9:6; Jn 1:10-12; 5:21-27; 10:25-33; 14:6; Ac 20:26-29; Ro 9:4-5; Mt 14:32-33; 26:63-64; Lk 7:48-50; Php 2:5-6; Heb 1:1-4; 2Cor 4:4; 1Jn 5:20; Tit 2:11.

Php 2:6-11 confirms the following facts:

1) Jesus was God while on Earth and at the same time was human.
2) Jesus was the only person who ever lived on Earth uniting the divine and human nature in a perfect way (cf Ro 1:3-4).
3) Jesus, being the only sinless human, was able to offer himself as a perfect sacrifice, dying on the cross for the sins of all those who believe and accept him.
4) This was the mission of Jesus and he was perfectly obedient to it.
5) Jesus receives the highest name ever; all people will have to bow to him and accept his authority.

❗ Conversation with a Muslim

Muslim: Jesus cannot be God; no human person can be God!
Christian: Is there anything impossible for God?
Muslim: No; God can do anything!
Christian: If God would decide today to walk in a human body in front of your house (and at the same time still control the whole universe), would you be able to prevent God to do so?
Muslim: No; nobody can hinder God to do what he pleases!
Christian: Well, God decided in history to appear in a human body form on Earth—and that person is called Jesus! How can you dare to say, this is not possible for God?

2.3.4 "Jesus was not crucified"

✂ Muslim objection

"Jesus was not crucified; it is impossible that Allah should allow a prophet to perish in this horrible way." (cf Sura 4:157).

The Qur'an denies three fundamental facts about Jesus Christ, namely his divinity, his function as the Saviour and his crucifixion. In this, Islam differs in its innermost core from Christianity. A "harmonizing" of both religions, as demanded by liberal theologians, is impossible without renouncing the fundamentals of the Christian faith. Jesus' death on the cross occupies an obscure position in the Qur'an. The statements are unclear and do not present a clear picture. The Qur'an mentions the actual crucifixion only in one place, where it is denied. Sura 4:157-158 says about the Jews:

وَقَوْلِهِمْ إِنَّا قَتَلْنَا ٱلْمَسِيحَ عِيسَى ٱبْنَ مَرْيَمَ رَسُولَ ٱللَّهِ وَمَا قَتَلُوهُ وَمَا صَلَبُوهُ وَلَٰكِن شُبِّهَ لَهُمْ وَإِنَّ ٱلَّذِينَ ٱخْتَلَفُوا۟ فِيهِ لَفِى شَكٍّ مِّنْهُ مَا لَهُم بِهِۦ مِنْ عِلْمٍ إِلَّا ٱتِّبَاعَ ٱلظَّنِّ وَمَا قَتَلُوهُ يَقِينًۢا ﴿١٥٧﴾ بَل رَّفَعَهُ ٱللَّهُ إِلَيْهِ وَكَانَ ٱللَّهُ عَزِيزًا حَكِيمًۢا ﴿١٥٨﴾	That they said (in boast), "We killed Christ Jesus the son of Mary, the Apostle of Allah"—but they killed him not, nor crucified him, but so it was made to appear to them, and those who differ therein are full of doubts, with no (certain) knowledge, but only conjecture to follow, for of a surety they killed him not. Nay, Allah raised him up unto Himself: and Allah is Exalted in Power, Wise.

Since the Qur'an denies the crucifixion, it is not surprising that it does not address the issue of the crucifixion as the means of salvation. The rejection of the crucifixion can be explained in that Muhammad met mostly heretical Christian sectarians, and thus never received a proper explanation of Jesus' redemptive work. The Qur'anic text contains ambiguities, and the words "made to appear to them" gave rise to different theories and speculations about what could have happened. Muslim theologians hold several views e.g.:[214]

- No one was crucified—it "appeared so" to the Jews, but no crucifixion happened.
- Jesus was crucified, but he did not die—the Jews and Romans thought Jesus was dead. However, Jesus recovered in the grave, and he managed to flee (this is an Ahmadiyyan interpretation).
- Another person was crucified in Jesus' place—Allah deceived the people.[215] Jesus was taken into heaven while still alive. It is not clear who replaced Jesus, and many different ideas about that replacement's identity (e.g. Judas) exist. Today, this theory is widespread.

The followers of the *Ahmadiyya* movement[216] assume that Jesus survived the crucifixion and emigrated to India, where he died a natural death.[217] Such a cruel death of a prophet is generally not accepted in Islam, where all prophets are considered to be successful. Allah would never allow the ignominy of a crucifixion. However, this is in contrast to the fate of prophets in the Old Testament.

---

[214] See also Gilchrist (1999:119-125).

[215] That Allah makes better plans i.e. may deceive people, is indicated in the Qur'an in Suras 3:54; 7:99 and 10:21.

[216] This movement is described in section 1.6.5.

[217] This theory is also called the "swoon theory" because Jesus allegedly merely fainted, but did not die, at his crucifixion. All those present were deceived. In the grave, Jesus recovered, rolled away the stone, and fled. This theory was developed already in the 18th and 19th centuries by theologians of the European rationalism. The *Ahmadiyyas* even think that they have found Jesus' grave in Kashmir (India).

To confound the situation further, the Qur'an says according to the translation by Yusuf Ali: "Behold! Allah said: O Jesus! I will take thee and raise thee to Myself." The original read quite differently. The word *"mutawaffi-ka"* means "I will cause thee to die". In his second edition, however, he changed it to "I will take thee", which is similarly deceiving. M.M.Pickthall translates: "I am gathering thee". Why this obvious deception? *"Tawaffi"* means "to die" (according to the following dictionaries: J.Catafago, EW Lane and ibn Mukarram). Ibn Abbas, one of the most esteemed companions of Muhammad, said: "mutawaffi-*ka* is *mumitu-ka*" i.e. "I will cause thee to die" *(Al-Bukhari)*.

Another passage hardens this evidence, saying of Jesus:
So peace is on me the day I was born, the day that I die, and the day that I shall be raised up to life (again). (Sura 19:33).

Many Muslims reason that his death will happen after Jesus' return to earth to defeat *al-Dajjal*, the Anti-Christ. After that, Jesus is expected to be buried next to Muhammad in Medina. This can hardly be a true interpretation, for almost the identical words are used in a verse just prior to the last quotation, this time referring to John the Baptist:
So peace on him the day he was born, the day that he dies, and the day that he will be raised up to life (again). (Sura 19:15).
Why would John the Baptist have died and not Jesus of whom it is said in almost identical words? It contradicts the repeatedly quoted verse Sura 4:157.

In the Christian view, Jesus' crucifixion is the centre and pinnacle of the entire biblical message. The crucifixion is part of Jesus' mission.[218] God demonstrated the greatness of his power when he resurrected Jesus as a living man from the grave. The crucifixion is an accepted fact in the Bible. There are, in addition, other historical witnesses on the subject. The evidence includes:
- The death of the Messiah was predicted by the Old Testament prophets (Is 53; Ps 22:1-8).
- Jesus' sacrificial death is the logical consequence and fulfilment of Old Testament teaching (Lk 24:26; 24:44). Jesus' one-time sacrificial death in the New Testament replaces the Old Testament sacrifices which had to be offered repeatedly (Heb 10:1-18).
- About a third of the Gospel is concerned with Jesus' last week on earth, his death and resurrection.
- Jesus predicted his own death (Lk 9:22; 22:37).
- There are several eyewitnesses' testimonies (2Pe 1:16-18; 1Jn 1:1-3; 1Co 15:3-8).
- Historians reported Jesus' death (e.g. Josephus and Cornelius Tacitus, first-century historians).
- The testimony of people whose lives were changed by Jesus (Ac 4:8-13; 7:56; 24:24).

---

[218] Jesus' mission was to die on the cross as the "final, perfect" sacrifice, so that all those who believe in him can receive forgiveness of sins and eternal life (Jn 3:16; 5:24; 14:6; 20:31).

The following table presents the amazing disparity of the status of the crucifixion among Christians, Jews, and Muslims:

Christianity	Judaism	Islam (according to the Qur'an)
Jesus **is** the Messiah, and he **did** die on the cross.	Jesus was **not** the Messiah, but he **did** die on the cross.	Jesus **was** the Messiah, but he did **not** die on the cross.

2.3.5 "The life of Muhammad was nobler than of Jesus"

 Muslim objection
"Muhammad is the final prophet of Allah and his life is of much nobler character that that of Jesus!"

Many Muslims are aware that Christians have the highest esteem for Jesus and even worship him. This is strange to them and they think that Christians have committed idolatry. In Islam, Muhammad is the final and greatest prophet of all, and of much nobler character than any other prophet, including Jesus.

Muslims often idealize Muhammad by ascribing things to him which he never did or said out of their desire to lift Muhammad higher than he really is. However, this attitude is closer to "wishful thinking" than to reality. Therefore, it is important for Christians to listen carefully to statements made by Muslims and ask them kindly for evidence to supports such claims. As said in section 2.3.1, Jesus is portrayed as superior to everyone else even in the Qur'an, including Muhammad. The following table illustrates striking comparisons between the life of Jesus and Muhammad:

Topic	Life of Jesus	Life of Muhammad
Marriage	God's concept of marriage is described in the creation narrative (Ge 1:27; 2:21-25). Jesus confirms this law that marriage is between one man and one woman (Mk 10:2-12).	Muhammad, as a model to all Muslims, had many wives. The Qur'an (Sura 4:3) allows every Muslim man to have up to four wives, which has caused much hardship to many women.
Authority to forgive sins	Jesus has the power and authority to forgive peoples sins! (Mt 9:1-8; Mk 2:1-12; Ro 10:9).	There is no claim in the Qur'an that Muhammad ever forgave peoples' sins in the name of Allah.
Table continues on next page.		

Topic	Life of Jesus	Life of Muhammad
Future kingdom and peace	Jesus proclaimed a spiritual kingdom based on truth, love, peace with God, joy, self denial, devotion and a life devoted to God (Mt 26:26-29; 1Pe 2:9-10, Rev 1:5-6).	The treaty which Muhammad made with the leaders of Medina (622 AD) was the foundation of his future political life and the basis for the military expansion of his empire. Today, it is the aim of radical Muslims to posses the whole world and introduce Islamic law on order to establish peace.
Self-interest and power	Jesus was aware of his mission and was obedient to his Father in heaven. Though Jesus knew that he would die on the cross in Jerusalem, he did not flee out of self-interest, but came willingly to Jerusalem to die as a sacrifice for all who believe in Him (Mt 20:17-19).	Muhammad emigrated from Mecca to Medina in 622 AD. He was persecuted by his own people in Mecca and chose to go where his personal security was granted! In Medina he established an army and grew rapidly in power and wealth.
Forgiveness	Jesus ordered his followers to forgive others willingly (Mt 6:14-15).	Muhammad practiced the law of "blood revenge" i.e. teeth for teeth. Muslims do not know unconditional forgiveness.
Successor	Jesus announced that, after his death, the Holy Spirit will come and guide all disciples (Jn 14-16).	Since Muhammad did not appoint a successor, after he died his followers quarrelled over who would be the future leader.

? Questions
- Why does the Qur'an say that Jesus is "a holy son" (Sura 19:19), whereas Muhammad was commanded by Allah to ask for forgiveness for his sins (Sura 48:2)?
- The Qur'an indicates (Suras 3:54; 7:99; 10:21) that Allah is quicker to make plans than mankind and may thus deceive people. If this is the case, how do you know for sure what in history is now deception or true?
- Why does the Qur'an reject the crucifixion in one verse (Sura 4:157) whereas it is a fact of history that it was indeed Jesus who was crucified?
- The statements in the Qur'an portrays Jesus higher than Muhammad. Why then do Muslims believe that Muhammad was the greatest prophet?
- Theological understanding is clear that the Messiah is the Son of God. Why then do Muslims accept Jesus as the Messiah but reject him as the Son of God?
- If Muhammad is the final prophet, then why was Jesus taken up to heaven (Sura 4:158)? Would not that make Jesus the seal and final prophet?

2.4 Muslim objections to Christian teaching

2.4.1 "God is portrayed wrongly in the Bible"

 Muslim objection
"Allah is the only true God, who created the universe. The Christian Bible pictures many characteristics of God with which Muslims cannot agree. Only in the Qur'an can one find the true description of God."

When Muslims call God by the Arabic name "Allah", they use a Semitic root that can also be found in the Hebrew *Elah, El* and *Elohim*. Arabic-speaking Christians today use the term "Allah" as indeed they did prior to the appearance of Islam.[219] Has the one God, who revealed himself in the Biblical history of salvation, also revealed himself in the Qur'an? Do the Biblical and the Qur'anic testimonies about God agree? The answer is absolutely *no!* A brief explanation is given in the following paragraphs.

Some Christians are inclined to say that all Muslims pray to a demon or a false god. This statement is simplistic and dangerous. People should hesitate to judge each other but rather leave judgment to God. One would only have to ask the question to which God did, for example, Cornelius pray (Ac 10:2): a demon or a false god? Cornelius, like many Muslims, prayed honestly to God, although he hardly knew him. He had yet to hear the message of Jesus, like the Muslims, to be capable of being reconciled with God. Only then could Cornelius truly know God.

! **True story**
A Muslim related the following story: "In the past I have prayed several personal prayers to Allah. However, since Allah is far away, my private prayer angel has to carry my requests on a long journey to Allah. None of my requests have so far been answered by Allah. I have the great suspicion that my angel does not do a good job. He most likely has never reached Allah but became tired and slept on his way, or met another angel and chatted with him and thus forgot to carry my requests to Allah! I am so frustrated and don't know what to do!"

Many Muslims have no assurance that their prayers ever reach Allah. Christians have thus a wonderful opportunity to explain the concept of God, who is always near us and hears us through his Spirit.

---

[219] In Arabic versions of the Bible, "God" is translated as "Allah". Although Arab Christians as well as Muslims say "Allah" when they talk about God, the understanding of that term is different.

How, then, is Allah described in the Qur'an? Some characteristics seem to be the same as those in the Bible e.g. God is the creator, he is merciful, almighty, omniscient, and eternal—but some of the most important characteristics are fundamentally different. When the complete description of God in the Bible is compared with the Qur'an, it becomes clear that the one and only God cannot have revealed himself both in the Bible and in the Qur'an. Serious differences are listed here:[220]

Characteristics	God in the Bible	Allah in the Qur'an
Relationship	Father to child (loving relationship).	Master to slave (employer-employee relationship).
Revelation	Reveals his will and himself.	Reveals only his will.
Salvation	Through Jesus only, with certainty of salvation.	By accumulating merit before Allah in the form of good works. There is no certainty of salvation.
Covenant	Covenant with guarantee that he will keep it; many promises.	No covenant, few promises, Allah is depicted as being capricious.
Peace	Upon accepting his gift of eternal life through Christ (inner peace).	When Islam is established on the whole Earth (political peace).
Nature	Trinity	Allah is one, without son or partner.

From this we conclude that the God in the Bible cannot be the same as Allah in the Qur'an. In the same way as Peter made the true God known to Cornelius (Ac 10), Christians are given the task today of making God and his biblical message in Jesus Christ known to Muslims.

2.4.2 "There is no Trinity"

 Muslim objection
"There is only one God! How can Christians believe in the 'Trinity'? These are three Gods—but Allah is only one!" (cf Suras 4:171; 5:75-76).

Who can give a description of the eternal God? Human minds are unable to fathom what is beyond our perception. For this reason God introduced Himself largely in metaphors until He revealed Himself on the human level in Jesus Christ. Muslims consider the doctrine of the Trinity,[221] as well as Jesus being the Son of

---

[220] For further explanations see Gilchrist (2003:137-140).

[221] The doctrine of the Trinity (see also Gilchrist 1999:70-89) is the result of continuous exploration by the Church of the biblical data, thrashed out in debate and treatises, and eventually formulated at the First Council of Nicaea in 325 AD in a way they believed was consistent with the biblical witness. It was further refined in later councils and writings. The most widely recognized Biblical foundations for the doctrine's formulation are in the Gospel of John.

God, a violation of the doctrine of the unity of God *(Tawhid)*. Muhammad, as far as can be concluded from the Qur'an, never knew the Biblical writings through which the one God reveals himself as being triune, consisting of Father, Son, and Holy Spirit. Curiously, the Bible gives no explanation regarding God's Trinity, but merely states the fact (Mt 28:19). However, Isaiah was given a vision which makes the Trinity feasible (Is 63:7-10): Jahveh (v 7) became the Saviour (v 8, Hebr. *Yeshua*, the actual name of Jesus when he walked the earth). Then it is said that the people rebelled against *Yeshua* and grieved his Holy Spirit (v 10).

It seems that Muhammad only knew about the Trinity by hearsay, which accounts for the statement in the Qur'an that Mary was part of it (cf Sura 5:119) which no Christian actually believes. The nature of this subject makes it imperative to treat it with reverence in the knowledge of the limitations of our minds. To believe in the triune nature of God will always be an act of faith, as is the perception of His oneness.

The three "personalities" of God are described in the Bible as follows:

- **As God the Father.**[222] The most common name for God in the New Testament (Mt 18:10; Lk 12:32; Jn 11:41; 14:12). The Bible portrays God as a person who relates to man in a personal way. The Lord of the universe is the God of relationships. In the Godhead, the Father, Son and Spirit relate to each other in perfect love. Because of His nature, God invites man to enter into a relationship with Him, and get to know him as Father.

- **As God the Son.** Jesus talked about his relationship to the heavenly Father in words that emphasized his complete uniqueness as the Son of God (Mt 11:27; Jn 17:1-5). Jesus came into this world from the Father, and he left the world by returning to the Father (Jn 16:28). Jesus was not created but pre-existed before his incarnation (Mic 5:2; Jn 1:1-2). It is important to emphasize such Biblical texts in discussions with Muslims, because they clearly show the internal and divine relationship between Father and Son.

- **As God the Holy Spirit.** The Holy Spirit announced by Jesus (Jn 14-16) comes from the Father and testifies to Jesus (Jn 15:26), convicts the world of sin, righteousness and judgment (Jn 16:8), will be with the believers forever and is the Spirit of Truth who lives in them (Jn 14:16-17). The Holy Spirit leads disciples into all truth and reminds them of what Jesus said (Jn 14:26).

In some places, the Bible mentions the three persons of the Godhead—Father, Son, and Holy Spirit—in one sentence (Mt 28:19; 2Co 13:14; Eph 2:18). These

---

[222] This title does not occur in Islam, and is therefore rejected.

verses can be quoted in discussions with Muslims, but Isaiah 63:7-10 is most explanatory. Examples from nature, too, show that "three in one" is possible:
• The sun manifests itself as matter, light and warmth.
• Water can appear in three states: as a liquid, solid, or gas.
• A coin can be viewed from three sides (top, bottom, and edge).
• Time consists of past, present, and future.
• A human person consists of body, soul and spirit.

Such illustrations can in part but not fully help towards a better understanding of the Trinity. It is important, though, to explain to Muslims that Christians believe in only one God (Dt 6:4) who reveals himself in three personalities.

2.4.3 "The way to paradise cannot be obtained by Jesus' death"

 Muslim objection
"To be accepted into paradise, one has to do good works, which are then rewarded by Allah. How can Jesus die for mankind so that their sins can be forgiven? That is impossible" (cf Sura 6:164).

Muslims reject Jesus' substitutional, sacrificial death on the cross. They have their own perception of how their sins can be forgiven. The following table explains the differences regarding salvation and the way to paradise between Christianity and Islam:

Christian teaching	Islamic teaching and popular Islam
Reconciliation means the restoration of communion with God. This was introduced by God in the Old Testament and completed in the New Testament. Both Testaments are based on the premise that sin separates a person from God. By that token, the offender is excluded from the presence of God in time and eternity. A remedy is offered by God to address this dilemma.	Besides clinging to a false concept of God, Muslims have a false understanding of sin and its consequences. Sin is not really seen as an affront towards God, but rather an action which blocks the way of the offender from the paradise. Purity of heart is seldom the issue. Muslims believe that on Judgment Day good deeds are weighed against bad deeds one has performed. If the good deeds are weightier, the sinner may go to paradise. For self-assessment purposes, Islamic theology has provided a list of the severity of sins: *Kkati'a* is termed a mistake, a stumbling.
Table continues on next page.	

Christian teaching	Islamic teaching and popular Islam
Someone else will be executed instead of the offender—sacrifice becomes the offender's substitute. In Lev 4 and 16, the sinner is commanded to sacrifice a particular animal as a substitute for himself. Because "the wages of sin is death" (Ro 6:23) and because the life of the flesh is in the blood, an offender can only be reconciled to the Lord by the shedding of blood (cf Lev 17:11). This sacrificial ritual of the Old Testament is completed in Jesus Christ who is "...the Lamb of God, who takes away the sin of the world!" (Jn 1:29). By Jesus' sacrificial death, a way of forgiveness and thus reconciliation with God was established for all people who accept this order of God in faith.[223] All animal sacrifices offered during the time of the OT pointed to Jesus, the only valid sacrifice (cf Heb 10:10-14). Jesus' death on the cross is therefore the only way by which people can be saved (Jn 14:6; Heb 10:1-18; 1Pe 3:18). God has, in his love, revealed to us one way of salvation; all are asked to return this love by accepting Jesus personally as their Saviour (Jn 3:16). As a result, God promises all those who accept him and his way of salvation the certainty of eternal life (1Jn 5:11-13; Jn 5:24). God offers salvation as a gift which cannot be obtained by good works (Eph 2:8-9; Ro 6:23). This divine concept of reconciliation is difficult to understand for many people, especially Muslims. It is comprehensible only when the Holy Spirit reveals it (Ac 10:44).	*Dhanb* is a fault, a crime. *Ithm* is a graver sin. *Shirk* and *kufr* are considered the most serious sin: such as to add a partner to Allah (faith in Christ is therefore *shirk*). "Light sins" can be compensated with good works. For heavier sins forgiveness *(istighfar)* is sought. *Shirk* and *kufr* require *taubah* i.e. repentance. Based on this understanding, Muslims see no need for a saviour. The Qur'an offers no clear message as to how sins can be forgiven, and there is no certainty of forgiveness.[224] Since the Qur'an does not contain a doctrine of salvation, several theories evolved in the course of time how one may be able to enter paradise. Below some of the most common ideas that Muslims hold regarding entrance to paradise (some arise from popular belief rather than formal Islamic theology): 1. Salvation through good works (cf Sura 7:7-9). Muslims try to please Allah by their own efforts to keep the Islamic law. 2. Salvation through Allah's mercy (cf. Sura 3:31). Many Muslims simply hope that Allah will somehow benevolently forgive their sins. 3. Salvation through predestination (cf Suras 5:23; 14:4; 30:29). Allah determines in advance whom he will, or will not, allow into paradise. 4. Many Muslims hope that Muhammad, the prophet of Islam, will speak up for them on Judgment Day. 5. Every person will be punished in hell for his sins for a limited time. After that, all Muslims hope to enter paradise. 6. The martyrs that fight and die for Islam in "holy war" *(jihad)* are promised to enter paradise immediately (cf Sura 9:20-22; 9:111). 7. Some Muslims believe that if they die on their pilgrimage to Mecca, they will enter paradise immediately.

---

[223] It has to be emphasized that only Jesus was able to achieve this, since he was the only one sinless and perfect (Heb 4:15).

[224] Even Muhammad did not seem to have assurance of where he would go after death (Sura 46:9; Mushkatu'l Masabih III, p118).

In conclusion:

Christianity	Islam
God has provided:	Allah has offered:
1) God provided Jesus to be the Saviour for all who seek forgiveness and pardon through him as their sacrifice for sin. Only one way of salvation is offered.	1) Salvation may be obtained by striving to do good deeds and to obey the *Shari'a*. People may choose from a variety of different ways of going to paradise.
2) God offers eternal life (heaven) as a gift. Everyone who accepts this gift will have their sins forgiven.	2) People may try these ways through their own efforts. Nobody can know for sure whether their sins are forgiven.
3) God guarantees that whoever accepts his way of salvation by faith will have eternal life and will enter heaven.	3) Allah offers no guarantee to anyone (though martyrs think they get to paradise).

2.4.4 "There is no original sin"

 Muslim objection

"We do not inherit sin. All people are born sinless and merely copy the sinful life of adults while they grow up. A person becomes a sinner by trespassing the *Shari'a*" (cf Sura 6:164).

Another difference between the two religions is the understanding of human sinfulness:

Christian teaching	Islamic teaching and popular Islam
The existence of sin in the world is traced back to the first sin of Adam and Eve in the garden. Adam was the first person to sin, and thereby sin entered the world (Ge 3). Since all mankind is descended from Adam, all are affected by the consequences of this sin and have inherited an inclination to sin (cf Ro 3:23; 5). This is called "original sin". Every child at birth is sinless (has not committed any sin yet), but has inherited a nature which is inclined to sin.	The Qur'an does not teach "original sin". Every human is born unburdened, pure and free (cf Sura 30:30). Man is thus not in a state of separation from Allah. Some Muslims believe that every person is born a Muslim and is only separated from Allah when he rejects Islam. Yet the Qur'an also contains a narrative of the fall. However, contrary to the Bible, Adam and his wife did not try to hide their sin, but immediately asked Allah for forgiveness: "They said: Our Lord! We have wronged our own souls ..." (Sura 7:23).
Table continues on next page.	

Christian teaching	Islamic teaching and popular Islam
Adam rebelled against God and ignored his instructions. This broke his fellowship with God. The consequence is that all descendants of Adam, in other words all mankind, are "spiritually dead" by nature and thus separated from God. God's love for us is of eternal constancy; he has therefore prepared a way for sins to be forgiven so that mankind can be reconciled with God (Jn 3:16; 14:6). God calls all men and women everywhere to repent (return to him), accept his offer of pardon and enter into a new relationship that includes purification from sins (Heb 8).	Thus, Adam and his wife did not sin primarily against Allah, but themselves. Their transgression of Allah's command changed neither their relationship to Allah nor to each other. They were banished from paradise by Allah, but he forgave their transgression, and therefore their sin had no further consequence for mankind. Islam teaches that humans are morally neutral creatures that can freely choose between good and bad. Although the Qur'an regrets the inclination to evil (cf Sura 100:6-8), human failure is not considered to be a serious misdeed.

Muslims hold the view that they do not need salvation and reconciliation with God through Jesus' death on the cross. They think that they can erase their sins by their own strength, by doing good works. The Bible declares that it is impossible to do good without God's enabling power. Moreover, all good works are not enough to pay for transgressions (Is 64:6). Therefore, humans cannot save themselves (cf Eph 2:8-9).

Muslims agree with Christians that Adam and his wife were expelled from paradise. Why then, were they expelled when God seemingly had forgiven them? Why were they, and all their descendants, sentenced to live and die on Earth? Islam has no answer to these crucial questions.

Muslims also believe that Jesus was the only one who ascended to heaven without dying. Why was this possible only for Jesus, and not for any other human being, including Adam and Muhammad? One should call Muslims' attention to the fact that Jesus said he would return to where he came from (Jn 3:13; 16:28). Jesus is the only way to eternal life (Jn 14:6; 5:24). Without his work of redemption, there is no way into heaven.

2.4.5 "The prayers of Christians are invalid"

Muslim objection
"The correct prayer ritual is the Islamic way! The prayer direction is towards Mecca. Allah will only accept these prayers!" (Sura 2:142-144).

The following table explains the difference of prayer in Christianity and Islam. It is important for Christians to understand the concept of prayer in both religions and be able to explain this to Muslims. However, first of all the knowledge gained should help to pose challenging questions.

Prayer in Christianity	Prayer in Islam
The Christian way of prayer is described in the Bible, where Jesus serves as a model (Lk 11:1-4). Various examples of wording or formulation and postures can be observed, but there is no ritual order to be rigidly observed. Jesus left us a model prayer, the so-called "Lords Prayer", which reflects basic components. Prayer is seen as the greatest spiritual weapon and is made through faith in the power of the Holy Spirit (Eph 6:18). Christians practice personal as well as communal prayer. Various denominations have different emphases in practice. The following types of prayers are distinguished. Essentially, prayer has at least some of these components: 1) Worship, adoration 2) Thanksgiving 3) Confession 4) Submission 5) Intercession 6) Petition[225] 7) Repentance Depending on the situation, Christians are free to choose their posture. The Lord's Prayer is the best known prayer: "Our Father in heaven, hallowed be your name, your kingdom come, your will be done, on earth as in heaven. Give us today our daily bread. Forgive us our sins as we forgive those who sin against us. Save us from the time of trial and deliver us from evil. For the kingdom, the power, and the glory are yours now and for ever. Amen."[226]	The Islamic prayer *(salat)* is basically a rigid prescribed ritual. It is a duty to pray and by performing it Muslims hope to accumulate blessings from Allah.[227] Guidelines for prayer are to be found in the Qur'an as well as in the *hadith*. There are small differences in the ritual among the different Islamic sects. The following points may be highlighted: 1) The Call to Prayer *(adhan)* is said always in the same format by the *mu'adhdhin*. 2) Muslims have to ritually wash themselves in order to be fit to stand before Allah. 3) The five daily prayers include the following prescribed points: • Muslims may perform the prayer alone, but it is recommended that it is done within the community. • The *imam* is at the front and leads the collective prayers. • The whole community (men and women pray separately) simply follows the directions of the *imam*. The prayers are recited audibly. • The words of prayer are equally prescribed and are to be spoken in Arabic. • The relevant postures are prescribed. • Prayer has to be directed towards Mecca; otherwise it is invalid. • Prayer times are set each day and are adjusted to the sunrise and sunset. During the five prayer times, Muslims say the following words in Arabic: Allah is very great *("Allahu Akbar")*; reciting the first chapter of the Qur'an; Glory be to my Lord Almighty; Allah hears those who call upon Him; Our Lord, praise be to You; Glory be to my Lord, the Most High; Peace be upon you and Allah's blessings".

[225] Prayer as petition to God: personal needs are prayed about in conjunction with concern for the well being of others.

[226] The translation of the English Language Liturgical Consultation (ELLC), an ecumenical translation.

[227] See also section 1.5.2. The Qur'an speaks on prayer, but it is not specifically written that Muslims need to pray five times a day: Suras 2:43; 11:114; 17:78f ; 30:17f; 20:130.

It is not that common that personal prayers *(du'a')* are offered as well, since for most Muslims the five ritual daily prayers are all that count. The difference in which prayer is performed within to the two faiths is striking. In Christianity it is a personal conversation between man and God, like a child to his father. Muslims see themselves as servants of Allah. In Islam, Muslims do not have assurance whether Allah has heard their prayers. Christians may therefore share with Muslims the experience of their own prayer life with God.

2.4.6 "Christians do not fast"

 Muslim objection
"The correct way of fasting is the Islamic way! Allah will only accept fasting during the month of Ramadan!" (Sura 2:185).

The following table explains the difference in fasting between Christianity and Islam. Christians need to understand the concept of fasting in both religions and be able to explain this to Muslims. The knowledge gained should help to pose challenging questions.

Christian teaching	Islamic teaching and popular Islam
Fasting generally means going without all food and drink for a period (e.g. Est 4:16), not merely refraining from certain foods. However, the following differences can be seen in practise: 1. No drinking or eating (Est 4:16; Ac 9:9), longest period three days and nights, except Ex 34:28. 2. Usually only not eating; drinking is essential to survive, (2Sa 12:16-17; Mt 4:2), 3. Eating and drinking at a reduced level (Da 10:3). Sometimes inner attitude was manifested by outward signs (Ne 9:1). **1. In the Old Testament** a) There were certain annual fasts. The Hebrews fasted on the Day of Atonement (Lev 16:29). After the Exile, four other annual fasts were observed (Zec 8:19)—all, according to the Talmud, marking disasters in Jewish history.	There are several Muslim fasts. The most important one is during the month of Ramadan, the ninth month of the Muslim calendar. It is obligatory to a Muslim (Sura 2:183-185). Verse 185 declares that the Qur'an was revealed in the month of Ramadan. Muslims believe (based on a reported saying of Muhammad) that during Ramadan the gates of paradise are open and the gates of hell are closed, and that all who keep the fast will be pardoned of all their past venial (excusable) sins. **1. Regulations for Ramadan** 1. It cannot begin until a Muslim is able to state that he has seen the new moon. 2. The fast must be kept from about the age of ten or twelve years (certain exemptions: sick, travellers etc.).

Table continues on next page. ⟶

Christian teaching	Islamic teaching and popular Islam
b) Occasional fasts: sometimes individual (e.g. 2Sa 12:22), or sometimes corporate (e.g. Jdg 20:26). **Purpose of fasting** • Expression of grief (1Sa 31:13; Est 4:3; Ps 35:13-14). • Penitence (1Sa 7:6; Da 9:3-4; Jnh 3:5-8) • A way by which men might humble themselves (Ezr 8:21). • Self-inflicted punishment. • Often directed towards securing the guidance of God. • On behalf of others (Ezr 10:6). Some thought that fasting would automatically gain man a hearing from God (Is 58:3-4) but the prophets declared that, without right conduct, fasting was in vain (Is 58:5-12; Jer 14:11-12; Zec 7). **2. In the New Testament** a) General Jewish practise: the Day of Atonement is the only annual fast referred to in the NT (Ac 27:9). Some strict Pharisees fasted every Monday and Thursday (Lk 18:12). Other devout Jews, like Anna, might fast often (Lk 2:37). b) Jesus: time of temptation (Mt 4:2), to prepare for his future ministry. Fasting must be Godward (Mt 6:16-18), and appropriate (Mt 9:14-17; Mk 2:18-22). c) In Acts: leaders of the church fast when choosing missionaries (Ac 13:2-3) and elders (Ac 14:23). **3. Today** In the New Testament, fasting is done out of freewill of individual Christians. However, the Roman Catholic Church made it a rule and law to gain merit for heaven.	3. It commences at dawn until sunset. During this period, not even one's own spittle should be swallowed. 4. An additional 20 *rak'a* are said after the night prayer. 5. The fast lasts for 30 days, the length of a Muslim month. 6. During the nighttime, a Muslim can eat as much as he likes and indulge in any lawful pleasure. 7. If a Muslim is unable to keep the fast, he is allowed to make it up later. **2. Benefits** (according to general Muslim belief) 1. Fasting enables one to become humble and fearful of Allah's punishment. 2. It is supposed to break one's lust and cravings. 3. It ensures sympathy, compassion and mercy, enabling one to enjoy giving alms to the poor. 4. It affords an opportunity for both the rich and the poor, the king and the servant, the mighty and the meek to experience hunger and for all to be on an equal footing. 5. It melts away unhealthy deposits in the body, specifically in the case of those who eat very rich food and rarely exercise. **3. Summary** • Every Muslim has to keep the fast and obey the regulations. • Done in public, they watch one another's observance of it.

Table continues on next page.

Christian teaching	Islamic teaching and popular Islam
The Reformation brought change in this matter, but failed to stress biblical fasting. The result today is that, in many churches, fasting is in the background or completely neglected.	• Muslims have certain hopes linked with this fast e.g. they hope to become more conscious of Allah, they desire happiness in this world as well as prosperity in the hereafter, forgiveness of sins, blessings and rewards from Allah, etc. However, Muslims have no assurance of any of this.
4. Benefits (see ref. above) • To come closer and to get to know God our Father better. • Before an important decision. • Out of repentance. • In connection with intercession (Mk 9:29).	• Some guidelines regarding the fast are found in the *hadith*, the Islamic traditions, but few specific regulations are found in the Qur'an.
5. Summary Fasting is generally done in secret, a matter between man and God. There are no strict laws or regulations. Directions for fasting, especially the teaching of Jesus, are only found in the Bible.	

In general, fasting among Christians it is not as rigidly practiced as in Islam. Muslims have no assurance whether Allah will give rewards and blessings to those who fast. Christians may therefore challenge Muslims on this and explain their own experience of fasting.

? Questions
• What do you know about Allah?
• Do you feel Allah is pleased with you?
• How does Allah show his love for you?
• Do you think Allah can do anything?
• Do you think it is possible for Allah to appear on Earth as a human and at the same time continue to rule the universe?
• How do you think that "sin" came into the world?
• What does "sin" mean to you?
• What is necessary to enter paradise?
• Do you think you fulfil these conditions to enter paradise?
• Why do you pray five times a day? Where exactly is it written?
• What benefits do you get by keeping the fast during Ramadan?
• Would you please show me the references where the fast during Ramadan is commanded?

2.5 Further Muslim Objections

2.5.1 "The Gospel of Barnabas is true"

>< **Muslim objection**
"The Bible contains four gospels, Matthew, Mark, Luke, and John. Jesus received only one Gospel, why are there now four? Why did Christians remove the Gospel of Barnabas?"

Muslims do not consider the four gospels as authentic. Many have heard about a "Gospel of Barnabas"[228] and are told that this is the true gospel. Muslims allege that it was written in the first century AD by the apostle Barnabas. The gospel first appeared in Holland in 1709. Muslims like to raise this topic, but Christians should confidently ask the Muslims for proofs.[229]

What is this Gospel? Its content betrays even to lay people that it is an Islamic forgery. It can quite accurately be dated to the 14th Century AD. The content is a grossly disfigured construction of the life of Christ and is made to coincide in many points with Islamic teaching. It is obviously aimed at persuading Christians of that time to turn to Islam. Some statements not only conflict with the Bible, but also the Qur'an.

The whole narrative is dense with problems:
- Some of the background culture does not reflect the first century, the time of the New Testament, but rather the Middle Ages e.g. duels between rivals in a love affair.
- The text contains citations from Dante (an Italian poet and politician, 1265–1321).
- The text contains grave geographical and cultural errors about the Holy Land as well as anachronisms. It is obvious that the writer had never been there. It is said (ch 20), for example, that Jesus sailed to Nazareth which is supposed to be on the shore of Lake Galilee. Nazareth is, however, about 20 kms away from the lake and is crested on a mountain. Jesus is said to walk *up* to Caparnaum (ch 21), which lies on the shores of Lake Galilee about 200m below sea level. No one can walk up to it! Further, Jesus keeps "Lent" (chs 91-92), which was introduced to the Church after the fourth Century AD, mentions casks (barrels) which were invented much later in Gall, mentions *three* Magi (ch 6; the Bible gives no number), a tradition introduced much later as well, lets Eve eat an apple (ch 40) which is again a later tradition, mentions coins (*minuti*, ch 54) which were first used in Spain in the seventh century AD and so on.

---

[228] See English Translation: The Gospel of Barnabas, Islamic Publications Ltd., Lahore, Pakistan.
[229] Muslims may also be challenged as to whether they regard the Gospel of Barnabas as the word of God, having the same authority as the Qur'an, and whether they believe in it.

- It says that Muhammad is the Messiah, not Jesus (chs 42; 82; 97); Jesus is insinuated to be the preparer (like John the Baptist for Jesus) for the coming of Muhammad (chs 82; 191). This contradicts both the Bible and the Qur'an.

Many more passages clearly show that the Gospel of Barnabas is a fake with no historic credibility.[230] Muslims should therefore be persuaded to set this document aside and to study the four true gospels in the Bible to learn the truth about Jesus.

2.5.2 "Muhammad is predicted in the Bible"

 Muslim objection
"Why do Christians reject the Islamic prophet Muhammad? After all, he was predicted in the Bible." (cf Sura 7:157).

Based on the statements in Suras 7:157 and 61:6,[231] Muslims assumed that Muhammad was predicted in the Bible and thought that these verses would be easy to find. They were disappointed to realize that the Bible's numerous predictions point to Jesus instead of Muhammad. Islamic scholars have searched the Bible eagerly to discover texts that point to Muhammad. Different views exist in the Islamic world as to which biblical texts refer to him. Many Muslims consider Deuteronomy 18:18 to be such evidence in the Old Testament and John chapters 14-16 in the New Testament. A closer examination of these texts quickly and clearly shows, however, that Jesus and the Holy Spirit respectively are referred in these scriptures, not Muhammad.

1) **The Old Testament text: Deuteronomy 18:18**
   I will raise up for them a prophet like you from among their brothers; I will put my words in his mouth, and he will tell them everything I command him.

Muslims assume that the prophet foretold by Moses is Muhammad. This Islamic claim is based on three reasons:
1. Muhammad had similar characteristics to Moses.[232]
2. The promise "my words in his mouth" was fulfilled when *Jibril* (Gabriel) passed on the Qur'an to Muhammad.
3. Muhammad came "from among their brothers", the Ishmaelites.

---

[230] For more details, see Gilchrist (1999:148-162).
[231] Sura 7:157: "Those who follow the Apostle, the unlettered Prophet, whom they find mentioned in their own (Scriptures),- in the Law and the Gospel ...". Sura 61:6: "...Jesus the son of Mary, said: O children of Israel! I am the apostle of Allah (sent) to you, confirming the Law (which came) before me, and giving glad Tidings of an Apostle to come after me, whose name shall be Ahmad ...". Ahmad has a similar meaning than the name Muhammad.
[232] This claim originates in the words "like you" of Dt 18:18. Muslims say, for example, that Muhammad led a normal life like Moses, that both were leaders of their people, both were married and that their descendants conquered Palestine.

At a first glance, these arguments appear reasonable. However, a look at the context leads to a different conclusion. First of all we must interpret the given text properly. The term "from among their brothers" is explained in the context of verse 15 in which it says *ad verbatim* in the Hebrew text: "Prophet from among you, from brothers of you like me he will raise up for you, Jahveh, God of you. To him you must listen." That alone settles the argument.

In addition, Acts 3:17-23 and 7:37 clearly state that this prophet is Jesus. Jesus himself implicitly did the same when he said (Jn 5:46-47):
> "If you believed Moses, you would believe me, for he wrote about me. But since you do not believe what he wrote, how are you going to believe what I say?"

Jesus is similar to Moses in many ways in which Muhammad is not. Only Jesus and Moses show the following unique characteristics, for example:[233]
- Both were mediators of a covenant between God and man.
- Both knew God face-to-face.
- Both worked great signs and miracles.

Muhammad was not a mediator of a covenant. He neither knew God face-to-face nor did he work great signs and wonders (cf Sura 28:48). Muslims want Christians to accept Muhammad as a prophet.[234] How shall Christians react to this? They should point out that a true prophet of God in the line of the Biblical prophets must meet certain criteria:[235]
- He should be able to prophesy, and his prophecies should come true.
- His prophecies and teachings should agree with the statements of God's other prophets.
- If challenged, he should also be able to work wonders, to prove that he comes from God.
- His teaching should contain new elements of God's message.

Muslims may then be challenged to find passages in the Qur'an where these Biblical criteria of a prophet[236] are met by Muhammad.

---

[233] For further elaboration, see Gilchrist (2003:71-80).
[234] As a reason, Muslims offer the fact that they accept Biblical prophets like Moses, Jesus, etc. So Christians (they say) should accept Muhammad in return too.
[235] See for instance Ex 7:8-10; Dt 18:21-22.
[236] The Bible contains several passages about this topic, e.g., Dt 13:5 and 18:19-22; Jer 14:14-16 and 23:16-22, etc.

2) The New Testament text: John 14-16

The New Testament statements which Muslims assume to refer to Muhammad are found in Jesus' references to the "Counsellor"[237]. Muslims hold that Muhammad is that "Counsellor", not the Holy Spirit as Christians believe. Their reasons are as follows:

1. Jesus' statement, "...he will guide you into all truth. He will not speak on his own; he will speak only what he hears, and he will tell you what is yet to come." (Jn 16:13), applies to Muhammad.

2. Since Jesus, when talking of this "Counsellor", uses the term "he" i.e. the male third person singular pronoun, Muslims argue that the Counsellor can only be a man, not a spirit.

3. Based on Jesus' statement, "Unless I go away, the Counsellor will not come to you; but if I go, I will send him to you" (Jn16:7), Muslims are convinced that this can only be Muhammad, "because", so they argue, "the Holy Spirit was always there."

Christians have a good opportunity to explain the text in its context, and introduce the true "Counsellor," the Holy Spirit, and his work. These New Testament texts point to the Holy Spirit who came 50 days after Jesus' resurrection (Ac 2:1-21). Christians can thus answer:

1. Reading the whole text about this "Counsellor", we learn that he is "The Spirit of Truth" (Jn 14:17), not a prophet or any other man, that he will be with us "forever" (Jn 14:16), that "he will be in you" (Jn 14:17) i.e. live in the believers, that he will glorify Jesus (Jn 16:14), that he will remind the disciples of Jesus' teachings (Jn 14:26 etc.) and "will tell what is yet to come" (Jn 16:13).This can only be the Holy Spirit, not Muhammad.

2. Jesus clearly says that the "Counsellor" is the Holy Spirit (Jn 14:26).

3. Jesus said that he would send the "Counsellor" to his disciples (Jn 16:7), not 600 years later to Muslims!

Muslims claim that Christians have changed the Greek word *periklytos* (the praised one) to *paracletos* ("Counsellor", cf Jn 14:16). Muslim scholars point out that the name "Muhammad", literally translated, means "the praised one". For Muslims, this is another hint that the person Jesus talks about in Jn 14-16 is supposed to be Muhammad. However, Muslims have absolutely no proof at all for this assumption.

---

[237] Many translations use the terms "Comforter" or "Helper".

Muslims can be asked to read the text (Jn 14:15-17; 14:26) themselves and replace "Counsellor" with the name "Muhammad". It can easily be recognized that this exchange does not suit the text. The following chart summarizes the argument:

Reference	Muslim argument that this is a prediction of Muhammad in the Bible	Christian answer that with these references Jesus or the Holy Spirit is predicted
Dt 18:18	• Muhammad had some characteristics of Moses. • Muhammad descended from their "brothers", namely the Ishmaelites.	• Jesus had many characteristics of Moses. • Other Scriptures show clearly that Jesus is the subject of this prophecy (Jn 5:46-47; Ac 3:17-23 and 7:37). • The "brothers" of Moses were the Israelites (Dt 18:15).
Jn 14-16	The "counsellor" in these chapters is Muhammad who is predicted by Jesus. Muhammad is the next prophet following Jesus.	• The passage clearly refers to a "Spirit" who will be with the disciples (Jn 14:17: 14:26; 16:7). • The context shows that the "Holy Spirit" is predicted by Jesus: (Jn 14:17; 16:7; Ac 2:1-21).

Nothing can be detected in these biblical texts that hints at an annunciation of the Islamic prophet Muhammad. The same is true for the rest of the biblical texts: there is no prediction of Muhammad in the Bible!

? Questions

- Do you think the "Gospel of Barnabas" is true?
- The "Gospel of Barnabas" states that Muhammad is the Messiah (ch 42). However, the Qur'an states that Jesus is the Messiah! So, do you believe in the Qur'an or the "Gospel of Barnabas"?
- If you believe that Muhammad is predicted in the Bible, can you show me the references?
- Would you mind to explain and read the passages with me where you think Muhammad has been predicted in the Bible?
- What do you think are the marks of a true prophet of God?
- According to your point of view, who is a prophet?
- What are the names of the prophets of God?

3. Encounters with Muslims

> **This chapter offers you**
> a) a Christian attitude towards Muslims
> b) basic knowledge for an actual meeting
> c) practical advice for helping converts and guiding them in their
>   new faith
> d) motivation for the Church to reach Muslims with the Good News
> e) information on political and social issues

Next to Christianity, Islam today is the second-largest religious community in the world. People in Africa, Asia and the West no longer have to travel to Islamic countries to meet Muslims—they are in almost every country on Earth. Christians and Muslims may meet each other everywhere, at work or at leisure. Many are of the same nationality.

Many Muslims in non-Islamic countries are largely secularized and no longer observe the requirements of their religion. Further, many Muslims from countries such as Iran are disappointed by their religion, and search for something different. In general, Christians have failed to address the large number of Muslims in the world. One reason for often little contact between Christians and Muslims is ignorance, breeding fear which leads to avoiding contact with Muslims. This book intends to help Christians to get to know Islam and Muslims and thus lose this fear and start asking challenging questions.

In their native Islamic countries, Muslims often have very little opportunity to learn anything about the gospel. However, in Africa, Asia and the West it should be easier since Christians and Muslims may meet more freely. Many a Muslim is searching for answers, because Islam does not meet the deepest needs of a person. All people seek acceptance by God, an assurance of forgiveness of sins and personal communion with God. In Christ one can find all that and more. Therefore, Christians need to be an example in lifestyle, since Muslims often pay careful attention to their behaviour. As a result of Christian witness in words, deeds and behavior, Muslims will become aware that Christians have a different kind of relationship with God.

Not every guideline of this chapter applies to every situation where Muslims and Christians meet. The reader needs wisdom concerning the practical implementation of recommended steps.

3.1 The Christian reaction to the Islamic challenge

3.1.1 What does the Bible say?

Islam is a challenge to Christians. In the Great Commission (Mt 28:18-20), Christians are called upon to meet that challenge. Preparations need to be in a twofold way. First, Christians best prepare themselves for this task by prayer and close communion with Jesus. Secondly, Christians need to practice Christian love and care by learning to properly communicate the Gospel wisely to people from a very different culture and thought. It is important to understand the Muslim neighbour, his religion, his reasoning, his hopes and longings in order to present the message of the Gospel to him in a way that makes sense.

1) **Prayer:** The importance of prayer is repeatedly emphasized in the Bible.[238] In addition, Christians should be ready to fast for special concerns (Ac 13:3; 14:23). In prayer God's will may be discerned. A good example is the story of Peter and Cornelius in Acts 10. During his prayer time, Peter was being prepared for the encounter with Cornelius, and God's spirit worked to bring about conversion (Ac 10:9-16; 10:44). Christians should pray that Muslims hear, understand, and accept the gospel. The Christian message may be spread by personal testimony, literature and other media. In addition, Christians should pray that the Holy Spirit will speak to Muslims via dreams and visions.[239] It is important to pray for other Christians to become aware of the need to witness to Muslims, join in prayer and witness to them.

2) **Spiritual warfare:** Christians are called to be ready for spiritual warfare, and to prepare themselves (Eph 6:10-18). Islam is an anti-Christian religion and Christians are strongly advised only to act under the guidance and protection of the Holy Spirit. Christians must use spiritual warfare as a means of God breaking the darkness of the *jinn* that Muslims deal with. The aim is to help Muslims find freedom in Christ through spiritual warfare. It must be emphasized that each Christian can be a witness, but better preparation means greater effectiveness among Muslims. Therefore, a reasonably good knowledge of the Bible is indispensable. Knowledge of Islam and apologetics are highly advantageous, too. Christians need to be ready to engage in ongoing study and to break new ground.[240]

3) **Meetings in love:** God has created all mankind and loves them all alike—including Muslims. 1John 4:8 says that God is love. Christians are called to pass on this love to Muslims without which everything is in vain (1Co 13). Christians need to grow in this love, so that it becomes more and more apparent in their everyday life (Php 1:9; 1Co 16:14). After each meeting, a Christian should ask himself, "Have I passed on God's love?"

---

[238] See, for example, Mk 14:38; Lk 21:36; Eph 6:18.

[239] "Dreams and visions" play an important role in the conversion process of Muslims. Many converts have confirmed this. See also section 3.6.1.

[240] This means mainly new ways of mission methods and communication.

3.1.2 Which is the proper attitude?

It is important, first of all, to make a distinction between Islam as a religion and Muslims as people. Christians are called to love Muslims as created by God while rejecting anything that is against Christ—as is the case with many Islamic doctrines. Several attitudes may be displayed in encounters with Muslims. In this book, the fourth one is considered to be the proper attitude:

1) **The liberal attitude:** Islam and Christianity are religions of almost equal value. Islam is as valid a way to God as Christianity. Mission among Muslims is therefore offensive and displays conceit. One meets Muslims mainly only at cultural events, or works together on humanitarian projects. Inter-religious church services can also take place.

2) **The adapting attitude:** Christians try to pass on the gospel to Muslims and, in doing so, adapt to them as far as possible. They wear Muslim clothes, follow their prayer rituals and keep the fast during Ramadan. Thus they hope to gain better access to Muslims. However, misunderstanding is often the result. Muslims may think that such a Christian wants to become a Muslim, or has used deceit to convert Muslims to Christianity or act as a spy.[241]

3) **The militant attitude:** Muslims are considered enemies. Those who hold to this attitude have a crusader mentality and view Muslims as foreign infiltrators to the indigenous culture that have to be removed. Evangelisation among Muslims is not an option.

4) **The missionary attitude:** The command to "go and make disciples of all nations" (Mt 28:19) provides no exemption for Muslims. They need be reached

"I remember: this is the church which has spoken against mission!"

---

[241] This is not to speak against contextualization which has its proper place (see section 3.8.3). But Christians always have to ask themselves: what kind of signals they are sending to Muslims in their behaviour and actions? How might Muslims possibly interpret this? It is, however, not easy to find the right balance of contextualization and setting limitations.

with the message of Jesus Christ, who also died for them, that they also should receive salvation and eternal life through him (Jn 3:16; 14:6). Christians meet Muslims in the love of God, and respect their culture while not compromising the Christian message. This demands that Christians "build bridges of friendship and trust rather than walls". Unless a Muslims knows and trusts a Christian, he is not likely to listen to the message. One needs to earn the right to speak. However, building trusting relationships requires patience and love!

3.1.3 How shall interaction take place?

Interaction may take place on three levels. All should aim to establish bridges of friendship and trust i.e. relationship:

1) **Conversational level:** Christians talk to Muslims so that both can get to know each other better on social or other issues, while respecting each other's view point. Conversation should be as objective as possible, and with a readiness to listen.

2) **Working level:** Christians and Muslims share responsibility for social and humanitarian projects. Both have concerns for social justice, peace and the conservation of our environment and can work together on such projects.

3) **Missionary level:** Christians bear witness to Muslims about Jesus Christ as the truth. It needs to be done in a sensitive way and so that Muslims can understand the message. This requires careful listening to Muslims, working hard to understand each other and an ongoing endeavour to understand Islam, its culture and history and, in the name of Jesus Christ, to "spiritually" overcome it.

The purpose of interaction is to become acquainted with Muslim men and women and to discover where Christians can and cannot co-operate. We interact to discover and acknowledge common ground as well as differences, not to fabricate a uniform religion. Christians owe it to Muslims to act as witnesses of their Lord Jesus Christ.

In addition, Christian mission must aim at getting below the surface to discover the views of Muslims in their complex, sometimes unpredictable and often hostile world, as well as the less publicly-known, parallel world of folk Islam.[242] This world can be discovered in the literature of the *hadith*, in customs of local communities, and in myths. It is visible in rites and critical life situations, such as birth, marriage and death. Islamic magazines and newspapers give us an understanding of the Muslims' daily life.

---

[242] See also section 1.6.10, and Musk (1989).

3.1.4 Non-threatening approach: asking questions

Most Muslims are trained from childhood not to doubt or ask questions about their own religion. Why are Muslims not allowed to question their own religion? Is it, because Muslims are convinced it is the truth and therefore beyond questioning? Or is it that questions may reveal many difficulties that Islam tries so hard to subdue? If something is true, then there is nothing to fear. You may ask as many questions as you like, but truth will remain.

In meeting Muslims, I have made the following observations:
1) Often Muslims make a statement about their religion.
2) When asked where it is written, in most cases they claim that it is written in the Qur'an.
3) However, often these things are *not* written in the Qur'an but elsewhere, betraying misinformation or wishful thinking.
4) Asking Muslims good questions challenges them to find the truth for themselves!

> **Testimony: the importance of asking questions**
> I once met a man from Alexandria (Egypt) who told me the following story: "I was brought up in Alexandria in a staunch Muslim family. As is the custom, I was trained not to question Islam. However, between the ages of 16 to 20 I met every year several tourists and had short conversations with them. Every time, they asked me challenging questions about Islam. As a good Muslim I tried to ignore these questions. However, when I was 20, I was no longer able to sleep well; these question circled in my mind. I decided to find answers.
> For the first time in my life, I did not merely recite the Qur'an but tried to understand it. I was very disappointed—the Qur'an is very difficult to understand and in most cases did not answer my questions. This provoked a great crisis in my life; I refused to be a Muslim any longer! Through my business I travelled to Britain, got to know Christians and studied the Bible. I realised that the Bible has the answers and I finally became a Christian. I wish I could find these tourists to say 'thank you' to them for asking me simple questions through which I found the truth in Jesus Christ! Most likely these tourists, of whom some were Christians, are not aware that this changed my life!"

One question I like to ask Muslims is, "Tell me: how you became a Muslim?" Most of the time they say " I was born a Muslim". I then ask them, "Well, if you were born in Japan then would you be a Buddhist or something else and not a Muslim?" This leads to more discussion. Often in the end they ask, "How did you become a Christian?"

Asking questions is advantageous especially in a country where you are not free to evangelize openly. If you are just asking a Muslim questions, and he asks you questions, no one can accuse you of proseltyzing.

Consider the following suggestions:
1) Learn as much as you can about Muslims and Islam.
2) Show a keen interest by getting to know them.
3) Listen carefully to what they say about themselves and Islam.
4) Ask challenging questions in a friendly way.

The approach of asking questions, instead of giving answers immediately was often used by Jesus. One example is Mk 11:29, after the teachers of the law posed a question to Jesus:[243]

Jesus replied, "I will ask you one question. Answer me, and I will tell you by what authority I am doing these things."

! Conclusion

- A person will not consider believing something outside his cultural norms and beliefs unless he has begun to question the integrity and trustworthiness of his own faith. It is therefore often imperative to lead a Muslim to the point where he discovers the untrustworthiness of his religion. Here in particular the asking of pertinent questions proves very effective. However, the right questions are the key, lest a conversation becomes offensive or irrelevant.
- Every Christian can be a witness to Muslims. The more you know about their religion and the way they think and practice it, the better you are able to ask effective and challenging questions.
- Asking appropriate questions is a non-threatening approach which can be used worldwide.
- Christians must be aware that asking questions is no substitute for sharing the Gospel.

3.2 Practical guidelines

John has talked about his school friend Omar more than once at home. Omar's entire family is Muslim. One day, the parents meet at a parent-teacher evening and get into conversation with each other. During their talk, Omar's father says that they have been living in England for eight years, but have no local friends. They are political refugees from Africa. He has long searched for a job where he does not have to deal with alcohol, which is not easy in the hotel sector. Now, he is a porter in a hotel and very happy with his work. His wife, too, mentions several things that show how difficult it was for her to blend into western society. John's parents promise to invite them for a meal in the near future. (Names have been changed).

---

[243] See also Mk 10:3 and Lk 20:3.

Daily life offers countless possibilities for Christians to socialize with Muslims and make friends[244] with them. Christians are challenged to use this great opportunity to make contact and be witnesses for Jesus.

3.2.1 Ten basic rules

1) **View Muslims as normal human beings**
   - Very few of them are radicals or violent fundamentalists.
   - Most prefer a quiet and happy life.
   - Most are simple people who desire to serve God.
   - They have desires, hopes, joys and pains like everyone else.

2) **View Muslim people as individuals**
   - Each Muslim is an individual who is different from others. Avoid viewing them in a stereotypical way.
   - Get to know them as individuals and to show a keen interest in them.
   - Each Muslim follows his own form of folk-Islam which he practices differently to others.

3) **Understand their inner tensions**
   - Many Muslims are insecure and ask themselves: "What is true Islam and how should I practice it?"
   - Muslim young people living in a largely liberal and decadent society in the West are often confused. They belong to mutually excluding societies: they have a cultural duty to follow Islam, but are tempted to live in a "liberated" world. The value systems of a liberal modern democracy are in stark contrast to a conservative Islamic theocracy.[245]

4) **Recognise the cultural differences**
   - Many Muslims are torn between western culture and their parents' original culture.
   - Especially great is the difference of treatment of women in Islamic countries in contrast to non-Islamic countries.
   - Christians should aim to understand this and be sensitive in any encounter.

5) **Do not fear Islam nor the Muslim people**
   - Muslims often appear self-confident outwardly but in their hearts are often insecure.

---

[244] Though the Qur'an is somewhat divided concerning advising Muslims to become friends with Christians (Sura 5:54 is negative; Sura 5:85 is positive), most Muslims I have met are happy to become a friend.

[245] A democracy is where the people of a state have the final vote for the country's laws whereas in a theocracy the laws are made mainly by the religious leaders. Many Islamic countries function as dictatorships or kingdoms. Others have introduced democratic elections to a certain degree.

- Islam is not a threat to Christians but a challenge! Consider: "All authority in heaven and on earth has been given to me", said Christ in his last words, and "... surely, I will be with you always, to the very end of the age." (Mt 28:18-20).
- Christians know the truth in Jesus Christ! What then do they have to fear?

6) Take the initiative to meet Muslims
- Christians are often too timid! Take courage and make an effort to meet Muslims.
- Often Muslims are isolated and lonely: take the initiative to establish friendship.
- Think and pray of new ways and methods of engaging with Muslims.

7) Pass on God's love to them
- God loves all people, including Muslims.
- Muslims do not know God's love through Jesus Christ.
- Christians are obliged to share the love of God with Muslims: first in practical care and secondly through sharing the Good News.

8) Listen first; then talk to their hearts
- Talk about daily matters which concern Muslims.
- Recognize and listen to their worries, fear and doubts.
- Ask if you may pray for them, either in their presence or privately.

9) Talk naturally and openly
- Explain what you believe and how you experience God's guidance in everyday life.
- Communicate in ways they can understand. Ask them if they have understood you.
- At the right time, you may share your personal conversion story.
- Muslims are very likely to engage you in arguments regarding the Christian faith. They perceive the Western, liberal lifestyle as seen on TV to be Christian. They are told the Bible has been corrupted and that Jesus is not the Son of God and did not die on the cross to make an atonement. As truthful witnesses, Christians have to respond to that challenge and repudiate all false allegations in a kindly and informed manner.

10) Explain the uniqueness of Jesus
- Do not talk denigrate Islam, but concentrate on the message of the Bible.
- First of all the uniqueness of Jesus should be explained: He is more than a prophet.
- Explain the names and titles of Jesus.

3.2.2 Cultural and religious issues

Cultural and religious rules of behaviour should be respected. These rules differ for Muslims from various countries, and whether they are orthodox or liberal. Some general practical rules are given:[246]

- First impressions are important. Am I shy, aggressive, defensive, or uninterested? Or am I friendly, interested, a good listener, open and honest?
- Being convincing: Christians should behave confidently because they have a convincing message!
- Listening with interest, being thankful and making positive remarks comes across as constructive.
- Show respect for the Bible and the Qur'an. Never put them on the floor, or place anything upon them. Use a "clean" Bible i.e. the Bible should be in a good condition and without notes or marked passages.
- Hospitality is important, but only food and drink acceptable for Muslims (i.e. *halal*) should be offered. It is best to ask guests in advance, and to be prepared.[247]
- Invitations by Muslims should be gratefully accepted.
- Generally speaking, conversations should occur only between people of the same sex, especially where no third person is present.
- Women should dress conservatively and be sensitive to local customs concerning clothes and cosmetica.
- Most Muslims are "conservative" to modern western styles e.g. long hair and earrings on men are frowned upon.
- Christians should observe the behaviour of Muslim body language.[248] If in doubt, it is advisable to ask what is proper behaviour and to accept correction.

3.2.3 Having a conversation

Pay attention to the development of conversations. Christians should remain calm and friendly, even when a discussion gets heated and blasphemous statements are made by Muslims. The following basic rules can help:

1. Listen attentively when the Muslim speaks. People who show real interest in the experiences and opinions of their friends will have an attentive listener later.
2. Certain words, particularly from the religious palette, carry an obscure or ambiguous message e.g. God, prayer, salvation, heaven and hell, prophet, sin and many more. When a Muslim asks a question, it is often better to clarify terms with a counter question, such as **"What do you mean by that?"**[249]

---

[246] This list is not meant to be complete. Christians always should try to act appropriately in every situation.

[247] Do not serve alcohol or pork. In addition, very orthodox Muslims do not eat food that was prepared with pots already used by Christians to prepare their meal.

[248] It is e.g. advisable not to cross the legs when sitting. Orthodox Muslims can be upset by this because they are reminded of the cross. You may cross your legs only if the Muslims themselves do so.

[249] When a Muslim asks, for example, "Are you a Christian?", you can use a counter question to find out what he means by the term "Christian", and then answer accordingly. This method of responding with a return question has been used by Jesus often in the NT (Mk 10:3; 11:27-33; Lk 20:3).

People from different cultures and religions often mean different things by the same word, particularly with religious terminology. Let your Muslim friends explain their understanding of a term so that you can grasp what they mean and avoid misunderstandings.

❗ The following points may be of further help

- The technique of asking interesting, thought-provoking questions can be learned. Of course, you cannot expect the Muslim to answer every question. Muslims should be encouraged to reflect on their own relationship to God. Some questions are: *Why do Muslims pray five times a day? How can our sins be forgiven? What were your experiences during the pilgrimage to Mecca? How can Muslims enter paradise?*[250] Whatever their reply, this should lead to further conversation to press home the point.
- When Muslims make religious statements, ask for references and proofs. One should then take the time to study these matters.
- Never criticize Islam or Muhammad! It is preferable to change the statements into questions. Further, never ridicule Muslims if they make statements or ask questions which sound strange.
- Express yourself clearly. Any Christian expressions should be carefully explained so that Muslims can understand them.
- Where applicable, specific literature should be offered that expands upon the discussion. It is essential, however, to read this literature yourself to determine its suitability before handing it to Muslims. Offer it in a way that allows them to graciously decline if they wish.

---

[250] More questions to Muslims are provided at the end of every main section of this book. You may also consult our website: www.aymf.net.

- If you do not know the answer to a Muslim's question, it is better to ac-knowledge this than to risk making inaccurate statements. You can then research the answer and plan a new meeting to give the reply. Since a lay person is not likely to have the resources or knowledge to find such answers, one needs a resource person to help.
- In some cases, objections and arguments can lead to a heated exchange of words, but you should try to remain calm and matter-of-fact. This is not a matter of "defeating" a Muslim with words!
- Christians are called to stand clearly by the truth. You should testify, at the appropriate time, where your faith and hope lies. You can also tell the story of your conversion, talk about your personal relationship with Jesus and your daily experience with God.

3.2.4 Visiting the mosque

Visiting people in the mosque is one way to meet Muslims. However, only those Christians who feel comfortable should do so. The rules of behaviour should be clarified in advance, and observed. The Muslim demand that one takes off one's shoes is simple courtesy, whereas limits must be set. Partaking in Islamic prayer can send a wrong signal to Muslims.

Step-by-step guidelines:
1. The Christian individual or group leader should make an appointment with the leader of the mosque and discuss the format of visits.
2. Give your reasons why you as a Christian want to visit the mosque i.e:
   - your interest in their religion and culture
   - to establish better relations between Muslims and Christians
   - find out what meetings the Muslims have during the week in the mosque, and which are open to you as a Christian
   - explain that you are ready to listen but also are prepared to discuss what you understand is the truth.
   - you may also want to study in their library
3. Visiting the mosque in a group: Ask beforehand how your group should be-have in the mosque and keep the rules (shoes off, clothing for men and women, special rules for women). Muslims expect you to observe their religious and cultural rules in the mosque, but that you as a Christian will not participate in prayer nor ritual washing. You may sit in the back and quietly watch and pray for them.
4. It is better to go in the name of an organization or your local church. Muslims can be wary of Christian missions and associate their activities with the Cru-saders or with attempts to gain converts by offering material help.
5. Be sensitive and ask for permission to do things. Always be friendly and po-lite.
6. Ask how long you may visit the mosque and leave at the agreed time.

7. Questions should only be asked on topics the Muslims have spoken about. Do not "preach" at them in the mosque (remember, Muslims usually do not show their true face in a group!). You may be more direct in a personal meeting with them later at home.
8. Listen carefully and show an interest in what they say. "Earn the right to say something."
9. You may give the biblical view at the appropriate time, but keep answers short and to the point.
10. At times you may politely ask for the references on statements they make (say that you have a Qur'an at home and would like to look it up yourself). - If they cannot answer your questions, do not press the matter.
11. Do not ask aggressive or insulting questions.
12. The Christian group should always follow their leader's instructions.
13. A Christian lady should only visit the mosque in the company of a man, unless she has established friendships with Muslim ladies.
14. Christians may also invite Muslims to visit their church e.g. to explain the facilities and give a talk on the message of the Bible.
15. Once you have established friendships, you may visit the mosque on a regular basis on your own.
16. However, if new to a mosque, always ask a Muslim guide to show you the mosque. They may feel insulted if you just step in. Inform yourself about the rules for further visits.
17. Never walk in front of praying Muslims.
18. Remember: "If you do not ask, you will not know!" Every mosque has a different set up and schedule.

3.2.5 Special issues concerning women
1) **When inviting Muslims or visiting them, make sure that a third person is present when two people of the opposite sex meet privately:**
   · Only women should visit each other. Invite Muslim women into your home; in return they often invite you as well.
   · Taking a small gift is customary (sweets, scripture, a book, DVD) and wrap it as a gift.
   · If they visit, be sure your home is a friendly and comfortable place. Give them a seat of honour.
   · No dog should be present nor any men, unless from your family.
   · Think about pictures or objects in the room which may offend and remove them beforehand.
   · Put the Bible in an appropriate place—not on the floor.
   · Think about what you will serve and be generous.
   · Listen to what they share. Show a keen interest in their everyday life, their culture and religion. Ask appropriate questions, but don't pressure them if they have no answer.

2) **Issues women are concerned about:** (these are needs and areas where you can come alongside and love them. Share how the Bible meets these needs).

- Children: Having a child is very important! Women with no children long intensely for them. To not have a boy may mean a woman is not as acceptable as those who do. Children are her responsibility for much of their care and training. She may fear losing her children if divorced.
- Marriage: Each girl wants the best husband, but fears who her parents may choose, or force her to marry. Girls today long to finish school, even university, before marriage.
  They hope the marriage will work well, and they will not divorce or have a co-wife.
- Clothing: Wear modest clothing, suited to the culture and people where you are living.
- Relationships: Some women have no one to have a close relationship with. Families do not always share and the woman may like a foreign friend, outside of her circle of family to share with. You as a Christian woman may want to help her as time goes on to know God as a close friend, so that she can have a personal relationship with him.
- Health needs: This can be an area of need, as they would not easily tell any medical person their needs, preferring to tell a woman and find women to help.

3) **How women see their faith and spiritual life**
The home and family is where Islam is practiced at birth, marriage, death, and the yearly festivals. The home is the woman's domain; she is the keeper of the faith in the home. She often is the one who teaches the children to pray and the *hadith* stories. She cooks Ramadan meals and prepares for 'Id celebrations.

4) **Christian witness to Muslim women**
   - Talk naturally and openly about spiritual issues.
   - Share with them your personal experiences with God in everyday life.
   - Share your conversion story but choose words they can understand. Make sure you differentiate between the time before conversion, the conversion process and what it is like today.
   - When she expresses a need, ask if you can pray for her. Call again and ask to pray again. If the need is met, then give thanks to God with her!
   - Teach by example: a) God loves them and cares about their needs; b) God hears prayer; c) God answers; d) God can be trusted and he keeps his word; e) Endeavour to move from physical needs into spiritual issues.

5) **Learn to tell stories**
Women enjoy learning orally. Most can read, but some still cannot. Women often do not read books for fun and enjoyment but do listen to stories and tell stories to each other.
   - Stories give them knowledge, arouse emotions and transmit universal truths in a form they enjoy, sharing them over and over again.
   - Tell and learn stories that fit their needs. Think about their belief, stories they know and agree with, what their beliefs are missing, stories about

people who loved and obeyed God, about people who would not listen and did not obey God, about fear or death.
- Share stories about basic Christian doctrine. Think of what a person needs to hear to have a relationship with God and be saved.
- Use drama, video, music and other modern media to communicate.

3.2.6 Encounters with Muslim children

Encounters with Muslim children are challenging and demand much devotion, patience, love and empathy from Christians. Children come from very different cultures and family backgrounds. Some have difficulties with different languages and cultures. Many children live a dual life: the liberal and modern culture in public compared to the often strict Islamic culture at home. For many children, this double lifestyle leads to conflicts. Further difficulties arise as students of modern teaching systems which demand independent work and critical questioning. In general Muslims are not allowed or trained to ask critical questions.

Often children will go to an Islamic centre where Quranic courses are held. They learn to read Arabic script, but usually do not understand what they read.[251] They are given an introduction into Islamic behaviour and thought which is often used to set the children against Christian teaching.

Therefore, children know little about Christianity, the Bible, and Jesus; what little knowledge they possess is mostly distorted and wrong. As a rule, they have no overall view of what Christianity is. Children from different countries of origin are raised differently, following the customs of their parents' Muslim communities. Christians working with Muslim children and youth are strongly advised to gather sufficient information and training via specific literature and seminaries.

Practical hints for group leaders conducting children clubs:
- The Christian congregation should support the leader of the children's group in every way possible, such as prayer and practical help.
- In a group for children, local children need to accept Muslim children in a friendly way, to love and also invite them to their homes if possible.
- The leader's contact with the parents is important. The leader will explain what the children learn and do. Regular visits to the parents' house are essential to gain the trust of both the children and their parents.

Telling biblical stories:
• Biblical stories should be told in a simple and understandable way. Christian expressions must be sufficiently explained.
• Be careful with popular missionary tales. The children may easily feel that they are merely objects for mission.

---

[251] Muslims whose native tongue is not Arabic, learn to read the Arabic Qur'an, but generally do not understand what they read. For Muslims, it is predominantly important to recite the Qur'an in Arabic, and not necessarily to understand it.

- Practical role-playing with illustrative material is highly recommended.
- Sing a lot with children's groups—sung words stay with children more easily than the spoken word.
- It is better to pray to "God" instead of to "Jesus". Prayers can be said standing. Eyes do not have to be closed; hands do not have to be folded.
- Bible texts should be learned by heart. Muslims are well trained at this.
- Children should be able to recognize by the behaviour and testimony of the leader that the Bible is the authority. The Bible should not be put carelessly on the floor.
- No one should pressure the children toward conversion. Christians share what they believe is the truth, but only God's power changes peoples' hearts.

Conversion and subsequent care:
- When a child wants to trust in Christ, ensure that he or she has understood what it means. Have they understood their sinfulness, that eternal life is received as a gift of God, and not by good works? What does following Jesus means in practice (reading the Bible, prayer, fellowship, consequences, possible persecution)?
- Children should know that they may face difficulties (do not frighten them!), but that Jesus will be especially near them and help them.
- If the child agrees, a conversion prayer can be said.
- The child should get a good, understandable translation of the Bible, as well as a Bible study guide.
- These children are in dire need of further teaching and company in their young Christian life. They need loving assistance especially in difficult times.

3.3 Explaining the gospel to Muslims

3.3.1 General guidelines
The Bible clearly states that sins can only be forgiven through a substitutional sacrifice. Jesus offered himself as this sacrifice on the cross and taught that all can be saved, and obtain eternal life, through faith in him. However, Jesus forces no one to accept his offer. Therefore, Christians must not put pressure on Muslims to convert.[252] The gospel is communicated by God's people, but only the Holy Spirit can bring about conversion to faith in Jesus Christ.

Because of love for our fellow men and women and in obedience to the command to mission, it would be selfish to keep this treasure to oneself. The truth of the gospel must be passed on to Muslims. When passing on the gospel to Muslims, observe the following rules:
- No general method of evangelism exists that guarantees success at all times; each situation, and each person, is different. Christians are open and honest and would never use shameful ways in their witness (cf. 2Co 4:1-2).

---

[252] Conversion in this context means that a person starts trusting and believing in Jesus Christ.

- It is important that what Christians say is not contradicted by what they are. Converts have confirmed that Muslims closely observe the moral conduct of Christians (cf. Ro 12:1-2; 1Th 2:8).
- We all have limits to our capacity to absorb ideas. Muslims are no exception. Do not drown your witness with too many aspects of the gospel. It is far better to get over one point at a time.
- To give Muslims food for thought, relevant topics can be presented in an indirect way. Christians should learn to share Biblical truths through parables, as Jesus himself did (Mt 13:3,34).[253]
- At the appropriate time, the Muslim should be encouraged to read the Bible.[254]

3.3.2 Gospel presentation methods

Someone once said: "In natural things be spiritual and in spiritual things be natural". The Christian faith constitutes the spiritual side of life, and yet it becomes a natural part of it, with no need for a grand display. Do not speak about the faith in an unnatural manner. Every Christian will explain the gospel a little differently using his own words, relating incidents that captivate minds to spiritual answers. Muslims, who are religious people, respond to a spiritual conversation much quicker than for instance the average European. There are many ways of presenting the gospel, one uses a Bible verse that points to the core of the gospel.[255] It is advantageous to learn as many of these verses by heart as possible, such as Ro 6:23:

Romans 6:23	Explanation
For the wages of sin is death	The seriousness of sin in the eyes of God must be explained. Each sin (thoughts, words, actions) means death which results in separation from God.
but the gift of God is eternal life	God gives eternal life only as a gift, it cannot be earned. A gift/present is received without payment! Eternal life means life in God's presence in heaven/paradise (cf Jn 5:24).
in Christ Jesus our Lord.	Jesus Christ is the Messiah whose task was to die on the cross for our sins in our stead, so that all who believe in him can live. Jesus is the perfect sacrifice designated by God (cf Jn 3:16; 14:6).

Christians should adopt an approach that comes naturally, according to circumstances. A selection of methods are summarized:
- Using individual verses or longer passages from the Bible (as shown above with Ro 6:23).

---

[253] See also section 3.3.4.
[254] The gospels of Luke or John are highly recommended to start with because they describe the life of Jesus in terms Muslims can understand. The *Jesus* video, based on the gospel of Luke, is also suitable for presentation. For more information see www.jesus.ch or www.cfc.ch.
[255] See, for example Jn 3:16; 1Ti 2:5-6; Ro 3:23-24; 5:12,21; Eph 2:8-9; 1Jn 4:9; 5:11; etc.

- Using stories and parables to explain Biblical truths.[256]
- Sharing Old Testament stories in the context of the New Testament.[257]
- Explaining how Old Testament prophecies are fulfilled in the New Testament—proof of the divine origin of the Bible. There is probably no better way to convict and convince any person of the fact that the Bible could not have been compiled by man, for no one could foreknow that Christ would come into this world by being born by a virgin in Bethlehem (Mic 5:2; Lk 2:4-7).[258]
- Taking up topics and texts mentioned in the Qur'an which are in agreement with the Bible, and explaining them according to the Bible.[259]

3.3.3 Special Bible studies

Evangelisation means first and foremost communicating information about God, Jesus, man, sin and making peace with God again. Due to his past, during which he has in many cases absorbed many anti-Christian ideas, a Muslim usually needs considerable time to understand the gospel. Once a genuine interest can be observed, it is helpful to conduct private, informal Bible studies with them. The following topics are foundational and should, if possible, be explained in the given order:[260]

1) **The Bible.** Many Muslims have been taught since childhood that the Bible has been falsified. Muslims need to learn how the Bible came to us and why it is trustworthy. Once they start trusting the Bible, they find it easier to accept the message of salvation. They need to spend time reading the Bible for themselves and wrestling with the truth.

2) **God.** Some Qur'anic statements about Allah seem to agree with the biblical portrait of God. Other fundamental statements, on the other hand, openly contradict biblical statements. Muslims need to know who God really is and what he says about himself, his law and his love. Muslims have to learn about God's love for mankind and see that he offers a way to all people by which they can accept him and receive eternal life as a gift.

3) **Mankind and sin.** The doctrine of the fall of man must be explained. Muslims need to understand the grievousness of sin in the sight of God and its consequences. They will not understand the necessity of a redeemer until they understand that they cannot free themselves from sin.

4) **Jesus.** Muslims need to understand who Jesus really is, and why he came. This presupposes an understanding of the meaning and purpose of sacrifices as of-

---

[256] See section 3.3.4.
[257] E.g. the topic of "Abraham" as shown in section 3.4.1 (without using the Qur'an as a stepping stone).
[258] For more references see section 2.2.2.
[259] See section 3.4.
[260] Examples of suitable courses can be requested from several organizations (see e.g. Nehls 1985). The seven points listed here are an outline of topics which need to be covered in a course.

fered during Old Testament times. This helps people to understand and more easily accept Jesus' death on the cross, and his resurrection on their behalf. Muslims need to get to know the true Jesus, who is more than a prophet; he is the true Messiah and the Son of God.

5) **God's kingdom.** Christians need to explain the necessity to be born again into God's kingdom. The differences between the Kingdom of God and the Islamic *umma* need explanation, as well as the Bible's teaching on how to live a Christian moral lifestyle and living in harmony with our Maker and Lord to bring honour to him.

6) **The Holy Spirit.** Muslims need to understand who the Holy Spirit is, what he does and how the doctrine of the Trinity can be comprehended.

7) **Mission and the future of mankind.** God calls all Christians to be his witnesses in the world, and promises always to be with his disciples. Muslims need to learn that God gives promises and keeps them, such as that the future of Christians is secure; God gives assurance of salvation to those who follow Jesus in faith.

3.3.4 Using illustrations, parables and stories

Stories are valuable aids to convey Biblical truths to Muslims. Jesus used parables to challenge his audience to reflect (Lk 6:39). In Arab culture, stories are an important part of daily life. Storytelling is a helpful art to practice, and useful stories should be collected, while recognizing that there are limits to this approach. A selection of short stories is presented:

The drowning man

Muslims are convinced that the Qur'an is the final and perfect revelation of God. Christians believe that Jesus is the perfect revelation of God. What is better for mankind, a book, or a person, as revelation of God? The following example can be used to deepen understanding:

Imagine that you are standing on a lakeshore, and see someone in the water, crying for help. What would you do? Would you go to the nearest bookstore and buy a book entitled *How to become a good swimmer*, and throw it at the one in the water? Or would you, as a good swimmer, jump into the lake and save the drowning person?

The spoilt egg

Muslims think that they can compensate for their bad works with good works, and that Allah will then let them into paradise—without Jesus' sin offering. Muslims must understand that God takes sin seriously, and that sins can only be forgiven according to God's plan. An example:

A housewife mixed dough using several eggs. She throws in a bad egg by mistake. What must she do now? Should she put in more good eggs, and hope that the bad one will not be noticed? No—everybody knows that one bad egg spoils the entire dough, regardless of the number of good eggs in the mixture. In the same way, a single sin spoils our whole life, and God cannot receive us in our sinful state unless we accept his way of forgiveness.

Jumping over a gorge

Muslims try to enter paradise through good works. This is, however, impossible by one's own strength; no one is perfect. Consider the following example:

To follow their path, a group of walkers has to cross a gorge 30 metres wide. Those who think they can make it, jump. Some manage to jump five metres, others jump farther, but no one reaches the other side—all fall into the gorge. The same happens to people who want to gain admittance into heaven. There is only one way to enter heaven, one bridge: God's bridge, named "Jesus".

Pay for the gift?

The Bible clearly states that God gives eternal life only as a gift. Those who want to buy paradise—as Muslims do with good works—actually try to buy something only available as a present. Christians do good works, of course—not to buy eternal life, but to thank God for the present they have received.

Imagine a poor man, invited to a party by a rich man. At the end of the party, the rich man offers the poor man a huge present: a new car! The poor man, however, does not want to accept the car as a present; he wants to pay at least a bit for it. Wouldn't the host be upset by that? He wanted to give the car as a present, just as God wants to give eternal life only as a present.

Four reports

Muslims have *one* book as highest authority, the Qur'an which contains statements about Muhammad. Christians have *four* gospels that describe Jesus' life from different points of view. Muslims find it difficult to accept the four gospels because they do not say literally the same thing. The following comparison emphasizes the importance of the four reports:

Four friends watch a traffic accident. The police arrive and ask the four witnesses, each by himself, to give a written eyewitness account. Let us suppose that each witness writes his report using his own words and style. The accounts are of different lengths. But then let us suppose instead that four identical texts, saying same word for word, are given to the police. Which is the more credible? The police will surely assume that something went wrong in the case of four identical reports; the witnesses have come to an agreement and settled for one version.

Two employers

Imagine you are looking for a job and you may choose between two offers. At the first factory, the boss offers you a contract signed by himself, in which he guarantees you a job and fixed salary which you will receive at the end of each month. At the second factory, the boss gives you no contract and no guarantee of receiving a salary. The boss indicates that you may work at your own risk and, if he as the boss is in a good mood, he may give you some payment.  Which job offer would you choose? Surely the first one! In Christianity God offers one way of salvation and guarantees paradise to all who accept his offer. In Islam, Allah offers many different ways of salvation but gives no guarantee.[261]

3.4 Common ground approach

When Christians meet Muslims who know the Qur'an and repeatedly refer to it, they should be prepared to study it with the Muslim and to use constructively in conversations. Similarities between Christianity and Islam can then be used to pass on Biblical truths.[262] However, Christians must avoid giving the impression that they accept the Qur'an as authoritative. Unless a Muslim mentions the Qur'an as a reference, there is no need for a Christian to do so, preferring instead to use the Bible as the main point of reference.

When a Muslim repeatedly mentions the Qur'an and quotes from it, a Christian should study the Qur'an and other necessary literature. Some Qur'anic statements agree with the Bible, but in general, only up to a certain point. It is important to know these similarities and differences.[263] This "common ground approach" means that Christians pick up a statement from the Qur'an which agrees with the Bible, and subsequently explain this to the Muslims according to the Bible. Some examples are suggested in the following sections.

3.4.1 Abraham, the friend of God

Abraham is the only prophet in the Bible and the Qur'an who receives the title "friend of God".[264] Christians can ask Muslims why only Abraham was given this unique title. Only the Bible contains an explanation:

Abraham is wonderfully guided by his trust in God. His obedience—the sacrifice he is asked to make—foreshadows what God will one day do through his own son, Jesus. Abraham thus foreshadows the gospel through this event. Abraham was able to perceive the message of God, His plan of salvation, through this experience

---

[261] See also on the topic 2.4.3: "The way to paradise..." .

[262] This was, for example, the method the apostle Paul used in Athens (see Ac 17:22-23).

[263] In section 2.1 some of the similarities and differences have already been listed.

[264] Bible: 2Ch 20:7; Is 41:8; Jas 2:23. Qur'an: Sura 4:125.

(Isaac was an image of Jesus, cf Jn 8:56; Ge 22:8):
• It happened through the son he loved.
• The son entered this world via an unusual birth.
• The sacrifice was a sin offering.
• The promise of blessing came through the son.

Jesus bore the wooden cross, just as Isaac bore the wood up the mountain. Jesus was bound, as was Isaac. In the end, Isaac was not sacrificed (God sent a lamb, Ge 22:11-13), but he served to teach Abraham a lesson of what God would do in the future through his own son. God reminded Abraham of the blessing (Ge 22:16-18). Abraham recognized that his true followers did not come by flesh, but by faith.

All who accept these facts, and thus the faith of Abraham, become Abraham's children and thereby children of God through the reality of this faith. This was also confirmed by the prophets (Is 53:7, 10) and John the Baptist (Jn 1:29). This is why Abraham was called the friend of God. A comparison of material in the Bible and the Qur'an:[265]

Statements	Bible	Qur'an
Abraham as the father and archetype of all true believers.	Jews: Lk 3:8; Jn 8:33, 39. Christians: Ro 4:16; Gal 3:7,9.	Archetype: Sura 2:124. Hanif: Suras 3:67;16:120.
God commends Abraham for his obedience in faith.	Gal 3:6-9.	Suras; 2:130; 2:135; 3:95; 6:161; 22:78.
Promise of a son.	Ge 17:15-16; Ro 4:18.	Suras 11:71; 37:112.
Command to sacrifice the son.[266]	Ge 22:1-13.	Sura 37:102.

---

[265] Only the most important references are listed.
[266] Muslims argue that it was Ishmael and not Isaac who was to be sacrificed. However, the Qur'an nowhere clearly states that it was Ishmael. On the contrary, the context points rather to Isaac. See Suras 15:53; 29:27; 37:100-113; 51:24-31. Muslims also believe that the sacrifice happened in Mina near Mecca.

Ask Muslims the following questions and, if appropriate, read the references together
- Why was Abraham called "the friend of God"?
- Why was Abraham the father of all true believers?
- What was Abraham's faith?
- Why was Abraham commanded to sacrifice his son?
- If you believe it was Ishmael who was to be sacrificed, can you show me where it says so?

3.4.2 The uniqueness of Jesus Christ

The Qur'an rejects Jesus' divinity and the crucifixion.[267] However, many other texts in the Qur'an regarding Jesus are positive, and partly agree with the Bible. These qur'anic statements are mostly vague indications not clearly explained, and can be explained according to the Bible. The following topics regarding Jesus are mentioned in the Qur'an, but explained and unfolded only in the Bible:

Statements	Bible	Qur'an
Jesus was born of the virgin Mary.	Lk 1:26-35	Suras 3:45-47; 19:17-21
Ascension into heaven.	Ac 1:9-11	Sura 4:157-158
Title: "Word".	Jn 1:1-14	Sura 4:171
Jesus returns on Judgment Day.[268]	Mt 25:31-32	Sura 43:61
Jesus' death.	Jn 19:28-37	Sura 19:33

When these statements and titles are explained according to the Bible, it can be shown that Jesus is the perfect revelation from God for mankind. We can receive God's salvation for mankind only through Jesus.

Ask and discuss the following questions with Muslims
- Why was Jesus born of a virgin?
- Who is the father of Jesus?
- Why did God allow Jesus and not Muhammad to ascend into heaven? What was God's reason?
- Why is the title "Word of God" only given to Jesus in the Qur'an?

---

[267] See Suras 4:157; 5:19, see also section 2.3.
[268] The Qur'an does not teach the second coming of Jesus as clearly as the Bible. But the Muslims generally hold that Sura 43:61 refers to the return of Jesus to earth.

3.4.3 The Messiah
Another topic mentioned in the Qur'an is the idea of a messiah. Several texts in the Qur'an give Jesus the title *al-Masih 'Isa* (Suras 3:45; 4:157,171). It is assumed that Muhammad adopted this title from Jews and Christians during the time in Medina. The title is always used with the definite article, "*the* Messiah". The Qur'an considers this title to be unique, applicable only to Jesus but without any explanations. Muslims should ask themselves, "What does the title Messiah mean?" Again, Christians have an opportunity to explain a topic for which only the Bible supplies the answer.

"Christ" is the Greek translation of "Messiah" and means "the anointed one" (cf Jn 1:41; 4:25). Anointing signifies the calling and equipping for a special task in God's service. The Anointed of the Lord is first and foremost the king of Israel. David was the Anointed of the Lord in a special way. His house was promised to bring forth the promised great "Ruler".[269] The prophecies referred to an apocalyptic messiah, who would be the culmination of God's revelation.[270] The expectation of this messiah, the redeemer, can be found in Jewish writings between the completion of the Old Testament and the appearance of Jesus. In the time of Jesus, this hope was strengthened and kept alive by the miserable political situation of the Jewish people. These promises of a messiah are fulfilled in Jesus. His claim to be the Messiah, the Christ of God, is made known to Mary when the angel announces his forthcoming birth and is confirmed before Caiaphas and the council, and through the insight of the disciples.[271] This claim of Jesus' messianic mission and his authority remains at the core of the church's preaching; and will do so until the final, complete acknowledgment of his sovereignty.[272]

Jesus' question to the Pharisees in Mt 22:42, "What do you think about the Christ? Whose son is he?", can be addressed to Muslims, too. The Biblical context makes it clear that the Messiah is the Son of God.[273] For the Jews, it was then and is now difficult to see their messianic hopes fulfilled in Jesus. It is likewise difficult for Muslims to accept the Biblical explanation for the title Jesus "the Messiah". It is therefore crucial to explain the meaning of this title.

Questions to ask Muslims
• Why does the Qur'an give the title "the Messiah" to Jesus?
• What does this significant title "Messiah" mean to you?

---

[269] See Da 9:25; Is 9:6-7; 11:1-5; 11:10; 42:1; 53.
[270] See prophecies: Zec 6:12; Mic 5:1; Da 7:13-14.
[271] See Lk 1:31-33; Mt 16:16; 26:63,64; Jn 1:41.
[272] See Ac 9:20,22; 10:36-38; Php 2:9-11.
[273] See Lk 4:41; Mt 16:16; 26:63-64; Jn 11:27; 20:31.

3.4.4 The Lamb of God

The Feast of Sacrifice (Arabic: 'Id al-adha, Turkish: kurban bayrami) is the greatest feast in Islam, when Muslims remember Abraham's sacrifice of his son.[274] Families slaughter a sacrificial animal, usually a sheep. After a short prayer, the neck artery is cut, and the sacrificial blood flows into a prepared ditch. The dead animal is then skinned and divided in three parts. One part is usually given to relatives, the second to the poor and the family keeps the third part.

The sacrifice is meant only as a remembrance of Abraham's sacrifice. The Qur'an denies all further spiritual meaning (Sura 22:32-37). In folk Islam, however, several further meanings have been added. Some think that the animal is slaughtered instead of the firstborn son, or as general thanks to Allah, or as a protection against evil spirits. Since the Qur'an has no clear answer to these questions, Christians have a good opportunity to explain the spiritual meaning from the Bible.[275] The Old Testament sacrifices are decreed by God. The animal serves as a substitute and is killed so that the person may live.

Symbolically, sins are transferred from the person to the sacrificial animal. According to the Bible, there is no forgiveness of sin without bloodshed (Heb 9:22). If someone repeatedly sinned, the Old Testament sacrifice had to be repeated. In the New Testament, God has instituted a new covenant through Jesus; Jesus died as a unique sacrifice for all sins (Heb 10:14). This puts an end to the slaughter of sacrificial animals, because Jesus is "...the Lamb of God, who takes away the sin of the world!" (Jn 1:29). Whoever accepts this sacrifice in faith, will be saved.[276]

> **? Questions to discuss with Muslims**
> • Why do Muslims still have to keep the 'Id al-adha (Feast of sacrifice) today?
> • How is the feast celebrated?
> • What is the meaning of "shedding the blood and eating the meat", of the sacrifice (sheep)?

3.4.5 Further subjects

There are many more topics which can be taken from the Qur'an and explained according to the Bible. A study of of topics which fall into this "common ground

---

[274] Contrary to the biblical story, most Muslims think that the son to be sacrificed was Ishmael, and not Isaac. See footnote in section 3.4.1.

[275] See also sections 2.3.4; 2.4.3 and 3.4.1.

[276] Important Bible verses regarding the sacrificial lamb are: Ge 4:4-7; 22:6-8; Ex 12:3-7,22,23; Lev 16; Is 53:4-8; Jn 1:29,36; Ac 8:26-39; 1Pe 1:18-21; Rev 5:6-8; 21:22.

approach" are explored in the book *Sharing the Gospel with Muslims* by Gilchrist (2003):

Old Testament Personalities	New Testament
Adam: The man of dust, the man from heaven	**Jesus:** Unique in the Qur'an and the Bible
Eve: Satan's three great temptations	
Noah: The first herald of righteousness	**The Son of God:** the Messiah, Spirit and Word
Abraham: The gospel that was preached to him	
Isaac: The reflection of the father's love	**Al-Masihu Isa:** God's anointed Messiah
Joseph: A symbol of the coming deliverer	
Moses: Law and grace in sharp contrast	**The love of God:** Father, Son and Holy Spirit
David: Prophecies of death and resurrection	
Solomon: Image of the true son of David	**Nuzul-l-Isa:** The second coming of Jesus
Isaiah: Behold the servant He has Chosen	

3.5 Implementing the vision in the local church

It is vital that the whole Christian community supports mission to Muslims. The following general guidelines, not strict rules, need to be adapted to the context of the relevant situation and culture. Considerations must be made in respect of how a church operates: a church in England has more religious freedom and therefore more evangelistic varieties at hand than a church in Egypt. The guidance of the Holy Spirit is necessary to formulate means of outreach suitable in each community.

By becoming active in Muslim evangelism, the church gains the following:
a. It will have a new perspective on how to reach Muslims for Christ.
b. The people of the church will be motivated to pray for new activities and the conversion of Muslims.
c. Christians will be educated and begin to lose their fear in approaching Muslims.
d. Christians will be more effective in witnessing to Muslims and new friendships will develop.
e. The knowledge of the Bible will be better grasped and Christians will learn how to share their faith in a way understandable to Muslims.
f. The basic knowledge of Islam will allow Christians to relate better to Muslims.
g. Converts from Islam will be cared for by trained Christians.

3.5.1 Motivation and education
The Great Commission says:
> Then Jesus came to them and said: All authority in heaven and on earth has been given to me. Therefore go and make disciple of all nations, baptizing them in the name of the Father and of the Son and of the Holy Spirit, and teaching them to obey everything I have commanded you. And surely I will be with you always, to the very end of the age. (Mt 28:18-20)

From this verse the following can be learned from Jesus:
- He has all authority. If you follow him, you are under the highest power. Nothing can harm you.
- He commands all Christians to reach all people (including Muslims) with the Good News.
- He also commands Christians to make disciples, baptize and teach them.
- Jesus does not just give orders and commands but also a wonderful promise: He will always be with you and help you.

It is important that the whole church community embraces that the Great Commission is directed to all people—including Muslims! Often Christians are fearful and timid to approach Muslims, yet Christians know the truth and this must be shared. Fear is often caused by ignorance; the antidote is to be well informed—by training church members on the following subjects:
1. **Introduction into Islam.** History, the life of Muhammad, Qur'an, *Shar'ia.* etc. As Christians know the faith of their Muslim friends, communications and relationships will improve.
2. **Apologetics.** To be able to respond wisely to objections Muslims have against the Christian faith.
3. **Practical guidelines:** How to meet Muslims in practical ways in everyday life.

3.5.2 Forming a special task group
As many Church members as possible should acquire a basic knowledge of Islam, apologetics and practical guidelines for interaction. However, a special group within the church body should receive more advanced training and coordinate prayer and outreach to Muslims.

The following steps are recommended:
1. Church leadership needs to agree that some kind of Christian mission to Muslims will be part of future activities.
2. The whole Christian community should be adequately informed on strategy and specific steps forward.
3. The church appoints 5—10 devoted Christians to a special task group with an appointed leader..
4. This group meets regularly for prayer, planning of activities and further training.

3.5.3 Responsibilities of the task group
The task group develops plans and makes decisions on developing contacts with the Muslim community in order to share the Good News. The task group has the following responsibilities:
- To take the initiative for new activities to meet Muslims in the neighbourhood.
- To conduct and coordinate activities.
- To inform church members to solicit prayer support.
- To plan and conduct ongoing training for the task group and the whole church.

- To care adequately for new converts.
- To explore possible contact to other churches and/or organisations with the same vision to reach Muslims for Christ (for encouragement, combined training, prayer).

This special task group needs constant training and encouragement. Continuous training is needed in Christian theology but also awareness of Islamic literature. Training sessions should conclude with evaluation and adjustments for the future.

An other important aspect is networking. The task group should, whenever possible, be in contact with other task groups of neighbouring churches and exchange information:
- To encourage and pray for one another.
- To coordinate and combine any further training.
- To enhance the exchange of experience from past activities.
- To plan and conduct combined activities in the future.

3.5.4 Possible activities
Through much prayer and discussion the church, but in particular the special task group, needs to discern appropriate activities that will enhance Christian witness, leading to sharing the gospel with Muslims in any given situation. Possible ideas are given here to stimulate ideas; Christians are encouraged to constantly develop new methods:
- Implement a systematic program to visit Muslims in their homes (e.g. with the help of a specially designed questionnaire).
- Visit Muslims in public places such as hospitals, prisons, etc.
- Visit them at the mosque and in return invite Muslims to your church.
- Distribute literature at public places with a booktable.
- At the end of the year, distribute Christian calendars which have a short devotion for each day.
- Offer courses on computer knowledge, language learning, and other desirable skills.
- Organize combined outreaches such as hiking, bike tours, or visiting museums.
- Organize special talks on agreed-upon topics.[277]
- Visit individuals on their birthday. Bring a gift and read a short passage from the Bible.
- Accept invitations to their special festivals and in return invite them to your special festivals in the church.
- Invite them to a special meal, individually or as a group, in your home or church. Offer a program with music, singing, reading from the Bible, showing a film, etc.

---

[277] See section 3.5.5.

- Distribute tracts to their houses or letter boxes and then call to ask them whether they have questions they want to discuss.[278]

Questionnaire approach

One approach to Muslims is through a specially designed questionnaire. There are many variations possible. Two or three Christians should go together to visit Muslim homes. The following suggest how it could be done:

At the door, the group introduces themselves:
- Good day, my name is... and this is my friend...We are coming from...and are conducting a survey on religious/social questions and are prepared to help everyone who is seeking God!
- We would appreciate your thoughts on a few questions. May I have a few minutes of your time? (if the person says YES you may continue; if the answer is NO, then try to enter a religious conversation without the questionnaire by saying things such as: "May I explain to you how I came to the certain knowledge of having eternal life?" if the person is not interested, say good-bye; if the time is not suitable, try to make an appointment at another date).

Suggested questions

Social:
1) How long have you lived in this place?
2) Are you happy in this community?
3) What would you like to change to make this a better place?

Religious:
1) What is your religious affiliation?
2) Do you belong to any particular religious group?
3) Do you belong to this religion through birth or personal decision?
4) How would you judge yourself concerning practical faith in everyday life: (very religious—occasional—seldom)
5) Why do you regard your faith as the true one?
6) Do you fear a) death? b) day of judgment? c) that God will not show mercy to you?
7) Are you sure that you will be with God in paradise one day?
8) Imagine if you would die today and stood before God and he asked you: Why should I let you into paradise? What would you answer?

After you have finished the questionnaire you may say:
- We have finished the questionnaire. Your answers are interesting! Thank you so much for your time!
- Would you like to know the result and evaluation of our survey?

---

[278] Tracts need to be specifically written for Muslim readers and be relevant to the situation.

- Do you have more time so that I can explain how I know that I will be in paradise with God after I die?
- Would you like to receive some Christian literature or DVDs?
- May I visit you another time?

Christians should keep records of visits with Muslims, as in the following example:

Place:		Address:
Name:		Tel:
Date/Who:	Literature given:	Observations:

3.5.5 Organizing special meetings with Muslims

There are many different ways for peaceful meetings between people of different faiths. Here is but one suggestion:

The aim of a "Meeting for better Understanding" is not criticism but to present different points of view on an agreed topic. Each side presents its faith and, as both parties are heard, some statements may be in agreement while others may be contradictory. A better understanding of each other's faith should create respect between the two faith communities leading to new friendships. Christians cannot convert Muslims—this is the work of God! Christians and Muslims both need to be aware and accept that some people may change their religion as a result of such meetings.[279] Some suggested guidelines:

1) Muslims and Christians meet alternatively in the church and in the mosque.
2) In preparatory meetings, the whole set up will be discussed in detail and agreed on by an organizing committee.
3) Each side has the same amount of time (e.g. 30 minutes) to present a talk on an agreed topic.
4) After the two presentations, another session of about 30 minutes of question/answer time will follow. An appointed moderator accepted by both parties will direct this session. Only questions related to the topic will be allowed. People should refrain from aggressive or insulting questions. Brief points of view, queries or answers may be given.
5) Another, more relaxed time of meeting should follow in a place that fosters individual conversations and discussions. At such times Christians may have an opportunity to share the gospel. Refreshments and light food should be served.

---

[279] Such meetings are only possible where there is religious freedom granted from both sides.

Topics chosen may be religious and social:

Religious	Social
1) The unity of God	1) Human rights and religious freedom
2) What is "sin"? How does man enter paradise?	2) Morality, honesty
3) Who is Jesus Christ? Who is Muhammad?	3) Family life: husband-wife-child relationships
4) Bible and Qur'an: origin and inspiration	4) Married life
5) Relationship of man to God	5) Upbringing of children in the local society
6) What are the marks of a true prophet?	6) Basic rules of friendship and neighbourhood
7) The attributes of God	7) What is the cause of terror?
8) Prayer and fasting	8) How could war be avoided?
9) What are the marks of a true Christian/Muslim?	9) Why is there so much corruption?
10) Definition of the "Church"/ "Umma"?	10) Cultural life
11) What happens on the day of judgment?	11) How can peaceful life between different races be achieved?

3.6 Conversion and discipleship

Since World War II, a new international economic situation, numerous local wars and persecution of certain ethnic, political or religious groups have caused a tremendous shift in the world population. Millions of people have moved from one country to another in search for safety, stability and work. As a result, Christians and Muslims meet daily in almost every corner of the world. The awareness that Christians and Muslims have of each other's faith has also grown extensively. One aspect common to Christianity and Islam is that they are missionary religions where believers actively invite other people to become adherents to their faith. This inviting attitude has its basis in their respective Scriptures:

Mt 11:28: Come to me, all you who are weary and burdened, and I will give you rest.[280]

Surah 16:125: Invite (all) to the way of thy Lord with wisdom and beautiful preaching; and argue with them in ways that are best and most gracious...

Some Christians and Muslims are dissatisfied and disillusioned with their own faith for various reasons. Such people look for an alternative to satisfy felt needs. It has become more common for people to change their allegiance from Christianity to Islam and from Islam to Christianity in recent times.

---

[280] It has to be emphasized that although Christians should bear witness to the truth, only the Holy Spirit can bring about conversion. (see, for example, Ac 10:44). Christians are called to teach converts how to follow Jesus (Mt 28:20).

I have personally witnessed this change of allegiance with many people, both in Africa and Europe. In 2000 there was a public event in Zürich (Switzerland) where Muslims presented their faith in an informal, attractive way. In speeches the relevance of Islam for the people in Europe was explained, literature was sold and oriental food was given free of charge. There were Swiss people who had already converted to Islam and many who found Islam very attractive but had not yet made a decision to embrace it formally. Most of these people told me that they grew up in a Christian environment and some professed to have been Christians before.

On the other hand, I met a business man from an Islamic state who had been a Muslim all his life but recently converted to Christianity. He had secretly obtained and read a Bible in his own language. As he travelled to Europe, visited churches and spoke to Christians, it became clear to him that becoming a Christian was the right step . For reasons of persecution and fear for his life, it was not possible for him to return to his home country as a Christian. He was prepared to pay the cost of his conversion, leave his family and business behind and start a completely new life in Europe. This businessman pointed out that he knows of many more people in his home country who are disillusioned with Islam.

3.6.1 Conversion motives

In my doctoral thesis I interviewed 20 converts, ten who converted from Christianity to Islam and ten from Islam to Christianity.[281] The narratives reveal that between two and four of the five motives I have identified played a role in each conversion process.[282] In the following I briefly outline five conversion motives which, according to my findings, are the most important. However, these are not the only ones.

Five conversion motives:

1) **Religious**

   This motive is sometimes called the "intellectual" motive for conversion, or traditionally the "true" motive. A person actively seeks knowledge about religious or spiritual issues via literature, television, lectures and other media. In my study it means that a person actively acquires knowledge of the Christian or Islamic faith.

   Some converts interviewed were seeking religious knowledge about Christianity or Islam because there was a problem or "crisis" with their experience of their original faith. The main reason given was that of not being able to "understand" teaching or rituals. Since such persons could no longer understand and agree with the teaching of their faith they felt "pushed" to leave it and

---

[281] See Maurer (1999).
[282] The narratives also reveal that conversion usually takes place over a rather long period of time—months or sometimes years.

explore alternatives. Since the new religion was experienced as "better" and more "understandable," it "pulled" the person to accept it.

2) Mystical

A mystical conversion experience "is generally a sudden and traumatic burst of insight, induced by vision, voices, or other paranormal experiences." A "paranormal phenomenon" is usually described as an experience which cannot be easily explained scientifically or rationally. The prototypical conversion in respect to mystical experience in the Bible is commonly attributed to Saul of Tarsus on his way to Damascus (Ac 9). In religious terminology it has therefore the understanding of the direct intervention of the spiritual divine power. In such conversions it is the Holy Spirit who "is at work in ways that pass human understanding."

The term "supernatural" is also sometimes used in this context,—that which "cannot be explained by natural or physical laws" and has its original cause in the "world of spirits." If people speak about supernatural experiences they usually refer to a significant dream, vision or impression, an extraordinary happening or event usually sudden and unexpected. The level of emotional arousal is extremely high, sometimes involving theophanic[283] ecstasies, awe, love, or even fear. A revelation is an extraordinary disclosure which a person receives. This extraordinary insight enables a person to make a step in a direction which would otherwise not have been easily taken, such as a change in religion. Dreams and visions can serve either to initiate conversion or to confirm it, or both.

3) Affection

It stresses interpersonal bonds as the decisive factor in the conversion process. A person experiences affection as being loved, nurtured and affirmed by another person or group. Interpersonal bonds are widely viewed as providing "fundamental support for recruitment". In my interviews this conversion motive appeared primarily in the form of affection for a person admired for his/her religious activities. Such a person was either a friend or a relative, from the same or the opposite sex. Negative affectionate factors are often traumatic events such as the death of a family member or a divorce, which constitutes a crisis in the life of a particular person and may push him/her into a conversion process.

4) Socio-political

This relates to the functioning of the individual within his or her socio-political group. A person is motivated for socio-political reasons to change his/her religious allegiance. This motive featured strongly in my interviews since many converts mentioned the socio-political situation as a reason for embracing another religion.

---

[283] "Theophanic": an appearance of God.

5) **Material**

Particularly important for my research, it was mentioned by various converts. Many poor people find themselves in such a desperate situation that they will change their religious allegiance if it can somehow improve their lot. Sometimes criticised as "impure", this conversion motive includes the desire for benefits such as food, clothes, gifts, housing, etc. I also viewed an offer of employment or a bursary for studies as a material motivation for conversion. Poverty constitutes a crisis which sometimes "pushes" a person into a conversion process leading to a change of religion.

3.6.2 Conversion from Islam to Christianity

A Muslim interested in the gospel and wanting to know more about the Christian faith needs special help. Christians should spare no effort to give this searcher the support he or she needs, particularly introducing them to an appropriate, easy-to-understand Bible class. In addition, Christian values and the way the local church functions should be explained in detail, with appropriate explanations of how the church draws its practices from God's Word, the Bible.

Usually, conversion to Christ is a long process and the result of several factors. Christians should follow up each convert with love and care in this often difficult stage in their life.[284] In most cases, the convert is heavily pressurized and suffers persecution because his family, as well as the local Muslim community, will do whatever they can to bring him back to Islam. This reaction of the Muslim community is based on the teaching that everyone who leaves Islam is a traitor and brings great disgrace to the family. If the convert does not change his mind and return to Islam, he will, in most cases, be expelled from his family and lose his inheritance. Sometimes, the convert is threatened with death.[285]

As a result, converts need a new family and community where they can begin their new life. It is essential that a Christian family or group adopts each convert and cares for them with much love. It is important that converts clearly understand what conversion means. They should fully understand the gospel. The most important points are as follows:

1. Transferring one's trust from Muhammad to Jesus (Jn 14:6).
2. Knowing the risen and living Jesus Christ as personal saviour and redeemer (Jn 1:12; Rev 3:20).
3. Knowing Christ as Lord, whom must be obeyed, under the guidance of the Holy Spirit (Jn 14:23-26).
4. All sins must be confessed (Ac 2:38; 1Jn 1:9). This includes renouncing any connections with dark powers and occult practices. Should problems arise in this area, an experienced Christian counsellor should be called in.

---

[284] Both spiritual and social needs must be addressed.
[285] According to orthodox Sunni belief, a Muslim who leaves Islam has three days to consider his position and come back to Islam, otherwise he faces the death penalty.

3.6.3 Discipleship

The following points must be kept in mind when caring for converts:[286]

- Sufficient time and care must be given in explaining Christian teachings from the Bible to the convert. Prayer and the Christian lifestyle in particular have to be thoroughly explained. The convert should then go on to study a suitable introductory Bible course.
- Christians have to be careful not to imprint an alien culture onto the convert.
- Converts need to be introduced into congregations and Christian groups where they are given the love and understanding they need. The way the congregation operates should be explained. Churches should be able to welcome and disciple such converts.[287]
- It is always helpful to bring converts into contact with others of a similar background who have also come to faith in Jesus Christ.
- Converts should not be regimented or subjected to a system of rules. They need sufficient freedom to develop and grow into independent and mature Christians.
- Converts, in consultation with the church leadership, should decide when they get baptized.
- It is imprudent to publish conversion stories too early. It is often unwise to let converts speak in public because that can make themselves targets for militant Muslims or may become conceited.
- Christians should abstain from giving money on a long-term basis to converts. This could create an unhelpful dependency. It is better to find work so that the convert is paid money as a salary, or to give a small loan that they have to pay back.

3.6.4 Conversion from Christianity to Islam

It is not unknown for people to turn away from Christianity and adopt another religion such as Islam.[288] In most cases, these people are shunned by the Christian community. Is this the correct Christian attitude towards them? How did Jesus react when his disciples turned away from him?[289] Jesus did not exert pressure on them; he let the disciples decide for themselves. He is ready to love them unconditionally and let them go if they decide to do so. Should not Christians assume the same attitude today?

Some practical guidelines:
1. Individual Christians and churches as a whole are called to follow up these people in love, and to try to understand why they made this decision.

---

[286] The PALM course is specially prepared for such people: www.takwin-masihi.org

[287] Christians should therefore be ready to inform and educate themselves thoroughly, studying suitable literature as well as attending appropriate training courses.

[288] "Born-again Christians" would call such people "nominal Christians". There are many people who have been brought up within a Christian environment and are seen as "Christians", but have never made a personal commitment to Jesus Christ.

[289] See for example Jn 6:60-71, and Mk 10:17-22.

2. Even if such a person insists on converting to Islam and following through on this conversion process, friendly contact should never be broken off.
3. The Christian community can gain from this open and friendly contact by learning from possible mistakes and trying to do better in the future.
4. Should the person change his mind, and return to Christianity, the community should welcome him with open arms.[290]

This friendly attitude is the right attitude for Christians to pass on God's love to others.

3.7 Political issues

3.7.1 *Shari'a*, democracy and human rights

Islamic fundamentalism's push for the introduction of *Shari'a* and an Islamic state for all countries has come into conflict with conceptions of the secular, democratic state. They are in contrast to the internationally supported Universal Declaration of Human Rights (UDHR). This conflict centres on the following issues:
• Rejection of fundamental human rights such as total religious freedom.
• Rejection of the equality of men and women.
• Rejection of the separation of religion and state.
• Rejection of religious rights, such as the right of Muslims to leave their religion.

Democracy means the rule of the people. This is done by way of elections. Every individual adult may make his choice of a candidate. The party that gains most votes becomes the ruling institution. Islam, on the other hand, seeks to institute a theocracy, a state ruled by God. In real terms, the clerics hold the power. It is therefore evident that fundamentalist Islam is not compatible with democracy.[291] Most existing countries of political Islam have so far grossly failed to accept any meaningful conception of democracy.

Several major, predominantly Muslim countries criticized the Universal Declaration of Human Rights for its perceived failure to take into account the cultural and religious context of non-Western countries. Iran claimed that the UDHR was a "a secular understanding of the Judeo-Christian tradition", which could not be implemented by Muslims without trespassing Islamic law. Therefore the Organization of the Islamic Conference adopted the Cairo Declaration of Human Rights in Islam, which diverges from the UDHR substantially, affirming *Shari'a* as the sole source of human rights. This Declaration was severely criticized by the In-

---

[290] Jesus says that all sins can be forgiven, except sin against the Holy Spirit (Mk 3:28-30; Lk 12:10; Mt 12:31-32). That means knowingly resisting the clear and unmistakable actions of the Holy Spirit and attributing his work to Satan.
[291] Democracy (literally "rule by the people", from the Greek demokratia *demos*, "people," and *kratos*, "rule") is a form of government by the will of the people. This means that the citizens vote on electing the ruling authority and on laws. The state's power is in the hands of the people and not a religious authority as in a theocracy. Theocracy from the Greek theokratia: government of a state by immediate divine guidance or by officials who are regarded as divinely guided.

ternational Commission of Jurists for allegedly gravely threatening inter-cultural consensus, introducing intolerable discrimination against both non-Muslims and women, the restrictive character in regard to fundamental rights and freedoms and attacking the integrity, and dignity of the human being.

The increasing application of *Shari'a* law is creating multiplied possibilities of persecution. In countries such as Saudi Arabia, Afghanistan and Pakistan the courts may sentence a national to death for becoming a Christian. In many Islamic countries relatives will sometimes murder those who become Christians. This has brought much hardship to many Christians worldwide. Christians are called to pray, fast and help each other by giving necessary assistance. More guidelines are given in the next section.

3.7.2 Violence and terrorism in Islam

There are fundamentalist Muslims who want to return to what they believe was original Islam as practiced by Muhammad and the early caliphs. These Muslims are largely led by the mullahs/Imams/religious leaders and base what they believe on meticulous study of the Qur'an, *hadith* and writings of Islamic scholars. They despise western education and believe all true knowledge comes from the Qur'an and *hadith*. They believe in physical *jihad*. Some are what is generally called "terrorists," who participate in bombings and suicidal attacks inside countries who do not believe as they do. Through these acts of mass destruction, both Muslims and non-Muslims lose their lives. These radicals believe they are practicing true Islam. In Pakistan, the Taliban and their supporters are very active in this group, and these radical/extremist Muslims are a fairly large minority of the population.

The other group is what is called the westernized, modernist Muslims. They believe Islam should be adjusted to and practiced within the modern world with its scientific, cultural and economic advances. Their leaders are western-educated scholars, scientists, and other political leaders. They believe in spiritual *jihad*, but do not want to be involved in a physical war unless they are attacked and forced to fight. They want to "live and let live". In Europe and other Western nations, the storm of radical Islam is breaking with a fury that is frightening. Secular Western societies are being confronted by the ideologies of fundamentalist Islam.

Is Islam the only religion with a doctrine, theology and legal system that mandates warfare against unbelievers? Is it true that 26 chapters of the Qur'an deal with *jihad*? That fight able-bodied believers are obligated to join (Sura 2:216: "Fighting is prescribed ..."), and that the text orders Muslims to "instil terror into the hearts of the unbeliever" and to "smite above their necks" (Sura 8:12) that is, cut off their heads? Generally speaking, those questions focus on whether the Qur'an does indeed promote violence against non-Muslims, and how many of the terrorists' ideas about violent *jihad*, self-immolation, kidnappings, even beheadings come right out of the text? Is the "test" of loyalty to Allah not good acts or faith in general, but martyrdom that results from fighting unbelievers—a kind of higher degree of salvation in Islam (cf Suras 4:74; 4:95; 9:111; 47:4)?

Further questions

- Are the sins of any Muslim who becomes a martyr forgiven by the very act of being killed while slaying the unbelievers (Sura 4:95)?
- Is it really true that martyrs are rewarded with virgins, among other carnal delights, in Paradise (Suras 38:52, 55:56; 56:22)?
- Are those unable to do *jihad*, such as women or the elderly, required to give "asylum and aid" to those who do fight unbelievers in the cause of Allah (Sura 8:74)?
- Does Islam advocate expansion by force? And is the final command of *jihad*, as revealed to Muhammad in the Qur'an, to conquer the world in the name of Islam (Sura 9:29)?
- Is Islam a religion that does not teach the "Golden Rule"[292] (Sura 48:29)?
- Does the Qur'an instead teach violence and hatred against non-Muslims, specifically Jews and Christians (Sura 5:54)?
- Does Allah, the almighty one, need puny little humans to protect Him and defend Him?
- Is Allah willing to depend on humans to defend him before others?

How should Christians respond?

I have occasionally experienced incidents when Muslims became violent:

I once visited a Muslim home with a Christian friend. During the conversation we got into an argument and my Christian friend said that "Muhammad was a liar". Our Muslim friend lost his temper, and ran to the kitchen to fetch a knife! We left the house very quickly and were never able to return.

On another occasion, while visiting a Muslim we were discussing religious matters. I explained what the Bible says regarding the right way of entering paradise. Suddenly he stopped me speaking and said that, if I continue sharing about my Christian belief, he needed to kill me. I was quite surprised, but decided from that moment to talk about anything *but* religion!

It is not only people of other faiths who are attacked by militant Muslims. Many liberal Muslims have had to flee their homes because of persecution. It is not only major Islamic groups such as the Shi'a who fight Sunni Muslims today; many minor Islamic groups use violence against other Islamic groups, taking property and life. The real threat comes from militant Muslims prepared to destroy others' lives and property to defend and spread their unique system of belief.

I have witnessed violence with my own eyes. One morning I visited a Muslim friend. To my surprise, I noticed that his house was burned. He was very sad, telling me that Muslims from another group had attacked his house with petrol bombs.

---

[292] The "Golden Rule" according to Christians: "In everything, do to others what you would have them do to you, for this sums up the Law and the Prophets" (Mt 7:12).

I will never forget a Muslim friend who, after a number of discussion meetings, said to me:

> "It is so nice to come together with you Christian people, since we enjoy discussing things with you. We notice our agreement but also our differences. The good thing is, that we can leave in peace after the meeting. We could not engage in such discussion with our Muslim brothers on these issues, since we would never be sure if they get violent after the meeting and perhaps destroy our property."

While travelling in many parts of the world, I have met many Christians who face severe persecution from Muslims. How should Christians in Nigeria or Indonesia respond when a Muslim mob approaches their church or their houses in order to burn and destroy them? How should they react when their lives are in danger? Should they just pray or should they physically defend their property and lives? These are difficult situations for which there is no general solution. Christians should pray, listen to the voice of God and act accordingly. God is in control at all times and the judge of all people and their actions!

Why do Muslims resort to violence? Why do they believe that they have to physically defend Islam and Muhammad?

- Militant Muslims find support for their actions from a variety of verses from the Qur'an, as shown above.
- The Qur'an is not written in chronological order; verses promoting violence stand side-by-side by verses promoting peace. Muslims tend to choose those verses which appeal to them; those they dislike will be ignored.
- Muhammad is the role model, and took property from others, killing people as he deemed fit in the name of Islam.
- Since its beginning, Islam appears to be a religion of convenience, changing its face as needs change, denying things when put on the spot, and re-affirming things when in power.

❗ Conclusion

- Never say anything against Muhammad or Islam. Put your statements into a question form.
- Instead of saying e.g. "I am convinced that..." rather say: "I have read in a book...or I have heard that...". This takes the attention of your Muslim friend away from you to the book. He can then refute what is written in the book without jeopardising your friendship.
- While speaking with a Muslim in private, he or she will be much more open and honest than if another Muslim is present. In the latter instance, the person feels a social obligation to defend Islam.

3.7.3 The crisis of Islam

There is tension within Islam between the two extremist Islamic ideologies, namely:

1) radical ideology: to live as Muhammad did and keep all Islamic laws
2) modernist views: to adapt to modern (Western) lifestyle

To accommodate modern people, Islam has taken divergent paths in recent times and will continue to do so. While fundamentalism attracts some adherents, many are turning toward a more personalized faith. One main proponent of this in the Arab world is Amr Khaled, a young Muslim preacher.[293] Khaled is not trained by a Muslim theological school but does proclaim a very personalized faith which seems to bring Allah closer to the Muslim than traditional Islam would normally allow. This is an example of Islam "morphing" or transitioning to keep pace with the times.

Another example of this "morphing" of Islam is Sami Yusuf[294] who has recorded contemporary Islamic music which greatly appeals to young people. The old guard of Islam—namely Al Azhar-trained clerics—are not favourable towards this morphed expression of Islam.

Islamic governments are becoming more and more secular as well. Tunisia is probably the primary example. Perhaps Turkey in its quest to join the European Union is another example. Which path will Islam follow in the future? Will it become a more contemporary and youthful faith, or will the leadership of the faith remain in the hands of the old guard? This may well be a key question of the 21st century. Will Islam be able to re-invent itself and modernize? Will it be able to come up with a contemporary understanding of *jihad*, for example? These questions seem to be critical.

Christians are again challenged when discussing these issues with Muslims. The following steps may serve as general guidelines:

1) Listen carefully and show a keen interest in radical or modern ideas Muslims may express about Islam.
2) Ask appropriate questions.
3) Endeavour to turn the conversation into a spiritual one by witnessing to your practical faith.
4) Be prepared to study these new ideologies and read the relevant websites.

3.7.4 Conspiracy theories and how to react

Many Christians in the Arab world face this phenomenon. When an Egypt Air flight crashed shortly after take off in New York (flight 990, Oct.31,1999), the theory was that either the CIA or Mossad had brought the plane down. Of course, this is preposterous; the investigators concluded that the pilot himself brought the plane down. However, Egyptians could not accept this.

---

[293] See www.amrkhaled.net
[294] See www.samiyusuf.com

Most Arabs are convinced that the Jews control the world through the powerful Jewish lobby in the USA. They point to Jewish presence in the media, the entertainment industry and politics, to show that Jews are well-placed in every sphere of life in order to control the world. In the Muslim mind, Jews are to blame for much of what is going on in the world.

How should Christians react to such theories? The following remarks may serve as guidelines:
- Christians should not react one-sided manner, as if all evil on Earth can be blamed on Islam.
- Try to see both sides and avoid quick judgment.
- Avoid aggressive statements which may attack Islam.
- Instead of taking one or the other side, challenge your Muslim friend with questions.
- Endeavour to turn your discussion into a spiritual conversation.

3.8 Social issues

3.8.1 Christian-Muslim marriages
Christian women should not marry Muslim men, nor should Christian men marry Muslim women. Belief, spiritual and practical life and the concept of marriage are too different.

Christians who live already in a Christian-Muslim marriage[295] should be able to remain members of a Christian congregation or church. The Christian community has to help such couples with counselling. The Christian partner should strive for a Christian education of the children. According to Islamic views, marriage is not basically a promise of a life-long unity with only one partner. Equal rights for women in comparison with men are certainly not given. According to Islamic law, a Muslim woman is not allowed to marry a Christian man, because the man has the right to decide about education and has custody of the children.

In marriages where not only the religions, but also the cultures of the partners are fundamentally different, problems are unavoidable. Even though liberal and tolerant Muslims exist, a Muslim man will often not hesitate, in the case of a conflict, to apply Islamic law in his favour. The precise legal situation regarding marriage and the custody of children needs to be examined for the countries of both marriage partners. Resources exist to help those involved in or contemplating cross-cultural marriage which can enable them to think through the issues involved.[296]

3.8.2 Integration of Muslims in non-Islamic countries
Many Muslim leave their Islamic home countries for various reasons and settle

---

[295] It is recommended to use a marriage contract. Examples can be obtained from:
Secretariat.isdc-dfjp@unil.ch
[296] See for instance Fraser (1993) on the subject of cross-cultural marriages.

in non-Islamic countries in order to have a better life.[297] These are often secular Western states with a democratic free society. For many Muslims, mainly liberal and non-practicing, the new lifestyle with its culture is initially difficult to adapt to but eventually they integrate well. Ensuing generations of Muslims, most of whom acquire citizenship feel more at home in their country of birth than in the Islamic country of their forefathers.

Practicing Muslims find it harder to adapt and often complain about the structure of public life which naturally does not support the Islamic way of life. They may even have the impression that existing laws are desined to make it difficult for Muslims. This is not true, since other minority religious groups and organisations have to keep the same rules and regulations. Some Muslims appear rather arrogant, demanding that the Western society should accept the demands of Muslims for practicing Islam! An increasing number of Muslims are complaining, though they most likely do not have the same freedom in their Islamic home country! One might ask them why they do not emigrate back to their Islamic country with much less freedom but with a structure that supports Islam? Emigrating to a new country presupposes an adaptation to new lifestyles, rules and laws of that country. As for the observation of religious festivals and other practices, Muslims need to make the necessary adjustments, accept compromises or simply submit to the existing laws of the country.

There are certain basic realities which Muslims coming to a non-Islamic country should be prepared to accept in order to integrate well:
1) All immigrants, including Muslims from Islamic states, should attend a course on integration and national/local language, which is the basis for proper integration.
2) Muslims should respect the existing laws of their host country, even when they differ from Islamic laws.[298] Islamic laws or traditions such as blood revenge, forced marriages, oppression of women (including beating of women as described in Sura 4:34), spreading Islam by any means of force, violence or terror must be laid aside.
3) No parallel societies will be tolerated. Muslims are not allowed to live with a ghetto mentality that would introduce a separate Islamic world within the secular state.
4) Muslims shall have the same rights and status as other religious groups in the country, but will not be allowed to demand special allowances.
5) Imams and any Islamic teacher should make their teaching public. The secular state has the authority to control and watch that all teachings conform to regulations. No teaching or statements against any other religion will be tolerated. Islamic teachers who do not submit to this standard must be expelled.

---

[297] Reasons may be: to have a job, to study at university, to enjoy a free society, to receive medical treatment, to propagate Islam, etc.

[298] This is one of the major problems: radical Muslims will eventually not submit to secular law, but will force Islamic law on all countries.

6) Mosques and their facilities should be open to all people, including non-Muslims. Muslims are asked to be transparent in all their activities.

7) Muslims, as any other religious community, should be allowed to practice their faith as long as it conforms to the laws of the secular state. Muslims may have their own cemeteries and be allowed to build mosques with minarets, but only in compliance with the building codes.

8) Boys and girls at schools should be treated equally. Private absence for religious reasons should not be allowed (exceptions are community festivals). Muslims must accept local traditions and culture!

9) In all other matters e.g. the wearing of the headscarf or any other Islamic clothing at work, Muslims have to submit to local regulations.

3.8.3 Contextualization

The term "contextualization" as a specific missionary term came to the fore in 1972 when the Theological Educational Fund (TEF), sponsored by the World Council of Churches (WCC), published its report *Ministry in Context,* in which churches were strongly urged to introduce radical reforms in theological education. These included Feminist Theology, Liberation Theology and the so-called Black Theology. Since then there has been heated controversy representing a wide divergence of opinion on the issue. Contextualization includes, in sum, all that is implied in indigenization and more. It comprises constructing or developing a national theology making Christianity relevant to a particular group of people.

Contextualization is a fairly new missionary term. However, its roots are found in the life and activity of the early Church. Paul in particular was a perfectly contextualized preacher who expressed a contextual theology and approach:

> Though I am free and belong to no man, I make myself a slave to everyone, to win as many as possible (1Co 9:19).

As the Jews were reluctant to give up their Law, Paul did not demand that they abandon it. Instead, he acknowledged their worldview and invited them to believe in Jesus without abandoning the Thora. He dealt with the Gentiles in a similar way when he took the gospel to them. The Law and other Jewish traditions were repugnant to the pagans, so Paul affirmed the moral law—with love as the supreme interpreting value—setting aside the ceremonial/sacrificial law for the sake of their conversion. He held that Biblical Christianity was not related to any particular culture. The basic Christian truth is one: faith in Christ. Whoever accepts this truth enters the Christian fold, whatever his culture.

General characteristics of contextualisation are:
- Not to bring any pressure to bear on people to change their manners and customs unless they are evidently contrary to religion and sound morals.
- Do not draw invidious contrasts between the customs of the people and your own.
- Do your utmost to adapt yourself to them while not compromising the message of the Bible.

The relationship between the two major world communities, Christians and Muslims, has been extremely strained in the past and at present, owing to several factors.[299] Questions facing Christians oncerning bringing the gospel to Muslims are: Which aspects of the Word of God and Christian practices are negotiable and which are not? What are the parameters? What kind of signals are sent to the local Muslim community by practicing "contextualization"?

When entering a foreign culture it is incumbent to adjust to the people within this group, dressing in an unoffensive manner or even wearing indigenous clothing. One has to learn the language, adjust to prevailing customs and make certain that one does not offend the host people with your behaviour.

In Islam many cultural forms carry religious connotations. How should a Christian react? Which of these clash with biblical customs and content? Which of the points in question have a spiritual significance and which are merely forms? Anything that compromises your testimony or biblical content cannot be practiced. Some missionaries have gone far beyond what I would be willing to accept. They do this with the intent to remove all stumbling blocks for locals to come to Christ. But what kind of believers are they going to be? Everyone has to make his or her own decisions before God in this regard. What then are the issues?

Some topics are outlined which require contextualization:
- **Identification of Christian believers:** Christians will neither deny the Lord Jesus nor their commitment to him. Some contextualists do not identify themselves as members of the body of Christ. They continue in the mosque, but may name themselves "Followers of Isa[300]". When are asked whether they are Christians, they will deny it.
- **Religious practices:** Certain contextualists will pray in the Islamic way, keep the Ramadan fast and other Islamic festivals, wear the skull cap, etc. By that token they identify themselves as Muslims.
- **Language:** Acquiring the language of the target people is indispensable for a contextual missionary, because effective communication of the gospel is impossible without linguistic proficiency.
- **Food:** Should Christians living in an Islamic context eat pork? May they drink beer or wine? Should they eat *halal* food? This is not a matter of taste, but of love: pork and alcohol should be banned from homes in that situation. One will hardly obtain food that is not *halal* (cf 1Cor 8:6-9 and 10:23-31).
- **Dress:** Contextual missionaries are often encouraged to wear local dress and to show appreciation for it. The question remains whether this is advisable in every situation. In the Gulf, for example, it is strictly forbidden.
- **Jesus Mosque** *(Masjid-e 'Isa)*: According to some contextual missionaries, Muslims are hostile to all things Christian and, unless this hostility is reduced to a

---

[299] Some factors are: the Palestinian and Jerusalem question, the Crusades, terrorism and violence caused by radical Muslims.
[300] It is customary that Muslims call Jesus *"Isa"*. By this they mean Jesus as portrayed in the Qur'an.

normal human relationship, no proper evangelism can take place. What irks Muslims most is a Christian church. Would it not be better, the contextualists propose, to call Christian churches "Jesus mosques" or even erect a church on the pattern of a mosque? However, does this not go too far? One could argue that this might be a hindrance to Muslims becoming true Christians, since they are still worshipping in the "mosque", part of the world of Islam.

- **Bible recitation:** It is Islamic practice to recite the Qur'an in a chanted form. In Qur'an schools quite a few Muslims learn to recite the whole of the Qur'an from memory. These are called *hafiz*. How sensible is it to imitate this with the Bible? It certainly is a good habit to memorize portions of the Bible, but not to brag about it.

- **Festivals:** Every population group in the world has religious, social and cultural festivals which are celebrated in a unique manner. It is suggested in Christian literature that contextualized missionaries should celebrate the two Muslim festivals (*'Id al-Fitr* and *'Id al-'adha*) as 'Christian' *'Ids*. To what extent should a Christian partake? It is not advisable, since Muslims may well conclude that these Christians are on their way to become Muslims! Christians are not ashamed of their Lord Jesus Christ and rather celebrate Easter, Pentecost and Christmas.

Experience shows that Muslims will not, as a rule, hesitate to confess their faith. If Christians do not do the same, they will be regarded by Muslims as cowards or unbelievers, which is anything but honouring the Lord Jesus.

In the light of what has been discussed on this topic, contextualization of the gospel demands first of all an in-depth study of worldview, value systems, culture and customs. What is neutral and what carries a religious message? Every religious ritual or symbol has a spiritual meaning. Christians need to be aware not to compromise the message of the gospel. There are no general answers which apply to every situation. On the contrary, every Christian has to make his or her own wise decision as to what extent contextualization is applied in any given situation.

3.8.4 The modern face of Islam

For a number of years, modernity has exerted its influence on the Church. It questions the validity, value, trustworthiness and reliability of the Bible and what it stands for. Bible critics have tried to tear the Scriptures to pieces. God is placed in the realm of a myth. The very existence of the historical Christ has been strongly questioned. Christians have been ridiculed as simple-minded and attacked as fundamentalists and fanatics. The teaching of the creation of the world is equally ridiculed and replaced with the theory of evolution, which lacks any scientific credibility. The Church may have been decimated, but the integrity of the Bible stands firm. Today, there are more true believers than ever before.

Islam has not as yet come to face modernism. It has not permitted critique of the Qur'an and the *hadith*. The Muslim public is now more indoctrinated and fanaticized than ever before, but Islam's exposure to the West and the formidable ideological forces of modernity will have consequences. Second- and third-generation Muslims in secularized societies are already being challenged and the day will come when the historicity and trustworthiness of Islamic Scriptures will be openly challenged, possibly with catastrophic results.

Westernization as a collection of ideas, or a set of symbols, is now the greatest challenge to the cultures of the Islamic world. Popular culture is dominated by television and the internet, which in turn is dominated by Western images and products. In some Middle Eastern cities, up to 100 TV channels or more are available. It is hard to find a single house in Cairo that doesn't have a TV. Computers are ubiquitous and more and more Muslims within Islamic states are gaining access to the world wide web in their living rooms.

This Westernizing force puts a strain on Islam and the Arab world. Ordinary, moderate Arabs believe their families to be more decent and honourable than their counterparts in the West. They consider themselves to be more God-fearing, their daughters more modest, their communities more cohesive. With good reason, ordinary Arabs are proud of their culture, its generosity, hospitality and honour.

The painful dilemma facing Islam and especially the Arab World, is how to stay true to its values amidst an onslaught of Western, secular and sometimes immoral values. The variety of responses range from a complete rejection of Islam and the Arab world to a rejection of Westernization, or an attempt to steer some middle course.

- Some emigrate physically, others emotionally, adopting what they imagine to be the lifestyle of the West without actually leaving Islam or the Arab world.
- Some seek escapisms common in the West: shopping, TV, internet, drugs, mysticism.
- Some turn to radical Islam.
- A few become Christians.
- And the rest, like most people in the West, simply muddle through the moral incoherence as best as they can.

One area which divides Muslims today is that of the rights and responsibilities of women. The Qur'an defined the roles of women quite precisely for the seventh century. How should the precepts of the Qur'an be applied to the twenty-first century? Questions of marriage and divorce, inheritance, and dress codes for women are hot issues in the Middle East. The revolutionary spirit among some Muslims today leads them to abandon the compromises made by their parents and ancestors, in an attempt to return to the basic beliefs and practices of Islam.

What does the future hold for the world of Islam? History gives us a picture of constant change in the nations and cultures of the *umma*. One certainty is continued volatility rather than stablity. The Middle East will likely be a focus of tensions and turmoil. One word points to the dream of peace, for which people of the Middle East have longed for centuries, a word which sounds almost the same in both Semitic languages: *salam* in Arabic, and *shalom* in Hebrew. Christians know that only one person can bring real peace—the greatest prophet who ever appeared: Jesus Christ, the Messiah and Son of God, who says:

"I have told you these things, so that in me you may have peace.
In this world you will have trouble. But take heart!
I have overcome the world."
Jn 16:33

4. Appendices

4.1 Bibliography and recommended reading

Adeney, M 2002. *Daughters of Islam – Building Bridges with Muslim Women.* Illinois: IVP.

Ali, A Yusuf (ed). 1946 (Printed: 4/1993). *The Holy Qur'an.* WIPE International.

Ali, N 1987. *Frontiers in Muslim-Christian Encounter.* Oxford: Regnum.

Al-Omari, J 2003. *The Arab Way—how to work more effectively with Arab Cultures.* Oxford.

Battle For The Hearts. 12 Episodes of interactive training. Trans World Radio and Life Challenge Africa 2001.

Beaumont, M 2005. *Christology in Dialogue with Muslims.* Waynesboro, GA: Paternoster.

Bell, S 2006. *The Journey from Fear to Faith.* Authentic Media.

Belteshazzar & Abednego, 2006. *The Mosque and its Role in Society.* Pilcrow Press.

Brooks, G 1995. *Nine Parts of Desire—the hidden World of Islamic Women.* London: Penguin.

Burge, G M 2003. *Whose Land? Whose Promise? What Christians are not being told about Israel and the Palestinians.* Cleveland: Pilgrim Press.

Campbell, W 1986. *The Qur'an and the Bible in the light of history and science.* Upper Darby: AWM.

Caner, E and Caner E F 2002. *Unveiling Islam.* Grand Rapids: Spectrum Books Lim.

Chacour, E 2003. *Blood Brothers.* Chosen Books.

Chapman, C 1995. *Cross and Crescent—Responding to the challenge of Islam.* Leicester: IVP.

Chapman, C 2004. *Whose Holy City? – Jerusalem and the Israeli-Palestinian Conflict.* Oxford: LION.

Cooper, A 2003. *Ishmael my Brother.* London: Monarch Books.

Crone & Cook, P & M 1977. *Hagarism: the Making of the Islamic World.* Cambridge: University Press.

Durie, M 2006. *Do we worship the same God?* Australia: Harvest Publication.

Endress, G 2002. *ISLAM—An Historical Introduction.* Edinburgh: University Press.

Esposito, J L & Voll J O 1996. *Islam and Democracy.* Oxford: University Press.

Fraser, J 1993. *Love across Latitudes—A Workbook on Cross-cultural Marriages.* Loughborough: AWM.

Free, J P 1992. *Archaeology and Bible History.* Zondervan.

Gabriel, M A 2002. I*slam and Terrorism.* Florida: Chrarisma House.

Gaudeul, J M 1999. *Called from Islam to Christ—why Muslims become Christians.* London: Monarch.

Geisler N L & Saleeb A 1993. *Answering Islam—the Crescent in the Light of the Cross.* Grand Rapids: Baker.

George, R 2000. *The Qur'an in the Light of Christ.* WIN International.

Gibb, H & Kramers, J 1953. *Shorter Encyclopaedia of Islam.* New York: Cornell University Press.

Gilchrist, J 1989. *Jam'Al-Qur'an—The Codification of the Qur'an Text.* Johannesburg: MERCSA.

Gilchrist, J 1994. *Muhammad—the Prophet of Islam.* Johannesburg: MERCSA.

Gilchrist, J 1995. *The Qur'an—the Scripture of Islam.* Johannesburg: MERCSA.

Gilchrist, J 1997. *Sufi Muslim Saints of India & South Africa.* Johannesburg: MERCSA.

Gilchrist, J 1999. *Facing the Muslim Challenge—a Handbook of Christian-Muslim Apologetics.* Johannesburg: MERCSA

Gilchrist, J 2003. *Sharing the Gospel with Muslims—a Handbook for Bible-based Muslim Evangelism.* Cape Town: Life Challenge Africa.

Glasser, I & N 1998. *Partners or Prisoners? Christian Thinking about Women and Islam.* Cumbria: Paternoster.

Glubb, J B 1979. *The Life and Times of Muhammad.* London: Hodder and Stoughton.

Goddard, H 2000. *A History of Christian-Muslim Relations.* Chicago: New Amsterdam Books.

Goldsmith, M 2004. *Islam and Christian Witness.* OM Publishing.

Goodwin, J 2003. *Price of Honor —Muslim Women lift the Veil of Silence on the Islamic World.* London: Penguin.

Greenlee, D 2005. *From the Straight Path to the Narrow Way: Journeys of Faith.* Waynesboro: Authentic.

Guillaume, A 1955. *The Life of Muhammad.* Oxford: University Press.

Haddad, Y & W Z 1995. *Christian-Muslim Encounters.* Gainsville, FL: University of Florida Press.

Hughes, T P 1982. *Dictionary of Islam.* New Delhi: COSMO.

Ibn Warraq, 1995. *Why I am not a Muslim.* Amherst, NY: Promotheus Books.

Jeffery, A 1975. *Materials for the History of the Text of the Qur'an.* New York: AMS Press.

Johnstone, P & Mandryk J 2001. *Operation World—when we pray God works.* Virginia: Paternoster.

Jonsson, D J 2005. *The Clash of Ideologies—the Making of the Christian and Islamic Worlds.* USA: Xulon.

Kateregga B D & Shenk D W 1980. *Islam and Christianity—a Muslim and a Christian in Dialogue.* Grand Rapids: Eerdmans.

Khan, M M 1996. *Summarized Sahih Al-Bukhari (Arabic-English).* Riyadh: Dar-us-Salam.

Khurshid, A 1976. *Islam—its meaning and message.* Leicester: Islamic Foundation.

Khursihd, A & Zafar, I A 1980. *Islamic Perspectives.* Leicester: Islamic Foundation.

Lewis, B 1995. *The Middle East—a brief History of the last 2000 Years.* New York: SCRIBNER.

Lewis, B 2003. *The Crisis of Islam—Holy War and Unholy Terror.* London: Phoenix.

Love, R 2000. *Muslims, Magic and the Kingdom of God—Church Planting among Folk Muslims.* California: William Carey.

Maqsood, R W 2006. *Islam—teach yourself.* London: Hodder Education.

Marshall, D 1999. *God, Muhammad and the Unbelievers.* London: Curzon.

Maurer, A 1999. *In Search of a New Life: Conversion Motives of Christians and Muslims.* Pretoria: UNISA.

Mernissi, F 1985. *Women and Islam, an Historical and Theological Enquiry.* Oxford: Blackwell.

Moucarry, C 2001. *Faith to Faith—Christianity & Islam in dialogue.* Leicester: IVP.

Muller, R 2000. *Tools for Muslim Evangelism.* Ontario: Essence.

Muller, R 2001. *Honor and Shame-Unlocking the Door.* Xlibris Corporation.

Muller, R 2004. *The Messenger, The Message & The Community—three critical Issues for the Cross-Cultural Church-Planter.* Ontario: Essence.

Musk, B 1989. *The Unseen Face of Islam—sharing the Gospel with ordinary Muslims.* London: MARC.

Musk, B 1995. *Touching the Soul of Islam—sharing the Gospel in Muslim Cultures.* Crowborough: MARC.

Musk, B 2003. *Holy War – why do some Muslims become Fundamentalists?* London: Monarch.

Musk, B 2005. *Kissing Cousins – Christians and Muslims face to face.* London: Monarch.

Nehls, G 1985. *Al-Kitab "The Book" – a Bible correspondence course for Muslims.* Wellington: Biblecor.

Nehls, G & Eric, W 2006. *Reach Out: What every Christian needs to know about Islam and Muslims.* Nairobi: Life Challenge Africa.

Nehls, G & Eric, W 2005. *Islam – Basic Aspects: Trainers Textbook 1.* Nairobi: Life Challenge Africa.

Nehls, G & Eric, W 2006. *Christian-Islamic Controversy: Trainers Textbook 2.* Nairobi: Life Challenge Africa.

Nehls, G & Eric, W 2006. *Practical-Tactical Approach: Trainers Textbook 3.* Nairobi: Life Challenge Africa.

Newbegin L, Sanneh L, Taylor J 2005. *Faith and Power – Christianity and Islam in "Secular" Britain.* Wipf & Stock Publishers.

Newman, N A 1993. *Early Christian-Muslim Dialogue: Collection of Documents (632-900 AD).* USA: IBRI.

Nydell, M K 1996. *Understanding Arabs – a Guide for Westerners.* USA: Intercultural Press.

Parrinder, E G 1965. *Jesus in the Qur'an.* London: Sheldon Press.

Parshall, P 1985. *Beyond the Mosque – Christians within Muslim Community.* Grand Rapids: Baker.

Parshall, P 1994. *Inside the Community – Understanding Muslims through Their Traditions.* Grand Rapids: Baker House.

Parshall, P & J 2002. *Lifting the Veil – the World of Muslim Women.* USA: Gabriel.

Parsons, M 2005. *Unveiling God – Contextualizing Christology for Islamic Culture.* Passadena: Carey.

Pietzsch, H 2004. *Welcome Home.* Cape Town: Life Challenge Africa.

Riddell, P G & Cotterell P. *Islam in Conflict – past, present and future.* Leicester: IVP.

Riddell, P G 2004. *Christians and Muslims – Pressures and potential in a post-9/11 world.* London: IVP.

Robinson, S 2003. *Mosques & Miracles – Revealing Islam and God's Grace.* Australia: City Harvest.

Roy, O 2006. *Globalized Islam: The Search for a new Ummah.* Columbia: University Press.

Saal, W J 1991. *Reaching Muslims for Christ.* Chicago: Moody.

Safa Reza F. 1996. *Inside Islam – Exposing and Reaching the World of Islam.* Charisma House.

Schimmel, A 1975. *Mystical Dimensions of Islam.* Chapel Hill: University of N. Carolina.

Schlorf, S 2006. *Missiological Models in Ministry to Muslims.* Pennsylvania: Middle East Recourses.

Shorrosh Dr. Anis A. 1988. *Islam Revealed – A Christian Arab's View of Islam.* Thomas Nelson Publishers.

Siddiqui, A H 1999. *The Life of Muhammad.* Malaysia: Islamic Book Trust.

Smith, M 2004. *Through her eyes – Perspectives on life from Christian women serving in the Muslim world.* Waynesboro: Authentic.

Sookhdeo, P 2001. *A Christian's Pocket Guide to Islam.* Scotland: Christian Focus.

Sookhdeo, P 2004. *Understanding Islamic Terrorism.* London: Isaac Publishing.

Steer, M 2003. *A Christian's Pocket Guide to Islam.* Oldham: FFM.

Stoner, P W 1969. *Science Speaks.* Moody Press.

Tabataba'i, A S M H 1975. *Shi'ite Islam.* New York: State University. (Translated from the Persian and edited by Seyyed Hossein Nasr).

Tucker, J E 1993. *Arab Women, Old Boundaries & New Frontiers.* Indianapolis: University Press.

Watt, M 1953. *Muhammad at Mecca and Muhammad at Medina.* New York: Oxford University Press.

Watt, W M 1964. *Muhammad—Prophet and Statesman.* Oxford: University Press.

Watt, W M 1980. *Islamic Political Thought.* Edinburgh: University Press.

Wehr, H 1979. *A Dictionary of modern written Arabic (Arabic-English).* Wiesbaden: Otto Harrassowitz.

Williams, J 1998. *Don't they know it's Friday? Cross-cultural considerations for business and life in the Gulf.* Dubai: Gulf Business Books.

Ye'or, B 1985. *Dhimmi: Jews and Christians under Islam.* 2nd ed. London: Ass. University Press.

Zebiri, K 1997. *Muslims and Christians Face to Face.* Oxford: One World.

Zeidan, D 2000. *The Fifth Pillar: A Spiritual Pilgrimage.* Carlisle, UK: Piquant.

Zeidan, D 2003. *Sword of Allah – Islamic Fundamentalism from an Evangelical Perspective.* Gabriel Publishing.

Zenjibari, M A 2002. *Islam and Christianity – a comparative Study.* Qum/Iran: Ansariyan.

Zwemer, S M 2006. *Raymond Lull – First Missionary to the Moslems.* Diggory Press Limited.

4.2 Resources

This book has been written to provide a basic understanding for Christians about Islam and how to start meaningful interaction with Muslims. In order to provide further help and advanced teaching you are invited to contact the following website:
· **www.aymf.net (www.ask-your-muslim-friend.net)**

This website is constantly being updated and provides additional resources in a structured way according to the topics of the book!
Although you may find much information on the website mentioned above, you may contact the following websites directly:
· www.answeringislam.net
· www.wikipedia.com

If you do not have access to the internet, you may write to the following address:
· Ask your Muslim Friend (IfI)
  P.O. Box 367
  8610 Uster 1
  Switzerland

4.3 Abbreviations

AD	=	Anno Domini (years after Christ)
AH	=	After Hijra (The Islamic calendar starts with the year when Muhammad emigrated from Mecca to Medina, 622 AD)
b	=	born
BC	=	Before Christ
ch	=	chapter
cf	=	cross reference
d	=	died
f	=	see also the following verse
ff	=	see also the following verses
MBB	=	Muslim Background Believers (people who were Muslims and have become Christians)
MERCSA	=	Muslim Evangelism Resource Centre Southern Africa
p	=	page
pp	=	pages
v	=	verse
Vol	=	Volume
WEA	=	World Evangelical Alliance

Books of the Bible

Old Testament (OT)

Am	Amos	Hos	Hosea	Mic	Micah
Ch	Chronicles	Is	Isaiah	Na	Nahum
Da	Daniel	Jer	Jeremiah	Ne	Nehemiah
Dt	Deuteronomy	Job	Job	Nu	Numbers
Ecc	Ecclesiastes	Joel	Joel	Ob	Obadiah
Est	Esther	Jnh	Jonah	Ps	Psalms
Ex	Exodus	Jos	Joshua	Pr	Proverbs
Eze	Ezekiel	Jdg	Judges	Ru	Ruth
Ezr	Ezra	Ki	Kings	Sa	Samuel
Ge	Genesis	La	Lamentations	SS	Song of Songs
Hab	Habakkuk	Lev	Leviticus	Zec	Zechariah
Hag	Haggai	Mal	Malachi	Zep	Zephaniah

New Testament (NT)

Ac	Acts	Jn	John	Php	Philippians
Col	Colossians	Jude	Jude	Rev	Revelation
Co	Corinthians	Lk	Luke	Ro	Romans
Eph	Ephesians	Mk	Mark	Th	Thessalonians
Gal	Galatians	Mt	Matthew	Ti	Timothy
Heb	Hebrews	Pe	Peter	Tit	Titus
Jas	James	Phm	Philemon		

4.4 Glossary of Arabic/Islamic terms

The following list consists of concepts derived from both Islam and Arab tradition which are expressed as words in the Arabic language. Separating concepts in Islam from concepts specific to Arab culture, or from the language itself, can be difficult. Many Arabic concepts have an Arabic secular meaning as well as an Islamic meaning. One example is the concept of *da'wa*. Among the complexities of the Arabic language is that a single word can have multiple meanings. The word "Islam" is itself a good example. Readers should also note that Arabic is written in its own alphabet, with letters, symbols, and orthographic conventions that do not have exact equivalents in the Latin alphabet (see Arabic alphabet).

This list is a transliteration of Arabic terms and phrases. Consequently, Muslims may transliterate certain Arabic words differently, such as *din* as opposed to *deen*. The spelling of Arabic words can differ in English texts. In this book, a system of transcription has been chosen which permits readers to pronounce the words more or less correctly. Hints how to pronounce a word are given, where necessary, in brackets. This is, of necessity, a simplification. Arabic sounds do not exactly correspond to the English equivalents. The Arabic language is constructed from roots consisting of three consonants. Vowels are added in different ways to make different parts of speech (adjectives, nouns, etc.). Arabic/Islamic words appear in *italics* in the text, with the only few exceptions being those words that are already established in English. Terms are listed here in alphabetical order (disregarding the articles *al, an, ar, as, ash, at, az*).

Transliteration	Arabic	Explanation
'abd	عَبْد	"Servant; worshipper; slave". Muslims consider themselves as servants and slaves of Allah. Muslims have names such as *'Abd Allah* (Servant of Allah).
adhan (aadhaan)	آذَان	Announcement; call to public prayer by the *mu'adhdhin*.
Ahl al-Kitab (Ahl al-Kitaab)	أَهْل الكِتَاب	"The People of the Book"; followers of pre-Islamic monotheistic religions with scripture believed to be of divine origin—mainly Jews and Christians.
Allah (Allaah)	الله	The Arabic word for "God".
Allahu akbar (Allaahu akbar)	أَكْبَر الله	"Allah is very great"; this exclamation introduces the daily liturgical prayers and is also said at funerals and at the slaughter of animals.
al-Ansar (al-Ansaar)	الأَنْصَار	"The Helpers". The Muslim converts at Medina who helped the Muslims from Mecca after the *Hijra*.
arkan al-Islam (arkaan al-Islaam)	أَرْكَان الإِسْلام	"The Pillars of Islam"; the five duties of Islam: creed, prayer, tax, fasting and pilgrimage.
'Ashura ('Aashooraa)	عَاشُورَاء	The 10th day of the month of Muharram. For Shiites the day of the mourning of the death of Husain at Karbela.
aslama	أَسْلَمَ	To capitulate; to surrender to Allah; to give in to Allah.
aya (aaya)	آية	"Sign; miracle; verse". Indicates both one of the 6200 verses of the Qur'an and a miracle.
Ayatu Allah (Aayatollaah)	آية الله	"The Sign of Allah", title of a very high spiritual leader in Shiite Islam (Ayatollah).

Transliteration	Arabic	Explanation
al-Baqara	البَقَرَة	"The cow"; the name of Sura 2 in the Qur'an.
baraka	بَرَكة	"Blessing"; the power of blessing.
al-basmala	البَسْمَلة	The formula "in the name of God, the Beneficent, the Merciful." It is used before every Sura in the Qur'an and many actions.
burqu'	بُرْقُع	The burka; a long veil or drape worn by women.
chador (chaadoor)	شَادُور	Persian "tent"; a black cloak covering body and head, but not the face.
da'i (daa'ee)	دَاعِي	"One who calls or invites". An Islamic missionary.
Dar al-Harb (Daar al-Harb)	دَار الحَرْب	"The House of war"; regions and countries that are not yet Islamic and that have to be conquered.
Dar al-Islam (Daar al-Islaam)	دَار الإِسْلام	"The House of Islam"; the region in which Islam rules.
da'wa	دَعْوَة	"Call, invitation" to Islam: mission.
Dervish (Derveesh)	دَرْوِيش	Persian "poor". An Islamic mystic who tries to come near Allah in ecstasy via dances and recitations.
dhikr	ذِكْر	"Remembrance". In mysticism, a remembrance of Allah by continuous repetition of certain phrases.
dhimmi (dhimmee)	ذِمِّي	Inhabitant of a Muslim territory, who has not accepted Islam for himself (such as a Jew or Christian). He has to pay a tax and sometimes carry out humiliating duties. Dhimmi is a word which appears in Sura 9:8-10.
din (deen)	دِين	"Religion"; religious practice in Islam.
du'a' (du'aa')	دُعَاء	Personal supplication prayer.

Transliteration	Arabic	Explanation
fana' (fanaa')	فَنَاء	"To pass away; to cease to exist". The complete denial of oneself and the realization of Allah that is one of the steps taken by the Muslim Sufi (mystic) toward the achievement of union with Allah. *Fana'* may be attained by constant meditation and contemplation on the attributes of Allah, coupled with the denunciation of human attributes.
al-Fatiha (al-Faatiha)	الفَاتِحَة	Name of the first Sura of the Qur'an.
fatwa (fatwaa)	فَتْوَى	Legal opinion; religious or judicial decision.
al-Fiqh	الفِقْه	The Islamic law.
firqa	فِرْقَة	Sects; groupings in Islam.
al-Furqan (al-Furqaan)	الفُرْقَان	The criterion (of right and wrong, true and false). Sometimes the Qur'an is described as *furqan*.
ghusl	غُسْل	"Washing". The full ablution of the whole body.
hadith (hadeeth)	حَدِيث	A "saying, report". Report of what Muhammad did, instructed and what was done in his presence. There are many collections of customs and traditions (plural: *ahadith*).
hafiz (haafiz)	حَافِظ	"Keeper; custodian". A Muslim who knows the entire Qur'an by heart.
al-hajj	الحَجّ	"The Pilgrimage" to Mecca (fifth pillar of Islam).
hajj (haajj)	حَاجّ	"Pilgrim". Name given to a Muslim who has performed the pilgrimage to Mecca.
halal (halaal)	حَلال	Ritually clean and therefore permitted to Muslims.
hanif (haneef)	حَنِيف	Allah-seeker; orthodox believer; confessor of Allah's uniqueness.
al-Haqq	الحَقّ	The truth; the right.

Transliteration	Arabic	Explanation
harām (haraam)	حَرَام	Taboo; ritually unclean and therefore forbidden.
haram	حَرَم	Sanctified, protected and forbidden place. Is used for great mosques and for the private quarters of the Islamic house.
hijab (hijaab)	حِجَاب	"Cover". The self-covering of the body for the purposes of modesty and dignity.
al-Hijra	الهِجْرَة	"Emigration; separation". Muhammad's and his follower's emigration from Mecca to Medina (622 AD).
hur (hoor)	حُور	"Houris". Beautiful virgin with almond-shaped eyes and fine skin, who will please male believers in paradise.
Iblis (Iblees)	إِبْليس	Name of the devil in the Qur'an.
'Id al-adha ('Eed al-Ad-haa)	الأَضْحَى عيد	"The Feast of sacrifice" in the month of pilgrimage, in remembrance of Abraham's willingness to sacrifice his son.
'Id al-Fitr ('Eed al-Fitr)	الفِطْر عيد	"The Feast of fast-breaking" at the end of Ramadan.
ijma' (ijmaa')	إِجْمَاع	"Consensus" of Islamic scholars on a legal issue.
ijtihad (ijtihaad)	إِجْتِهَاد	"Striving". The finding of justice by rational thought; a way to adapt Islamic legislation to new developments.
imam (imaam)	إمَام	"Leader", e.g. the leader of prayer in a mosque.
al-iman (al-eemaan)	الإِيمَان	"Belief".
al-Injil (al-Injeel)	الإِنْجيل	"The Gospel". The name of the book Muslims claim Allah gave to Jesus.
in sha' Allah (in shaa' Allaah)	الله شَاء إن	"If it is Allah's will". An exclamation, mostly meaning "hopefully".
iqra'	إقرَأ	"Read! Recite!".
irtidad (irtidaad)	إِرْتدَاد	Apostasy from Islam.

Transliteration	Arabic	Explanation
'Isa ('Eesaa)	عِيسَى	The name of Jesus in the Qur'an.
al-Islam (al-Islaam)	الإسْلام	"The submission" to the will of Allah. The followers of this religion are called *Muslims*.
isnad (isnaad)	إِسْنَاد	Chain of witnesses of a *hadith*.
Jahannam	جَهَنَّم	Hell.
al-Jahiliyya (al-Jaahiliyya)	الجَاهِلِيَّة	"The age of ignorance". The time before Muhammad is so called by Muslims since the Arabs worshipped many idols at that time!
al-Janna	الجَنَّة	"The Garden"; Paradise.
Jibril (Jibreel)	جبْرِيل	"Gabriel". The angel Gabriel or a ghost who is said to have been the medium of revelation of the Qur'an to Muhammad.
jihad (jihaad)	جهَاد	"Effort" in the way of Allah. The fight of Muslims both against their own bad sides and against the unbelievers for the propagation of Islam, the so-called "holy war".
jinn	جنّ	Demons; ghosts; invisible beings of fiery origins.
jizya	جِزْيَة	Capitation or "head tax" for Jews and Christians in a Muslim state. Term used in Sura 9:29.
jum'a	جُمْعَة	Prayer at Friday noon.
al-Ka'ba	الكَعْبَة	"The Cube". A cubic building in Mecca, the central sanctuary of Islam (was supposedly built by Abraham) that contains the Black Stone. Muslims try to kiss this stone during the pilgrimage.
kafir (kaafir)	كَافِر	"Unbeliever". Someone who does not belong to the Islamic faith, someone guilty of *kufr*.
kalima	كَلِمَة	"Word".
al-khalifa (al-khaleefa)	الخَلِيفَة	"The successor" of Muhammad; the caliph; the leader of Islam.

Transliteration	Arabic	Explanation
khilafa (khilaafa)	خِلَافة	The caliphate; the rule or realm of a caliph.
khutba	خُطْبة	Sermon delivered on Friday during noon prayer in the mosque.
al-Kiswa	الكِسْوَة	"The Cape". The black cloth that enwraps the Ka'ba in Mecca.
kitab (kitaab)	كِتَاب	"Writ; book". This can be used for the Qur'an or another "holy writing".
kufr	كُفْر	"Disbelief"; blasphemy; to deny Allah.
Laylat al-Qadr	لَيْلَة القَدْر	"The Night of Power". Feast towards the end of Ramadan, when Muhammad is said to have received the first revelation of the Qur'an.
al-Madina (al-Madeena)	المَدِينة	Medina; in Muhammad's time, this city was named *Yathrib* (Sura 33:13). It is the city to which Muhammad emigrated in the year 622 AD. The city is located about 400 km north of Mecca. It was later named *al-Madina* (literally: "the City"), after it had become famous. It is today revered as Muhammad's city of burial. Only Muslims are allowed to enter this city.
madrasa	مَدْرَسَة	"School"; previously a theological high school.
al-Mahdi (al-Mahdee)	المَهْدي	"The Rightly Guided"; expected by Muslims in the last days.
Makka	مَكَّة	Mecca, the holy city of Islam, Muhammad's place of birth. Only Muslims are allowed to enter this city.
malak (malaak)	مَلَاك	"Angel"; Muslims believe that angels were created out of light.
manara (manaara)	مَنَارَة	The minaret; the tower of a mosque. From this tower Muslims are called to prayer.
mansukh (mansookh)	مَنْسُوخ	"Something abrogated". A verse of the Qur'an that was invalidated by a later revelation in the Qur'an.
masbaha	مَسْبَحَة	The Muslim prayer chain (rosary) consists of 99 or 33 pearls, and is used to recite the 99 names or attributes of Allah and in addition the "essential name of Allah".

Transliteration	Arabic	Explanation
al-Masih (al-Maseeh)	المَسيح	"The Messiah"; used in the Qur'an to denote Jesus.
masjid	مَسْجِد	Place of prayer; mosque.
matn	مَتْن	The "text" proper of a *hadith*.
mawla (mawlaa)	مَوْلَى	"Lord, mullah; mollah". A title of Islamic clergy and scholars.
mawlana (mawlaanaa)	مَوْلَانَا	Literally "our lord; our master". Mostly used as a title preceding the name of a respected religious leader (maulana).
mihrab (mihraab)	مِحْرَاب	Niche in a mosque that denotes the direction of prayer *(qibla)*.
minbar	مِنْبَر	The pulpit in a mosque.
al-Mi'raj (al-Mi'raaj)	المِعْرَاج	"The Ascension". Muhammad's voyage to the seven heavens during the "Night Journey".
al-Mizan (al-Meezaan)	المِيزَان	"The Scale". A large scale to weigh a person's good deeds against his bad deeds on the "Day of Judgment".
mu'adhdhin	مُؤَذِّن	The caller to prayer; *muezzin*.
mufti (muftee)	مُفْتِي	Legal specialist; someone who is allowed to issue legal opinions, a *fatwa*.
Muhammad	مُحَمَّد	The "Praised One". Muhammad, the founder of the Islamic religion.
mujahidin (mujaahideen)	مُجَاهِدِين	Fighters; Muslim warriors fighting in the *jihad*.
murtadd	مُرْتَدّ	A Muslim who declares *kufr*; unbelief in Islam.
musalla (musallaa)	مُصَلَّى	A "prayer place". The small rug a Muslim uses for prayer.
mushrik	مُشْرِك	"Idolater"; someone guilty of *shirk*, i.e. of associating other beings with Allah as additional divine beings.
Muslim	مُسْلِم	A Muslim; a follower of Islam. The term "Mohammedan" is old fashioned and should not be used.

Transliteration	Arabic	Explanation
mut'a	مُتْعَة	"Enjoyment". A temporary marriage with payment and contract, in Shiite law.
nabi (nabiyy)	نَبِيّ	"Prophet" who received a message by inspiration from God (through angels, inspiration or dreams).
an-Nar (an-Naar)	النَّار	"The Fire"; the hell-fire.
nasikh (naasikh)	نَاسِخ	Verse of the Qur'an that replaces an earlier section (mansukh).
al-Qadar	القَدَر	Fate; predestination.
qadi (qaadee)	قَاضِي	"Judge".
qibla	قِبْلَة	Direction of prayer—namely towards Mecca.
qiyas (qiyaas)	قِيَاس	Comparison; conclusion by analogy.
Quraish	قُرَيْش	Name of the Arabic tribe to which Muhammad belonged. This tribe played an important role in the Qur'an and in the history of Islam.
al-Qur'an (al-Qur'aan)	القُرآن	"The Recitation, the Reading". The holy book of Islam.
ar-Rabb	الرَّبّ	"The Lord", i.e. God.
rak'a	رَكْعَة	Bowing; revering; prostrating in ritual prayer. Plural: ruku' (rokoo').
Ramadan (Ramadaan)	رَمَضَان	Month of fasting (9th month).
rasul (rasool)	رَسُول	"Messenger; ambassador; apostle". One who brings a scripture to humanity. In Islam, Moses, David, Jesus and Muhammad are considered messengers. A messenger with a scripture (book) is more important than a Prophet (nabi), who only brings a message.
ruh (rooh)	رُوح	"Soul; spirit"; the divine breath which Allah blew into the clay of Adam.

Transliteration	Arabic	Explanation
as-salamu 'alai-kum (as-salaamu 'alaikum)	عَلَيْكُم السَّلامُ	The Islamic greeting; literally "Peace be upon you".
salat (salaat)	صَلاة	Ritual prayer.
sawm	صَوْم	"Fasting" in the month of Ramadan.
ash-Shahada (ash-Shahaada)	الشَّهَادَة	Muslim profession of faith: "There is no god but Allah and Muhammad is the messenger of Allah." (1st Pillar of Islam.)
shahid (shaheed)	شَهِيد	"Witness; martyr".
shaikh	شَيْخ	"Old man". Patriarch in Arabian countries; teacher of Islam; worthy old man.
ash-Shaitan (ash-Shaitaan)	الشَّيْطَان	"Satan; Devil"; also known as *Iblis*.
ash-Shari'a (ash-Sharee'a)	الشَّرِيعَة	"The law". The Islamic religious law.
ash-Shi'a (ash-Shee'a)	الشّيعَة	The Shi'a (literally "the Party" of 'Ali); main sect of Islam; originally of a political nature. They believe 'Ali (Muhammad's son in law) should have been the first caliph. Most Shiites live in Iran and Iraq.
shirk	شِرْك	Idolatry; associating other beings with Allah. This sin cannot be forgiven.
as-Sira (as-Seera)	السِيرَة	"The life or the biography" of Muhammad.
as-Sirat (as-Siraat)	السِّرَاط	The narrow, razor-sharp bridge leading to paradise. Only the righteous (faithful Muslims) are able to cross it, all others fall into the abyss.
Sufi (Soofee)	صُوفِي	Follower of Sufism; an ascetic-mystic branch of Islam.
as-Sunna	السُّنَّة	"The Path". Custom, tradition, way of life; the tradition of how Muhammad and his followers lived.
Sunni (Sunnee)	سُنِّي	Sunnites; about 85% of all Muslims.

Transliteration	Arabic	Explanation
Sura (Soora)	سُورَة	A chapter of the Qur'an; 114 in total.
tafsir (tafseer)	تَفْسِير	"Interpretation; exegesis; explanation". A commentary on the Qur'an.
tahrif (tahreef)	تَحْرِيف	"Corruption; falsification; forgery". Muslims believe the Bible was corrupted but the Qur'an is in its original form.
takfir (takfeer)	تَكْفِير	Declare a person an unbeliever (kafir), in particular those who leave Islam.
tanzil (tanzeel)	تَنْزِيل	"Revelation". The Muslim understanding of the revelation of the Qur'an is that it has read by Gabriel to Muhammad.
taqiyya	تَقِيَّة	"Caution; fear; disguise." It refers to the concept of allowing Muslims to conceal their faith when under threat or persecution.
at-Taurat (at-Tawraat)	التَّوْرَاة	"The Thora". The Pentateuch. Muslims believe Allah revealed the Pentateuch to Moses.
Tawhid (Tawheed)	تَوْحِيد	"Monotheism", confessing the unity and uniqueness of Allah, that Allah is one.
al-'ulama' (al-'ulamaa')	العُلَمَاء	"Those who know". The scholars of Islamic law and religion; the representatives of religious knowledge: the leaders of the Muslim society.
al-umma (al-umma)	الأُمَّة	"The nation". The community of all Muslims.
al-'umra (al-'umra)	العُمْرَة	The small pilgrimage. Unlike the hajj, it can be undertaken at any time. It is restricted to the Ka'ba and its direct surroundings.
wahy	وَحْي	"Inspiration".
wudu' (wudoo')	وُضُوء	"Ritual washing" before ritual prayer.
Yathrib	يَثْرِب	At the time of Muhammad, the city of Medina was called Yathrib.
az-Zabur (az-Zaboor)	الزَّبُور	"The Psalms"; the book revealed to King David.
az-zakat (az-zakaat)	الزَّكَاة	Mandatory alms tax (3rd Pillar of Islam).
Zamzam	زَمْزَم	The holy well in the area of the mosque in Mecca. Muslims claim it was Hagar's well.

4.5 Index

The index consists of some chosen words which are significant. It does not claim to be complete. Words followed by an asterisk (*) are described in the Glossary.